The Growing Child in Competitive Sport

ERRATUM

Due to an oversight the reference to the origin of the figures in the contribution by N. C. Craig Sharp, "Some Aspects of the Exercise Physiology of Children" pp. 110-112 has been omitted. All the figures in this contribution are from O. Bar-Or: *Paediatric Sports Medicine*, New York: Springer Verlag, 1983.

The Growing Child
in
Competitive Sport

Edited by

Geof Gleeson

HODDER AND STOUGHTON
LONDON SYDNEY AUCKLAND TORONTO

Acknowledgments

The publishers would like to thank the following for permission to reproduce illustrations:

Biological Review 1965 ('Structure and Function of Mammalian Tendon', pp 392–421, Cambridge University Press) page 114; Stanley Paul and Co. Ltd, pp 72–3; W. B. Saunders Company (The Physiological Basis of Physical Education and Athletics, Matthews D. K., Fox E. L., 1976) page 116; John Wiley & Sons, Inc. (Basic Anatomy and Physiology of the Human Body, McClintic J. R., 1975) page 114.

Chapters 2, 4 and 12 adapted by permission from the 1987 Medical and Health Annual, copyright © 1986 by Encyclopaedia Britannica, Inc., Chicago.

British Library Cataloguing in Publication Data

The Growing child in competitive sport
　1. Sports for children
　I. Gleeson, G. R.
　796'.088054　　　GV709.2

　ISBN 0 340 40755 7

First published 1986

Printed in Great Britain for Hodder and Stoughton Educational,
a division of Hodder and Stoughton Ltd,
Mill Road, Dunton Green, Sevenoaks, Kent,
by Richard Clay Ltd, Bungay, Suffolk

Photoset by Rowland Phototypesetting Ltd,
Bury St Edmunds, Suffolk

Contents

Contributors

Peter Coe Trained as an engineer; coach to Sebastian Coe.

F. W. Dick Director of coaching, British Amateur Athletic Board; Chief Coach, Athletics, for Great Britain in Olympic Games, 1980, 1984; President, European Athletics Coaches Association; Chairman, British Association of National Coaches.

Paddy Garratt Amateur Swimming Association Senior Coach; Swimming Coach to Millfield School.

Richard Glasstone Head of Choreographic Studies, The Royal Ballet School.

Geof Gleeson Executive Secretary, British Association of National Coaches; sometime Chief National Coach, British Judo Association.

Lew Hardy Lecturer in Sports Psychology and Research Methodology, University College of North Wales, Bangor.

Max Jones National Coach, British Amateur Athletic Board; Chief Coach for Throws and Combined Events.

Nick Juba Coach to the Esso-England International Youth and Swimming Squad.

J. E. Kane Principal, West London Institute of Higher Education; President, Physical Education Association; World President, International Council of Health, Physical Education and Recreation.

Martin J. Lee Director, Children's Sports Study Centre, Bedford College of Higher Education, Bedford.

Tom McNab Physical educationist, former British Amateur Athletic Board Nation Coach; Coach with British Olympic Athletics and Bobsleigh teams.

Sheila McQuattie Lecturer in Music Department, West London Institute of Higher Education.

Jim Riordan Chairman of Russian Studies, University of Bradford; Olympic attaché.

Glyn C. Roberts Sports Psychologist, Motor Behavior Laboratory, Institute for Child Behavior and Development, University of Illinois.

Stephen Rowley Project Officer, Training Young Athletes Study, Institute of Child Health, University of London.

Keith Russell Associate Professor, Department of Physical Education, University of Saskatchewan; National Coach to Canadian Gymnastics Federation, 1978–82.

N. C. Craig Sharp Co-Director of Human Motor Performance Laboratory, and Senior Lecturer in Exercise Physiology, Department of Physical Education and Sport Science, University of Birmingham.

Jacqueline Smith Principal Lecturer, London College of Dance and Drama, Bedford.

James Watkins Lecturer in Kinesiology and Biochemics, Scottish School of Physical Education, Jordanhill College, Glasgow.

Jean Whitehead Principal Lecturer in Human Movement Studies, Bedford College of Higher Education, Bedford.

Ray Williams Secretary, Welsh Rugby Union; President, British Association of National Coaches.

1

Introduction

Geof Gleeson

History of BANC

What is BANC? The British Association of National Coaches was founded between the summers of 1964 and 1965. In the early 'sixties, national coaches could be counted on the fingers of two hands (well, and a couple of toes). Before BANC they would meet from time to time, like wandering Bedouin, in the great sand pits. Their oases were the national sports centres, like Lilleshall and Bisham Abbey. During fleeting moments of conviviality over a cup of coffee there would be sagacious discussion of their unique problems. How do you teach originality to an enthusiastic mob of novices? How do you teach complex skills to a gang of incompetent beginners? How do you convince long-serving and well-intentioned part-time coaches that they still have a lot to learn? How do you convince sports governing bodies that coaching is a very serious business and is essential to the future growth of their organisations? The first amazing discovery emerging from these tête-à-têtes was that the problems were not unique, but were the common property of all national coaches. Unexpectedly, even the technical problems, such as skill analyses, were shared by everyone. Yet each coach had solved a part of the problem in his/her own way. When these part solutions were shared, they helped everyone tremendously. Several people were suddenly excited by the implications of such a mutual benefit society: here was the potential for a coach education plan which could shake Britain. It deserved an association to complement the idea – an association of national coaches providing regular opportunities for exchanging experiences and discussing and experimenting with new ways of doing old jobs.

In the spring of 1965, an inaugural meeting was called at the new Crystal Palace Sports Centre in London. The coaches who attended were an enthusiastic bunch of pioneers. They quickly saw the advantages of such an association and voted enthusiastically for its launching. A council was appointed, a draft constitution was prepared and the new body was christened 'The British Association of National Coaches'. The first honorary general secretary was Bob Anderson (fencing), a fitting appointment, for it was he who had tenaciously clung on to the idea of a national organisation and had been the actual convener of that inaugural meeting. The chairman was Alan Wade (football).

Evolution was slow, in spite of members' enthusiasm. As pioneers they were extremely busy, explaining as well as building. No one had any real idea of what a national coach looked like, or what he or she should be doing. Of course, the original concept went back to before the First World War, when the first ever national coach, V. R. Knox, was appointed in 1913. He was followed by the philoprogenitive Geoff Dyson in 1947, but that hardly constituted a job specification. The great stimulus for the profession of national coaching was the Wolfenden Report of 1960.[1] The map it drew for sport development was, and is, a very impressive one, and it could still be studied fruitfully; the vital clauses relating to coaching were as follows:

> 'We should like to see coaching opportunities in this country im-
> proved and extended . . . When a Governing Body decides to
> support a coaching scheme, it should regard the appointment of
> national coaches as the key to the scheme. Preferably these coaches
> should be individuals who have experienced top class competition
> and also had some relevant academic or professional training . . .
> Because in our view, 'national coaches' are the vital key to a scheme,
> they should command a range of salary and prospects comparable
> with those of training college lecturers.'

On the basis of that plan, coaches were appointed, sustained by grant aid from government through the Central Council for Physical Recreation. Governing bodies of sport had to support the innovation, but, it has to be admitted, were more interested in the money than in the proposed coaching service. So they appropriated the government grant and sent the national coach off round the country purveying pearls of dubious wisdom.

The general response was very mixed. The conservative sports-people did not want to be organised, did not want to think about different ways of doing things. Others seized the opportunity with great excitement; they saw the national coach as the peripatetic salesman of freedom, the excuse to cast off the crippling restrictions of musty custom. The coach had somehow to cope with all these responses. He/she was himself experimenting with teaching methods of all kinds, some lifted straight out of textbooks, some derived from personal experience. Some inspirations failed miserably, but others developed into success stories. These were demonstrated at governing bodies' technical conferences, and at BANC conferences. Heads were shaken in disbelief at what was happening. The coaches seemed to be attacking viciously the tried and true methods of long-established sport tradition. They were iconoclastic, destructive. Hubris would surely bring them down!

The critics of the national coaches did not appreciate the mental traumas coaches themselves were suffering. They had their doubts, too. Were they doing the right thing, they asked themselves? Like their critics, they had been nurtured in the schools of rigid technicality: either you performed a technique correctly, or you were wrong. There was no equivocation: if you modified the historical model, for whatever reason, it was incorrect. But experience had suggested to coaches that there must be other ways of learning complex skills; now they were encouraging the novice to devise his/her *own way* of doing things. The coach was there to help when necessary, but the onus of learning was thrown heavily on the performer.

It was a coaching revolution. Governing bodies could see nothing but heresy and anarchy, which made them think that their earlier suspicions of the scheme were justified. The 'establishment' reacted. Several top national coaches were pushed out of their jobs – because they were too avant-garde and too successful. Some of the amateur bodies could not, would not, see what the national coaches were trying to do. An ossified tradition was limiting development. The coaches were trying to cut through constraints and allow a whole new phase of development to begin, a phase encouraging individual growth and the expression of trained spontaneity. They were trying to show that coaching not only could but should go beyond the implanting of ever better physical skills and teach an improved understanding of life through those skills.

Was it surprising, therefore, when in those early days BANC was accused of being a trade union, a trouble-maker? It was accused of threatening to provoke labour problems. The Wolfenden Report had stated that national coaches should be paid well – they certainly were not, so that would be BANC's excuse for action. It was imagined that somehow BANC intended to overthrow the sport 'establishment' and undermine the status quo. The administrators could not see that national coaches were actually trying to strengthen the position of governing bodies by making sport a more influential part of society. (Some administrators have now admitted that they made misjudgements in those early days and wish things could have been different.)

Although progress was slow, BANC was moving forward. In addition to help from some generous altruistic small patrons, BANC's aspirations attracted a major sponsor, Adidas, in 1976. Its very generous contribution enabled BANC to have a semi-professional office administration under the cautious eye of John Crooke, then honorary general secretary. Services to the membership were improved and the annual conference enlarged to encompass a greater number of authoritative speakers. This expansion gave rise to a paradoxical problem. How do you organise a specialist to deliver information to a group of specialists who know more about the specialism than the specialist? It is a problem unique in education.

By the end of the 1970s the Sports Council recognised the need to construct a national educational scheme for coaches. As a first step, it gave some grant aid to BANC to improve further its organisational and advisory capacity, and to increase its coach education programme. In reply, BANC, as well as thanking the Sports Council, suggested there should be some form of national agency that would underpin a nation-wide coach education programme. Eventually the Council accepted the notion and asked BANC to draft plans. BANC set up its own small research programme to look into the suitability of educational institutes undertaking the education of coaches. The results were not encouraging. Institute lecturers did not appear to be able to modify their approach to suit the type of student they would then have to face. Coaches would have to be their own coaches. Academic knowledge would need to supplement, not dominate, pragmatic experience.

During this incubation period, the Southern Region of the Sports Council wanted to start up its own regional coach education scheme. It contacted BANC's executive secretary and invited him to join its discussions on how such a scheme could be implemented. During debate he produced a concept containing two major elements: one was the 'market stall' approach to direct teaching (Figure 1), the other a nuclear model of educational institutes to service that market stall. (See Figure 2.)

Traditional education dictated that the promulgating agency would decide the subjects to be learned and the students would learn them. Students were not asked what they wanted or needed – they were simply told. The market stall approach declared that the agency would supply a whole range of subjects related to coaching, and the 'student' (the coach) would be allowed to select whatever he/she wanted. The various educational institutes within the orbit of the local agency (the Regional Sports Councils) would be contacted and invited to provide the presentation of the subjects – *in the form the coach needed*. It was a very revolutionary approach to coach education and well within the short tradition of BANC.

The concept was accepted with some hesitation. Not only did it assume that the coach had sufficient knowledge to choose, but it would demand a fiendish amount of work to organise it all. Thanks to the great enthusiasm and dedication of David Dolman of the Sports Council's Southern Region, it did all come about, and with great success.

Meanwhile, BANC was rallying its resources to supply a draft plan for what it was calling a National Coaching Unit: a unit because it was seen as having some kind of organisational attachment to the Sports Council, but operated by BANC. The research carried out by BANC agreed with the successful scheme of the Council's Southern Region, so the concepts provided by the executive secretary of BANC for the

Figure 1.1 *A National and Regional Plan for Coach Training*
A 'market stall' approach

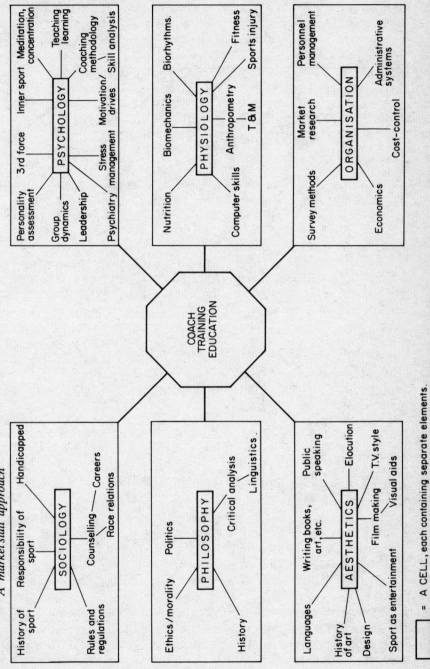

= A CELL, each containing separate elements.

A PACKAGE = 10 elements composed of :— 1 element from each cell and up to a maximum of 4 from any one cell to make up the total

Devised by G.R.Gleeson, April 1982

Figure 1.2 *A National Coach Education Grid*

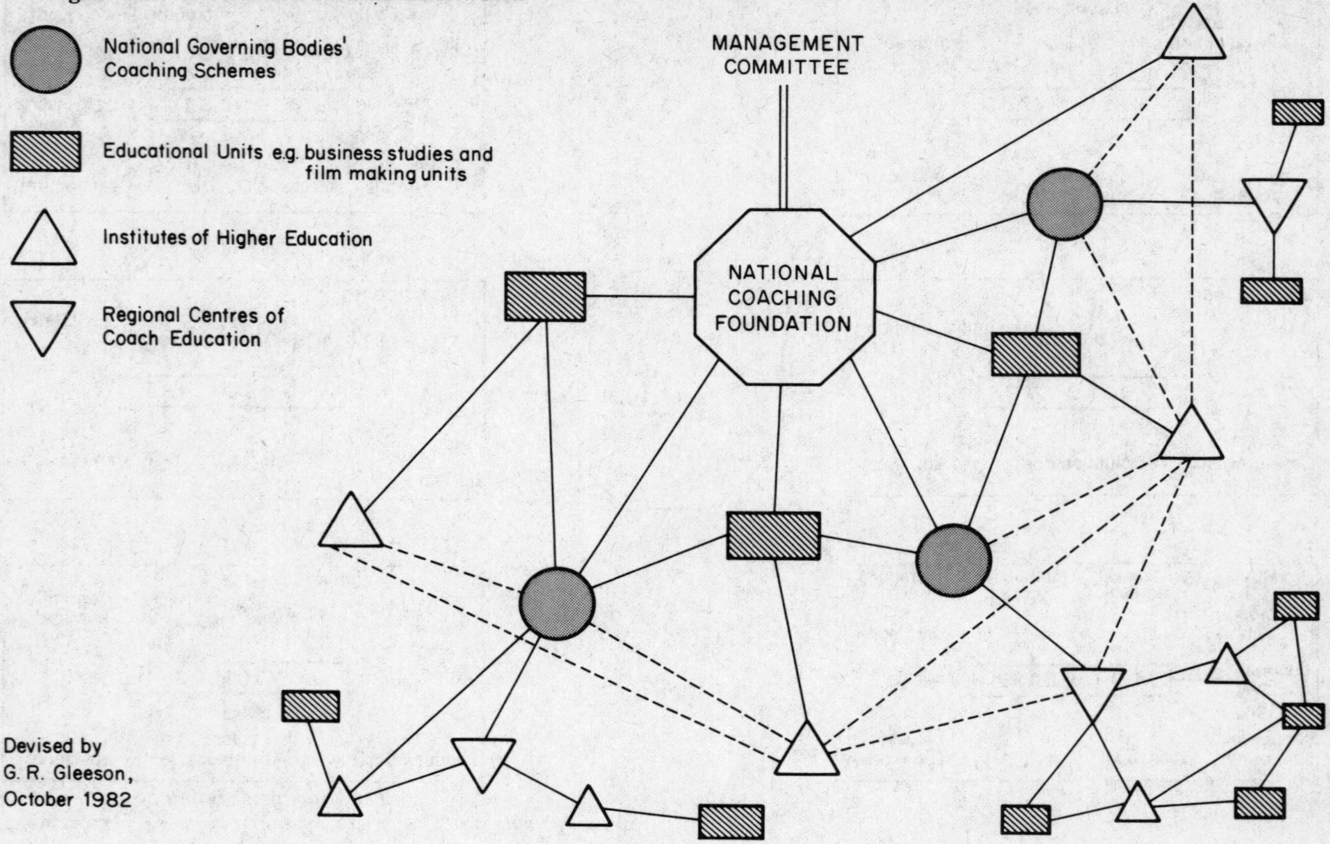

MANAGEMENT COMMITTEE

NATIONAL COACHING FOUNDATION

National Governing Bodies' Coaching Schemes

Educational Units e.g. business studies and film making units

Institutes of Higher Education

Regional Centres of Coach Education

Devised by
G. R. Gleeson,
October 1982

Southern Region became the main thrust of its suggested development to the Sports Council.

Subsequently, in conjunction with the Sports Council, BANC held a one-day seminar at Bisham Abbey National Sports Centre (19 October 1982). The audience comprised coaches of many different sports, teachers and lecturers in physical education, sports administrators, and others with close attachments to sport. BANC's scheme, consisting of the market stall and network structures, was outlined and explained to the delegates. Discussion followed, and subsequently the whole scheme was accepted unanimously, a proud moment for BANC.

The Sports Council decided that the coaching agency should have independent charitable status, so it was called The National Coaching Foundation (NCF). The Bisham Abbey agreement was adopted totally as the servicing structure of the Foundation. Since that time BANC and the NCF have worked very closely together.

How the International Congress came about

This brief history of BANC has been biased towards its innovatory capability. It has shown how the coaches who make up BANC cannot only initiate concepts and schemes within their own sports, but can also produce plans that embrace nation-wide developments.

To some people, this may come as something of a surprise. For them, the word 'coach' suggests a little subservient man in well-worn sports kit or old raincoat standing on the edge of track or field, making occasional incomprehensible gestures or mumbling shamanistic slogans. Perhaps coaches of that type once existed in days when sportspeople were not expected to know or even care what they were doing. Gradually it was realised that the coach did know what he was doing, and that was to win. Yet to train for winning was unsporting, and so the coach became an object of condescension. (A sport worth doing was worth doing badly – well, why not?) 'Winning is not everything, it is the only thing' became the slogan; some coaches and administrators reluctantly admitted adherence to the spirit of the slogan, and at one point the Sports Council even considered bringing coaches in from overseas, to be paid large salaries – but on results. BANC was much opposed to this idea: it would disembowel home-grown coaching schemes and do British coaching a great disservice, and it would threaten the whole ethical structure of sport. If winning was so important, it would be easy enough to cut corners for the sake of victory. Morality in sport could become obsolete. BANC's concern was for the wider issues in coaching and sport.

After the 1972 Olympic Games, those BANC members who were also Olympic coaches were very disturbed and concerned about the use

of drugs amongst the world's top athletes. The Council of BANC
called a one-day seminar on drug abuse at the Holme Pierrepoint
Water Sports Centre very soon after the Games had ended. The matter
was debated at great length and finally a statement was drawn up. This
statement was circulated to all major sports organisations – International Olympic Committee, British Olympic Committee, Sports
Council, Central Council for Physical Recreation, and so on. For the
sake of the record it has been included here.

DOPING AND SPORT

1 Sport without fairplay is not sport and honours won without
  fairplay can have no real value.

2 Methods of enforcement of doping laws must be given priority.
  Long before steroid detection tests had been devised it was
  possible for international federations to decide upon methods of
  enforcement. Their failure to do so must cast serious doubt on
  their will to rigorously apply whatever tests are ultimately devised. Punishment must be immediate and severe if doping is not
  to become a way of life in international sport.

3 Sports Council should advise national bodies to press for a
  standing international doping research unit, so that federations
  can be level or ahead of pharmacological developments.

4 Sports Council should put it to governing bodies that if the
  problem of doping proves insoluble grant aid to international
  sport will be discontinued, as this would, in effect, be government
  subsidy of British involvement in corrupt competition. Sports
  Council should press governing bodies towards opting out of
  polluted international competition, therefore, in effect, opting
  into fairplay.

The statement was signed by Tom McNab, then chairman of BANC,
and was issued to the press. It was the first public statement by a sports
organisation against the use of drugs. Unfortunately, it received very
little attention from the established sports organisations for it talked
about things that were best not talked about. It was uncomfortable.
Ignore it! But the drugs problem did not go away. If BANC's statement
had been heeded then, when the problem was small enough to handle
easily, perhaps something could have been done. Now it is taking
massive international sports legislation even to hold it in check.
    Some coaches, like many practical people, have an odd antipathy
towards the word 'philosophy'. They seem to imagine that it is all to do
with time-wasting abstraction, divorced from the real business of
living. This is odd, because, as the examples above show, they themselves are very practical philosophers. They have not turned their

backs on social obligations; they have given much thought to what is their role in both sport and society and then have acted upon their conclusions. If that is not the best example of true philosophy, what is?

The Wolfenden Report stated as long ago as 1960 that the national coach must be responsible for the national coaching scheme. The coach is called upon to mould the three elements recommended in the Report into a comprehensive, workable and acceptable package (with particular emphasis on the word *acceptable*). Since that time, many coaches have converted that final statement into a practical training system. The three elements are:

1 the analysis of skills;
2 the human function;
3 'an attitude of mind which sees sport as one aspect of human activity and while according it all the admiration and enthusiasm which it can at times so richly deserve, nevertheless recognises its limitations as well as its values'.

Of course, architects of such schemes must have a philosophy, so why do some coaches deride it so? Is it because they are afraid to be seen spreading their concern too widely? As it is, they must look at their sport from a social perspective, both for what happens within it and for how it relates to the community surrounding it. Emerging from those social considerations there is a concern for children. Not only are children the present future of sport, they are frequently the present now of sport – to say nothing of the future past, which is the culture of a nation. Educate the child, educate the adult.

So what kind of people are national coaches? They all do the same job, but every one of them is different. Their duties are many and various, the range being contingent on the history of the sport and the sum total of all those expectations generated by the people who have dominated that sport since the beginning. They may or may not run national squads, they may or may not train children, but they will be fully aware of the needs of those two extremes of their caring responsibilities. When the coach comes to deal with children, his/her professional perspicacity will ensure that he will learn to understand them because that is the way he works. He/she may begin by treating them as small adults, but he will soon discover that this is what they are not. They are different, each is unique. They have their own standards and their own values, but these are fragile because they are not supported by experience. Children are therefore susceptible to manipulation by adults who claim they know better because of their experience. Such people, if sincere, are foolish; if conniving, are vandals.

Some coaches, certainly the coaches on the council of BANC, are very aware of the dangers implicit in the seemingly altruistic training of young children. They know how the enthusiastic support of the parents is converted into fanatical bullying of their own and other people's children; they know how the care of the protective teacher becomes the ego trip of the school impresario, how the knowledge of the coach becomes the dictatorship of the puppet-master. Therefore, when discussing with the councillors of the City of Birmingham in 1984 how that city could benefit sport, BANC suggested the possibility of holding there a major international congress on the subject of children in sport. The City of Birmingham thought it was an exclent idea and agreed to support it. A deal was made, and a title created: 'The Growing Child in Competitive Sport'.

The Organisation of the Congress

In a project of this size there were many political and financial matters to resolve. The most challenging question was the programme itself. First, it was decided to have a four-day event. Any longer, and the whole conference would become tedious no matter what the quality; any shorter and the necessary ground could not be covered. A small organising group was set up – how would it function? Would the group plan all four days, or would one person plan and organise one day? The latter approach was adopted as being the most effective. The small group became a four-person organising team; a theme was set for each day and each member chose a theme to organise. There was a theme behind the themes: the congress was to expose the many problems of children in sport, and to do this in the most original way possible. That would be in the revolutionary tradition of BANC.

The final programme was as follows:

DAY 1   Performance and Preparation
         Organiser: Frank Dick, Chairman of BANC; Director of Coaching, British Amateur Athletic Board

DAY 2   Clinical Implications
         Organiser: John Atkinson, member of BANC; Director of Coaching, British Amateur Gymnastic Association

DAY 3   Selection and Utilisation of Talent
         Organiser: Geof Gleeson, Executive Secretary, BANC, and a founder-member

DAY 4   Youth Sport and Social Aspects
         Organiser: Alma Thomas, member of BANC; Head of the School of Human Movement Studies, Bedford College of Higher Education

Every planner approached his or her day with vision and interest.

The first day revolved around athletics, with Professor Keith Russell from Canada making a strong link between the first two days through the theme of preparation and overuse. Day 2 focused tightly on flexibility and overuse, both causes of concern in the world of gymnastics in particular. Dr Per Renstrom of Sweden gave an overview of youth and damage in sport. The third organiser likes to link the performing arts with sport, so the day did just that. The last day was almost given over to the child study unit at Bedford College of Higher Education, with an excellent 'flyer' in the person of Dr Glyn Roberts from the University of Illinois.

Each day raised its own peculiar points of controversy, but perhaps the third day was the most questionable. Some asked the obvious question: what were the performing arts doing in a sports congress? Others found these sessions the most illuminating of the whole congress. The similarity between sport and art is always a fascinating topic. Is sport art? If I say sport is art, then sport is art; who is to disagree? Most coaches would accept that, for when it comes to teasing a world performance out of an individual then coaching certainly is an art. However, when they want to measure or quantify a part of a performance, coaches will just as quickly confirm that sport is a science.

Kandinsky wrote much about form and content, concepts that are very close to the coach's line of business. When coaching, where does form take precedent over content – and vice versa? Matisse was concerned with line and hence with drawing. He proposed that the skill of drawing (the technique of doing) is essential for the developing artist (coach). Yet paradoxically he quotes, and fully approves of, the dying Toulouse-Lautrec, who said, 'At last, I do not know how to draw any more.' Is it not the same with the coach? He starts with line, technique, knowing that it is all-important, but then realises, after much application, that he no longer needs it. The coach and the artist have much in common; they should talk to each other more.

Matisse recognised the obvious danger that coaches recognise. 'I fear, therefore, that the painter who risks himself in the field of the literary man may be regarded with disapproval; in any case, I myself am fully convinced that the best explanation an artist can give of his aims and ability is afforded by his work' – and a coach, by the performance he or she produces.

The safeguard against this danger, he added, is the talent of the creative painter, and a comparison can be made with the talent of the creative coach. If talent is there, it will emerge in a creative performance. The coach's job is to recognise that talent. For that reason the performing arts were discussed during the Birmingham Congress: to offer an alternative approach to the skill of talent-spotting, which is an essential skill for any creative teacher. The search for talent in art has had a much longer history than in sport. If coaching is an art, and who can doubt this, the coach must absorb himself (herself) in many art forms in order to discover the diversity of creative talent and how to recognise it.

The coach needs to be a person of many parts. No wonder that Plato would not have the artist in his Utopia. He is too curious, too sceptical, too perceptive – in short, a very uncomfortable person to have around. The same should apply to the coach, but regrettably it is not always so. Too often he or she is quite prepared to accept hand-me-down platitudes and coaching clichés of the utmost banality – mere reflectors of untutored taste. What is needed is sport Dadaism!

The afternoon of that third day was an attempt to look at another form of talent selection. Whereas the morning had dealt with how to squeeze talent out of the individual by the individual, the afternoon was to do with talent being expressed through a group facility. The Birmingham Athletic Institute is a very well-provisioned sport and recreational centre, built in the middle of a massive urban development. Its purpose is magnetic – to draw all the unattached people with leisure into its many activities. Once in, individuals seem to coagulate into specific, goal-centred groups, groups that will allow the individual's own particular talent to blossom.

In this situation, the coach has to concentrate on the group and ensure that it provides the right kind of opportunity for the individual to express his or her talent so that it benefits the person, the group, and the community of which all are a part. Such an approach to talent development has many singular problems, and the various groups visited in the Birmingham Athletic Institute demonstrated both some of the problems and some of the solutions.

The Finale – the Opening!

On the opening day there were delegates from many parts of the world and from all over the United Kingdom. First came the welcoming banquet, and then talk, talk and more talk, into the early hours of each successive day. The speakers were sensible, provocative and worried – worried about the future of young children in highly competitive sport. At the risk of gross misrepresentation, perhaps their concern could be summed up in the four following sentences:

1 Do not let children specialise too young – certainly not before puberty.
2 Train children for life, not just for sport.
3 Beware of overuse: children's structures are not intended to have 50 years of heavy exercises thrust upon them in no more than five years.
4 Beware of complacent leaders, be they parents, teachers, coaches, or administrators – there is a difference between an open mind and a hole in the head!

No doubt the many and varied problems and concerns regarding children in competitive sport had existed before the BANC Congress: concern that generated much discussion in corners, and in rooms, throughout the physical education world and beyond. But the BANC Congress focused that concern and brought it under the bright light of organised public debate. Since the winter of 1985–6, many organisations have set up their own investigatory committees, the direct descendants of the International Congress. The Sports Council has a group involved with the problem of children in sport; the Physical Education Association has a committee looking at the implications for the teaching profession; the Central Council for Physical Recreation has a special group looking into the same problem; and the National Association for School Sport is adding its effort to analyse what is happening to children in schools.

So we in BANC feel we have achieved much in organising this International Congress which has initiated such a considerable amount of effort. We are proud of it. Not only have we uncovered much information about children in sport, but now we have started an organised investigation into the exploitation of children in competitive sport. That must be a good thing. It will be interesting to see what emerges from these developments.

Reference

1   CENTRAL COUNCIL FOR PHYSICAL RECREATION (1960) *Sport and the Community. The Report of the Wolfenden Committee on Sport.* London: Central Council for Physical Recreation.

Training

2

Training Theory and the Young Athlete

F. W. Dick

This chapter introduces the theme of the growing child in competitive sport and discusses key areas of training theory as they apply to such children.

I Competitive Sport and the Growing Child

At the Los Angeles Olympics in 1984, almost 30% of track and field athletes were 20 years of age or less. In some sports, the percentage of Olympians under 21 years was even higher. This means that preparation for competition at the highest level is starting for many athletes in their early teens.

Clearly, such preparation is successful in pursuit of short- and medium-term objectives. Many of these athletes achieve high standards of performance, reaching finals or even the victory rostrum. This suggests that growing children can accept training loads compatible with performances required for success at world level.

For some athletes, Los Angeles was their first Olympic competition and their preparation was part of a programme for long-term objectives. For others, Los Angeles was their only Olympic competition. Whilst several factors could contribute to a falling-off of interest, or a drop in performance, there are athletes in this one-off group whose preparation was married to expediency. This underlines how readily both sport and children can be abused by the over-ambitious and the irresponsible.

The growing child is easily motivated in the early years, and the gifted young athlete has in several sports many advantages over older competitors. What fertile territory for national and commercial ambition to reap a rich harvest, and for the dreams of athletes, coaches and parents to be accelerated towards reality.

The situation begs question of personal and social ethics; it brings into critical focus the knowledge and experience of coaches in working with young people; it demands extraordinary maturity in interpretation of perspective; and throws into stark relief the true dimension of accepting responsibility for coaching the growing child.

This work looks at several threads in the broad tapestry of this fascinating and sensitive theme. The authors present authoritative commentaries of quite outstanding quality, suggesting codes of practice on the one hand and a basis for a youth policy review on the other.

Because the focus of a youth programme must vary according to the demands of each sport, it is inappropriate that coverage should be confined to a specific age group. Rather, age groups are referred to as occasion requires, and, wherever possible, principles are advanced for interpretation according to the needs of each individual coach's athletes and sport.

Without doubt, there are problems for the coach when working with the growing child. These must be drawn out into the open and discussed. Our role, however, must not stop at identifying problems or proclaiming apparent advantages and disadvantages of our respective situations. We must look to solutions, and to recommendations for a future course of action. This must be seen in the perspective of these early years as part of the preparation for peak competitive achievement in the third, fourth and even fifth decades of these young people's lives. More than this, these years are preparation for a healthful lifetime of physical activity; for enjoying sport's highest values; and for enhancing the quality of life through participation and involvement.

Sport experience and performance development for school-age children is surely the centre of our thinking here. Each culture affords such experience and development according to its own needs and traditions. In the United Kingdom, school sport has been the vintage vehicle of tradition which has served to meet our needs. However, school sport has failed its MOT and the parts are no longer available to put it back on the road.

We cannot permit this situation to eliminate sport for school-age children. We would be less than responsible if we fail to look at what is a major problem for sport, for children and for physical education in the UK. We must review the contribution of those who have key roles in educating for and through sport. This, in turn, must help colleagues from overseas to review the situation for school-age athletes in their own countries.

The need will be seen as all the more urgent when one considers that the practice of sport as a profession comes in a concentrated early period of life. We gave modern sport and its values to the world. We must look most urgently at how to ensure that our children – our future – also receive that gift; and that it is a gift of the highest quality.

To summarise:

– The growing child can accept loadings compatible with success at the highest level in sport.

– This acceptance *can* be abused, damaging children and the development of sport.

- On the other hand, this acceptance can be the first stage in development towards competitive achievement in adult years, and healthful activity throughout life.

- Topics ranging from coaching in practice, through clinical implications, to talent selection and the social aspects of sport will be examined here, with a view to recommending a future course of action for policy and practice in coaching the growing child.

- Education for and through sport must now be reviewed in the UK in terms of shared responsibility by schools (education) and clubs (governing bodies and local community).

II   Training Theory and the Growing Child

Each sport has its own starting point for age-group development. For example, track and field athletics might be considered as having four broad age-range divisions as athletes proceed from 'cradle to gravy'!

Age	Focus	Examples of Planning Emphases
8–13	Participation	Introduction to techniques Performance-oriented Enjoyment
14–15 to 16	Preparation	Link with coach/club Performance/result-oriented Routine/discipline – enjoyment
16, 17–18 to 19	Competition	Key competition experience Result/performance-oriented Commitment
19 to 20–22	Monitoring/ competition	Junior–Senior bridging Result/performance-orientated Management – commitment

This said, it should be pointed out that, irrespective of starting point or numbers of divisions in progression, there are several common problems. These we should consider under six topic headings.

1   Motivational Climate

Success in an age-group is normally due to high ability and talent levels and the athlete's premature receptiveness to training compared with his/her peers. There is little problem in creating a good climate of motivation for this athlete. Achievement levels are high, failures are negligible. These athletes have not had to develop resilience to defeat.

The slightly lower-ranked athletes in this age-group are normally less gifted in terms of ability and talent. They will train hard and may or may not gain maximum value from training. They have worked to help create a good climate of motivation, developing substantial resilience to defeat.

The scenario for these two distinct sections within a given age-group is quite different as athletes progress from this to subsequent older age-groups till they eventually achieve Senior/Open status. Resilience to defeat and with it a determination to succeed next time has increasing significance in establishing a positive – winning – motivational climate.

The early achievers may have problems as their 'wanting to win' attitude slips towards 'not wanting to lose'.

Age-group high fliers must have their achievements played down or put in perspective. A balance of win–loss situations is critical in order to afford opportunities for learning how to handle the pursuit of competitive advantage in subsequent age-groups, and eventually in the Senior arena. The balance clearly must be positive, but little advance will be made towards creating the *right* individual climate if the athlete has no experience of the negative side. There are pointers here for structuring competition programmes.

2   Recovery

Growing is a very exhausting business! There is an immense drain on energy resources as the athlete adapts to the stresses of growing and of the tempest of change he or she experiences and causes. This puts a different perspective on the cumulative effect of training on young people compared with senior/adult athletes. It becomes more relevant to consider the cumulative effect of training and life-style.

The coach must therefore consider carefully the structures of loading and 'training ratios' used. To be more specific, the coach must review the *recovery* portion of the load. The stimulus itself is seldom an area of concern.

'Recovery' embraces all those vehicles available to enhance the residual and cumulative effects of training. They include:

- *Activity* (e.g. jogging, walking, lying down, reduced intensity version of the stimulus, etc.)
- *Unit* (e.g. psycho-regulative general training, etc.)
- *Physical Application* (e.g. massage, sauna, hydrotherapy, etc.)
- *Environment* (e.g. climatic, aesthetic, etc.)

Training microcycles must include, as an essential feature when working with growing children, more recovery at all points in the year plan, and more recovery within units, compared with adult programmes. This may be interpreted as shorter but more units in a weekly microcycle.

3   Balance

Pursuit of results in the short-term of a given season demands specificity of training to a very high level. This must result in biased loading of
the athlete both structurally and functionally. Of course, this is bad
irrespective of an athlete's age, but during the growing years the
damage can be so severe as to expunge all hope of achieving long-term
objectives.

Loading in these years must lean towards the general, the all-round,
the balanced. Whilst this will in all probability inhibit the athlete in
producing maximum performance in the growing years, it will ensure
that the right foundation exists for the pursuit of exceptional maximum
performance in the long-term. The problem, then, becomes one of
motivation through these years. How the coach defines achievements
and projects a winning motivational environment will solve the problem – or render it beyond solution!

The responsible coach of the growing child must be sure in his or her
mind that the athlete is performing within potential maximum. There
must always be confidence that in the preparation programme this or
that specific avenue is yet to be fully explored. The question to which
the coach must know the answer is: 'What is the final objective of the
programme when the athlete is at maturity?' If you do not know your
destination, how can you plan your journey?

4   Energy

Energy training programmes might be considered under two broad
headings:

(a) Training to *produce* energy (e.g. endurance training)

(b) Training to *express* energy (e.g. strength, technique and mobility
training)

It is an unfortunate fact that many coaches focus the programme for
young athletes more on the production side than is necessary. Concentration on endurance development can and should wait till late teens at
the earliest. Range of movement in all joint actions, all-round balanced strength, and sound basic technical models executed at progressing speed but within the limits of technical stability, are more the
order of these days. *Endurance* training is necessary only to a level
which will permit adequate numbers of repetitions for sound technical
models to be developed. *Strength* development systems should look to
body weight work and light resistance work, with weight-training
being introduced, if at all, late in the teens.

The challenge to the coach of creating strength systems for the
growing athlete is severe, and will demand much thought and inven-

tiveness. A growing catalogue of exercises must be worked on, with the coach following the simple rule that progression is in one of three directions (or a combination of them): resistance (strength); duration/repetitions (endurance); speed.

Technique training is the central feature of the growing child's programme. The conditioning aspects are geared to avoiding any compensatory features.

Speed might be considered as a sophistication of technique, or as a progression of basic technique.

Mobility must be worked on to ensure that range of movement is not a limiting factor to sound technique, or prelude to injury. But what of endurance-based events or sports? Selection for these events should not be based on endurance in early teens, nor should sports afford endurance competitions at the longer adult distances. The temptation then would be to train for endurance development to ensure selection. This would not normally be a satisfactory basis for progression. Again, energy expression rather than production must be the starting point. Endurance training and competition for the growing child should be enjoyable over distances which do not test endurance capabilities to the extreme.

5   Ebb and Flow

'Adaptation–Application–Recuperation' – this rhythm must commence in the growing years at the microcycle and macrocycle or training phase level. It must be married to the concept of alternation between *accelerated progress* and *building stability*. Performance progression should not be conceived as a linear affair. Achievement of maximum results at Senior level requires that progress to this point is achieved in a series of jumps. The coach must develop a method and system to ensure that this is the case from the outset.

6   Life-style Management

The performance of an athlete in his or her sport is the product of a very complex and unique capsule. That capsule is the athlete's life-style and all the factors which influence that life-style. The coach cannot possibly ignore a responsibility for helping the athlete to establish a clear overview of the capsule and management of its key areas. It rests with the coach to establish perspectives for the athlete in pursuit of sport objectives, by looking not only at how the athlete can express himself or herself totally through a chosen sport, but also how to manage the pursuit of non-sporting objectives. The focus, then, is on the athlete as a person, *not* just as an object in a tracksuit. Inextricably linked to such an approach is the responsibility for creating a winning attitude, for building a positive motivational climate. This of course, brings us back to point 1.

Training theory and the growing child must be viewed as part of an over-all application of training principles from the moment the child is introduced to sport till completion of his or her involvement. Because the growing years can be interpreted in as many ways as there are coaches, by examining several avenues of growth and development, it becomes essential that coaches define clearly the 'growing years territory' for their sports. Having done this, break these years down into stages where clear objectives can be pursued, and build progression through these stages into a national coaching and performance plan. The six topics discussed are each worth exhaustive exploration beyond the scope of this chapter.

3

Strength-training and the Young Athlete

Max Jones

Sport has an increasing influence on our daily lives and its importance to children and parents has increased dramatically. Competitive sport now reaches the very young. Leagues and championships are no longer confined to the late teens. The motivation of winning has brought organised training to the very young and the previously taboo area of strength-training is now likely to be accepted by the enthusiastic coach or parent in order to ensure success. Is this desirable? Are there dangers? Do we modify adult programmes?

Strength-training, whether it is for men, women, or children, follows the same well-tried principles:

1 *Overload* – the muscle must be forced to work hard for the cross-sectional area to increase and for strength to increase with it. Performing light weights easily will not produce strength gains.

2 *Reversibility* – the muscle must be regularly stimulated to ensure strength gains and, by the same token, if that muscle is left unstimulated, strength will be lost.

3 *Specificity* – exercise must be specific to the type of strength required and must therefore be related to the demands of the event.

Can these principles be applied to a very young athlete? A look must be taken at the young physique.

'Lifting heavy weights will stunt your growth'

There is no evidence that this 'old wives' tale' is true – a Soviet study[1] comparing swimmers with weight-lifters in the 14–17 age range found that the growth patterns were the same in both sports. It is true that weight-lifters tend to be shorter, but this is a natural selection process because shorter levers are mechanically more efficient at lifting heavy weights. Tall, thin boys will quickly leave the sport through lack of success.

'Weight-lifting will cause joint injury'

The bones of the young are more elastic, yet have less bending strength than those in the adult skeleton. The effect on bone growth of moderate training is clearly positive, but *excessively* biased loading may have a damaging effect. It is questionable whether weight-training would affect growth as the amount of time spent actually *lifting* weights is calculated at only 0.0011% of a week. Since growth plate damage *may* be caused by overuse, the more rigorous and continuous pastimes of team games may be potentially more dangerous. Recent studies indicate that epiphyseal zones are relatively immune to damage from overuse. However, it still remains to be seen if this sensitive area of children's anatomy remains immune to the increasingly rigorous training to which the young are subjected.

Potentially the spine and related areas are more at risk through heavy lifting as the support given to this complicated structure by the torso muscles is somewhat lacking in the young. Torso strength develops late in the growth cycle and loads carried above the head or on the shoulders may lead to injury if the technique is not correctly performed.

'Strength is for men, not boys'

There seems to be a firm basis for this statement. Research indicates[2] that specific strength can only be effective in post-pubescent age. It is because of the relative absence of the androgenic hormones (male hormones) that little strength gain can be made by the very young. It is interesting to note that in Figure 3.1, whilst the strength of the limbs did not change, torso strength did. This is possibly due to the lack of

Figure 3.1(a) *Percentage of changes in strength after 8 weeks of training*

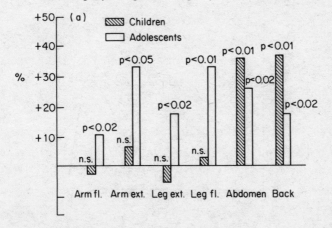

Figure 3.1(b)   *Percentage of changes in muscle surface area after 8 weeks of training*

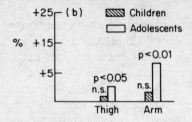

use made of this muscle group by the very young and the stimulus of exercise bringing the torso muscles up to the level of the legs and arms. It highlights the need to strengthen the torso region of the pre-puberty age group in preparation for adult sport.

A 15-year-old has 27% muscle mass as compared to the 44% of a 19-year-old and therefore loadings should be adjusted to take into account the lack of muscle in the young physique.

Figure 3.2   *Mean growth rates (in cm per year)* (Bayley, from *Prader*)

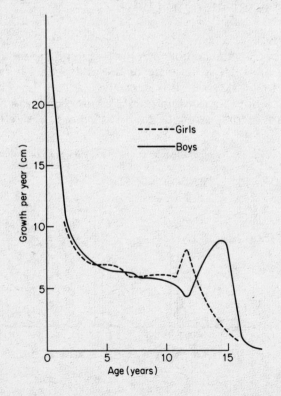

'Strength-training is unsuitable for girls'

Girls develop faster and stop growing earlier (Figure 3.2). They are approximately two years in advance of boys in development and therefore can be introduced to formalised strength-training earlier. Women have narrower shoulders and broader hips than men. Different angles of tendon attachment to, and of muscle alignment with, bone reduces the efficiency of muscle pull and increases injury potential. Strength-training can be introduced in an organised way as soon as a girl finishes her adolescent growth spurt. Strength-training should be progressed more gently than for men. Since girls have a weaker support system and less skeletal muscle mass than boys, the loadings given should reflect this deficiency.

Basic rules

Strength development of young athletes should be based on the established principles of basic training aiming for a many-sided technical and physical development. Specific strength improvement to force the performance level of a particular event is not recommended. The development of strength must fit into the framework of an all-round training procedure and is not to be singled out for preferential attention. Considerable attention in training should be directed at development of those muscles which stabilise the spine on the pelvis (abdominals and lower back) and the rotation of the spine.

Until the growing has stabilised in bone-joint development, it is inadvisable to load the spine when exercising. Unless the athlete has an extensive background of general strength work which has systematically developed the musculature supporting the spine, heavy weights should not be taken on the shoulders or held above the head.

It is essential that all strength exercises are performed correctly and it is therefore essential that competent coaching is given during the early skill-learning phase. The number of exercises attempted should be restricted to ensure that good technique is acquired. In acquiring good technique, it is necessary to embark upon a learning period where the load is light and the repetitions numerous. Initially the strength units should be short in duration with adequate recovery allowed between exercises. This will encourage good exercise technique.

Encourage the routine of warming up for strength work – injuries occur through either lack of warm-up, or incorrect technique, or a combination of both.

Extreme passive mobility or endurance work should not follow an extensive strength work-out as this will increase the possibility of connective tissue injury.

Certain exercises should be avoided when involving the young, growing physique, notably heavy conventional sit-ups or leg raises; deep knee-bending; good morning exercises; jarring work, especially on hard surfaces.

Developing a programme

When considering the design of a programme for an athlete, the coach must think about the type of strength required (elastic, absolute, endurance) and the type of muscle activity (concentric, isometric, eccentric). Before such factors are taken into account, the athlete must go through a period of general strengthening work that will build a base upon with specialised strength work can safely be attempted.

It is a mistake to assume that the only avenue for strength development is the barbell and dumb-bell. The principles of 'overload' can operate in a variety of activities.

Strengthening activities

Weights – the most generally used form of strength work, but heavy weights are generally unsuitable for the sub-16 age group where barbell and dumb-bell work should be limited to *light* technique work.
Multi-gym, or similar apparatus – an excellent lead-in to weight-training with little or no danger of injury and little technique needed. The majority of the stations (exercises) do not involve loading the spine and therefore leg work can be attempted.
Running – spring starts, uphill sprints, harness-work: all develop explosive, elastic strength.
Jumping – a large variety of jumps can be attempted and measured (motivation), but remember that the landing area should have 'give' (e.g. gym mats, grass). Correct technique should be taught.
Depth jumping (plyometrics) – should be avoided by the very young age groups since it places a great load upon the knees. When introduced it should be gradual with heights not exceeding 80 cm and the landing area having 'give' (gym mats).
Bodyweight exercises – old stand-bys such as the press-up and the sit-up are excellent for forming a basis of strength. By increasing/decreasing the leverage, exercises can be progressive. Gymnastic apparatus exercises are very effective strength builders.
Circuit-training – an excellent activity for increasing both fitness and strength. It is an essential part of the development of the young athlete and enables the coach to direct a session for a large group wtih little or no apparatus.
Isometrics – not too relevant to the dynamic sport of athletics. Strengthening in a specific static position may be useful for the mature athlete (e.g. the torso position in the long jump take-off).

Throwing – using shots, medicine balls and so on can provide an enjoyable method of developing explosive strength in the rotational direction.

Phase one

Pre-puberty (under-11 girls, under-12 boys)
The nine to 11 age group can be approached in the same manner for boys and girls, although boys will move to more advanced work a little later than girls.

AIM – all-round strength development in a fun environment.

EXERCISES – mainly partner and bodyweight exercises: pushing/pulling, hopping, climbing, games with light medicine balls, exercises on gymnastic forms, boxes and simple apparatus (Figure 3). The choice of exercises should be varied to avoid boredom, but limited to the extent that exercises must be well performed.

Figure 3.3

FREQUENCY – one strength unit per week (twice per week for advanced youngsters).

PROGRESSION – Callisthenics can be introduced later with single set many repetitions practised. Again, exercises should be correctly performed.

Phase two

12–14 girls, 13–15 boys
Children are moving into a period of growth spurt and it is essential that all-round development is stressed. Emphasis should be placed upon torso development in order that stability is ensured for more advanced/specialised work to follow.

AIM – all-round strength; torso development; good technical model.

METHOD – Sessions previously practised can be continued, but strength circuits can be introduced (Figure 3).

CIRCUITS – In a club/school environment the best method of developing strength in the young athlete is through circuit training. Bodyweight only should be used and the exercises practised and established before putting them into the circuit. The variations of circuit are many and varied and the circuits given are examples taken from *Training Theory* by F. W. Dick (Figure 4) and by Dr Hans-Peter Loffler (GDR) (Figure 5).

Phase three

15–16 girls, 16–17 boys
In this post-puberty period more specialised work can commence, although all-round development is still the key element.

ENDURANCE EVENTS
1st year
Circuits, but with resistance being used. Multi-gyms are excellent for such work because they are safe and exercises are easily learned. No attempt should be made to divert away from general exercises.

2nd year
Progression on to timed circuits to develop strength endurance.

EXPLOSIVE EVENTS
1st year
(i) Using multi-gym the athlete would use a simple set method (3 sets of 10) using basic exercises.
(ii) Barbells and dumb-bells used with light weights, high repetitions (technique emphasised).
(iii) Multiple jumps, bounding.

2nd year
Progression on to conventional weights, but restricted to exercises that *do not* load the spine (see below).
Depth jumping introduced.

Figure 3.4   *Organisation of Circuit and Stage Training*

TESTING OR DOSAGE SETTING

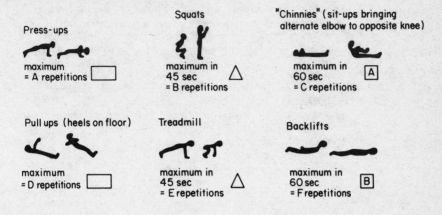

Press-ups

maximum
= A repetitions

Squats

maximum in
45 sec
= B repetitions

"Chinnies" (sit-ups bringing
alternate elbow to opposite knee)

maximum in
60 sec
= C repetitions   A

Pull ups (heels on floor)

maximum
= D repetitions

Treadmill

maximum in
45 sec
= E repetitions

Backlifts

maximum in
60 sec
= F repetitions   B

CIRCUIT TRAINING

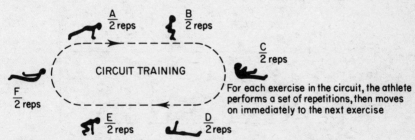

$\frac{A}{2}$ reps $\frac{B}{2}$ reps

$\frac{C}{2}$ reps

CIRCUIT TRAINING

$\frac{F}{2}$ reps

$\frac{E}{2}$ reps $\frac{D}{2}$ reps

For each exercise in the circuit, the athlete
performs a set of repetitions, then moves
on immediately to the next exercise

If more than one circuit is to be attempted then there should be 2 mins recovery
between circuits

Normal number 3-5 circuits

STAGE TRAINING

At each exercise the athlete performs
all sets of repetitions, with 30 sec
recovery between sets then moves on
to the next exercise 'stage'. 30 sec
recovery is taken between stages,
until all are completed

Normal number = 5-10 sets of
repetitions at each stage

Testing or re-setting of dosage should be done at 4 weekly
intervals to ensure progression of training

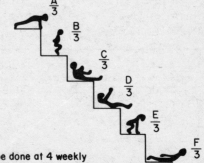

$\frac{A}{3}$

$\frac{B}{3}$

$\frac{C}{3}$

$\frac{D}{3}$

$\frac{E}{3}$

$\frac{F}{3}$

Figure 3.5

1 Double-leg take-off jumps on and off a bench (20 to 40cm) (legs and feet).

2 Knee lifts on a wall ladder (abdominal).

3 Push-ups with feet elevated on a bench (arm extensors).

4 Jumping on and off a gymnastic box (60cm) (leg extensors).

5 Sit-ups into V-position (abdominal).

6 Trunk and arm lifts on a box with feet supported (back).

7 Front support jumps into crouch position and then upwards (complex).

8 Twisting sit-ups with feet supported (abdominal).

9 Double-arm and over head medicine ball throws against the wall from 2.5m (8'2½") distance (shoulders, arms, chest).

10 Double-legged skipping (legs and feet).

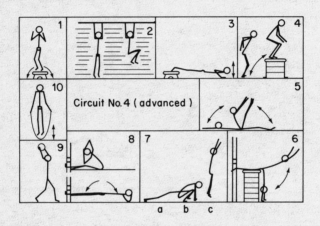

Circuit No. 4 (advanced)

Number of Exercises	Exercise Time (Sec)	Recoveries between exercises (sec) rounds (min)		Total time for	
			2	3	4 rounds
3	15	30 (sec)	3 (min) 6.30	11.15	16.00
4	15	30	3 8.00	13.30	19.00
5	15	30	3 9.30	15.45	22.00
6	15	30	3 11.00	18.00	25.00
7	15	30	3 12.30	20.15	28.00
8	15	30	3 14.00	22.30	31.00
9	15	30	3 15.30	24.45	34.00
10	15	30	3 17.00	27.00	37.00

3rd year
(i) circuits continued – barbells used if weakness is a limiting factor for an athlete.

3rd year
Conventional weights used – spine load-bearing exercises are restricted to high repetitions, fast movement, which limit the amount of weight being used (e.g. 10 reps in 20 sec).

EXAMPLE – PHASE THREE: *Year Two* (explosive events)

	Weight programme		*Effect*
	Power clean	8 – 6 – 6 – 6	(complex – legs/back)
	Bench press	10 – 8 – 6 – 6	(chest/shoulders)
	Dumb-bell jump squat	10 – 10 – 10	(legs)
Super set	Lateral raise	10 – 10	(shoulders)
	Curls	8 – 8	
Super set	Dumb-bell calf raise	15 – 15	
	Hyper raises	10 – 10	
	Partial sit-ups	15 – 15 – 15	
	Leg raises	15 – 15 – 15	

Duration – 50 min/60 min

From the progressions shown an athlete can specialise from this base of firm, all-round conditioning.

References

1 KURACHENKOV, A. I. (1958) 'Deformation of the bones and joints of young sportsmen'. *Physical Culture and Sport* (Moscow).
2 Johnson (1961); Iwanow (1964, 1965); Hebbelinck (1964); Bottger (1964); Bergler (1965); Matthias and Rufung (1966); Szabo (1969); Hollman and Bouchard (1970); Beunen (1972); Vrijens (1978).

4

Endurance Training and the Growing Child

Peter Coe

Introduction

This chapter on endurance training could be seen as giving more reasons against training the young for endurance than for pursuing a course of training for that particular purpose. I have always been aware that it is so much easier to fail than to succeed; although I have always sought the major share of the spoils of victory for my athlete – and his record shows just that – these 17 long years of dedication to this task have not been without set-backs, such as illness, or accidental traumatic injury (not necessarily the fault of coach or athlete).

As a coach, my thought is always to preserve the athlete. No method of training for stamina is likely to be the last word on the subject, but it is incontrovertible that injured athletes cannot train properly. In Sebastian Coe's own words, 'The single most important element in training is consistency.' Without this, all other efforts are seriously reduced. Programmes of training may differ, but without consistency no athlete will ever reach the top.

Talent is a very delicate quality; it does not flower without careful nurturing. Having athletic talent does not necessarily mean being able to deliver *the performance* now. It is much safer to consider talent as the ability to produce great performances later. Unlike music or chess, in athletics there are no equivalents of child prodigies or juvenile grand masters. A great achievement in athletics is directly related to the physical status of the performer. In sport, sufficient time must be allowed for youngsters to develop the whole body to the standard of fitness necessary for top-level performances.

A holistic approach is necessary, not only to keep the limbs and the agonistic and antagonistic muscles in balance, but also to develop the mind to cope with the mental pressures of high-level competition. It is only in the hothouse atmosphere of big events and championships that this talent can be developed, honed and proven.

Elsewhere I have frequently stressed that good coaching has a large management content. Wasting your principal assets for a quick profit or a short-term gain is a sure and speedy road to bankruptcy. A good manager exploits his assets carefully for the future; he does not consume them as fast as he can and take stupid risks.

For young athletes, the prime requirement is good coaching while the whole organism is allowed to mature. Remember that, while loading promotes growth, overloading not only stunts growth but may even deform. Even today, despite the triumphs of my own athletes and the personal satisfaction I have derived from them, for me the words 'Endurance Training' have a cold iron ring about them.

Collins's *English Dictionary* defines *endure* as '. . . to undergo hardship, strain, privation without yielding', and *endurance* as the 'capacity, state of enduring'. Enough, you might be forgiven for thinking, to get the young person put into care. So what do I mean by endurance training for the young athlete and to which actual age group am I referring?

I am talking about young athletes between 12 and 16 years of age. Before I break these years down into two separate periods, consider this Seb Coe story. In my search for the speed element in speed endurance it became very clear that his very slight physique *demanded* weight training to develop the strength needed to generate the power required for a fast 400 metres time. But, *before* he started weight training, he did a lot of conditioning work to get him strong enough to handle the weights! In other words, he was *prepared in advance* for the change in his training, which is only an extension of common sense practice in other areas – for example, not making sudden increases in mileage, or racing in untried shoes. In physical training, as in so many other areas, change in itself is not harmful, it is often needed. The danger lies in the *rate* of change. Please note: this careful approach was necessary not at 12, 14, or 16 but at *19 years* of age.

Similarly, it is much wiser to prepare the young person for endurance training than it is to launch him or her suddenly into heavy mileage or hard tempo training.

I realise that not all young people mature at the same rate, and that some may safely absorb a somewhat heavier training load than others, but it is not only the level of physical development that is important. Mental toughness and resilience are also required and these must be developed in parallel with their physical development. Endurance demands as much concentration as the more technical elements of sport, and for longer periods. It is only the foundation for endurance training you can safely attempt to put down in the early years between 12 and 14. Not until 15 and 16 should endurance in the middle distance sense be commenced, and then with care.

Successful athletes are not so unique that they do not conform to some of the statistical means of their events. They may represent a deviation from the mean in height, or in weight, but not in every way. They will conform mainly to the means of their adult peer group and any coach will be well advised to consider the statistics for the event –

the most important being, I believe, the age at which the top ten achieve their best performances. To argue from the particular to the general is very risky, but, as I am using the early training schedules of Sebastian Coe as examples of the softer approach to endurance training, it is fair to point out that he too conforms to, more than he differs from, the top ten.

Consider for a moment the average age of the best male 800/1500 metres runners. The average age is around 24 years at the time they produced their best performances, and this figure also applies to Olympic finalists in middle distance events. Thus we are talking about keeping a 12-year-old in the sport for another 12 years – that is, half his lifetime when he is at his best! Just think, 12 long years in a sport like middle distance running where the greatest risk is an over-use injury!

Seb joined the Hallamshire Harriers when he was 12 years of age. *Eleven* years later he won his first Olympic Gold Medal. *Twelve* years later he broke the world mile record for the third time. *Fifteen* years later he took the second of his unique two-in-a-row Olympic titles.

But what of the earlier years? As we go back in time we approach the heart of the matter. When still 18 years of age he won a bronze medal in the European Junior Championships on an average of 28 miles per week for that year. (The winner, although one year younger, was already on 70 miles per week but he never made it to the top although he is still running, in a modest way.) Two years later, in 1977, at the European Indoor Championships, he won the gold at 800 metres and followed this up in 1978 with a bronze medal at 800 metres in the European Championships in Prague – still only averaging 35 miles per week. Not until the winter of 1979, in the course of his 1980 Olympic build-up, did he get into higher mileages for the winter months (65 to 75 mpw).

It does beg the question: where do they go and what happens to all the young National and World age-best record holders? I think they are simply worn out too soon. When talking of physical maturity, particularly when discussing girl athletes, it always seems to centre on the onset of puberty – women, they say, mature earlier than men. But do they as athletes? Is this single physiological fact a good guide to real maturity, and is this earlier puberty of any real significance for endurance? It may be for learning skills and techniques and for strength development, but not for endurance. From the sprints to the marathons, just look at the current crop of greats such as Gohr, Koch, Wockel, through to Kazankina, Puica, Decker-Slaney, Waitz and Christiansen, women who have matured and continued to improve – women whose ages are 27, 35 and more! Kazenkina was born in 1951 and had reached the age of 25 before achieving her first big win; then she set about slaughtering the middle distance records.

Compare that with what happened to young Lindsay McDonald. For me she is one of the prime examples of wasted talent. Today,

16-year-olds are not considered as children any more, but in terms of athletic training they most certainly still are. For me, Lindsay stands out as an example not merely of athletics misuse but more of athletic child abuse. What was a small, frail girl doing in a harness, dragging a heavy car tyre around while carrying weights in each hand and shod in heavy pit boots? Not to mention pursuing a training schedule for a four-minute miler! Perhaps what happened to her explains the disappearance of so many of our young wonders. Also over-racing is nearly as destructive as overtraining and would seem to me to account for the eclipse of some of our best young male 800/1500 metres talent in 1985. Thirty to 40 races in a season seems to be their common experience. It is not enough to say that an athlete is out with injury; attention must be given to why and how he or she appeared on the sick list.

In order to keep young athletes in the sport long enough to profit from proper coaching and training and reach their best, I suggest the following rules must be obeyed:

1 Make a careful selection of the intermediate and long-term goals. (See Appendix 1, pages 00–00.)
2 Plan and train to reach those objectives on the *least* amount of work necessary to achieve them.
3 In the early stages of an athletic career, once the objective(s) for that year is achieved, do not seek to push on beyond it, even if it occurs early in the season. Be satisfied.
4 Look for maximum performances only when it is reasonable to suppose the athlete is at his/her best.
5 Keep the young out of too much involvement in highly structured sport.

Between 1979 and 1984 Sebastian Coe broke 12 World records or World bests, and acquired two Olympic Golds and an Olympic record, *without* once appearing on a National or World age-best record list as a boy or youth. He was certainly better than average (or how else would his potential have been recognised?), but his progress was made slowly and safely. By 1979, the date of his first World record, he had been in the sport for 10 years already. The most important aspect of endurance is *endurance in the sport*, simply staying whole long enough to develop your full potential (or, as Woody Allen said, 'Success is 99% just turning up!').

One aspect of coaching the young that must be borne in mind is that, once you commit them to training for competition, then competition is what they are going to need. Do not think that you can start someone off training for running without that child wanting and needing to race. The young person must see an objective which is concrete, rather than always being in a state of preparation for some unspecified date in the distant future. One or two years flash by for adults; for the young it is hard enough to envisage two years on, never mind actually waiting that length of time! As we say, the dog must see the rabbit. The art is to give children enough competition to keep up his or her interest, and the occasional win to maintain credibility in the coach and themselves, yet avoid being drawn into the athletic rat race. This problem is best reduced to manageable proportions by explaining carefully to your young charge why you are approaching his or her training in this fashion.

Training can be broken down into two parts, mental training and physical training. Although these two complementary parts are inextricably woven together, and their interaction one upon the other is complex, for simplicity we can discuss their requirements separately.

Mental conditioning

Mental conditioning should start as soon as training commences. It is necessary to withstand the pressures of the big event. A great danger here is over-racing. Over-racing will either trivialise the event by way of overexposure (not infrequently seen on the international circuit), or, especially in the young, tend to crush athletes under a mental burden with which they are as yet untrained to cope. A firm rule here is to keep the very young out of highly structured sport. Like physical stress, mental stress has to be applied in small amounts so that some degree of immunity can be acquired, otherwise the young athlete breaks down. I firmly believe in the theory that all stressors draw from a common reserve of anti-stressors, and any mental depletion of this reserve will lessen the ability to stand up to physical training. The greatest pressure an athlete will have to withstand is going to the line mentally prepared and staying alert throughout the final of a major championship, though that is not to say that some pre-race tension is not necessary in order to get the adrenalin flowing and the competitive spirit fully aroused.

What should be avoided is unnecessary stress. It is better to have to cope only with the unavoidables rather than the inessentials. Find out as early as possible what upsets the young athlete and if this can be avoided. As an example, when Sebastian first started running, I began to observe the opposition, and the first thing I noticed was their pre-race behaviour. It was their tendency to flock together as if for some mutual comfort, but at the same time to start earnestly discussing, sometimes almost in whispers, the latest exploits, often exaggerated, of their contemporaries – both present and elsewhere. Consequently they often ran the race mentally several times before the actual start, with the result that they became over-nervous, lost confidence and ran poorly.

This was easily avoided by not hanging around the track side. We registered, got Sebastian's numbers and pins, and retreated to a quiet refuge away from the others, not reappearing until the time of the race. He then came to the line rested, warmed up and prepared, only to disappear afterwards as quickly as possible. I soon discovered that if the event involved a lot of travel, the best plan was to arrive early, to allow recovery from the long tiring journey and get in a refreshing sleep. Save for upsetting circadian rhythms, a problem often exaggerated, sleep is ideal. While sleeping, youngsters cannot be worrying and chewing their fingernails. This is a practice Sebastian has always followed and maintained to this day. Yes, he even sleeps before an Olympic final.

The coach needs the young athlete to race occasionally to see how he is progressing and how he is responding to mental and physical conditioning. The athlete needs races to feel he or she is achieving something. A win just now and then keeps hopes and interest alive. Prepare the athlete in advance by showing him (her) your proposed racing programme. This programme should have the minimum number of races that are necessary to progress from one level to another and to reach the goal for the year. Let him understand that competition gets harder the farther he progresses. The sooner he understands the increasing difficulty of competition, the longer he has to learn to live with it and accept it. (See Appendix 2, page 46.)

In the early days, defeat is more common than victory, so there will be plenty of opportunity to learn to overcome the depression of defeat while never, never accepting it totally.

Mere relaxation is not the complete answer to pressure. The contradiction is that the athlete must always be on guard against complacency and being too laid back. His task is to stay aware of anything and everything in a race.

Physical conditioning

Let us begin with a description of the very early training of Sebastian Coe.

In his childhood he lived in rural Warwickshire, and it was very obvious from his earliest years that his greatest enjoyment came from just running wherever and whenever he could. Therefore it did not need much imagination to combine his pleasure in healthy exercise with the enhancement of his already competitive spirit. For example, any errand that he ran, say to a village shop, was always a time trial, and his first words on returning were, 'Was I quicker than last time?' An area much favoured by the family for outings and picnics was crossed by unfenced but gated roads. Seb would enjoy getting out of the car at the beginning of this area to start his 'Tempo Runs'! These consisted of opening the first gate and closing it behind the car, beating the car to the next gate and opening that one in time and so on, quitting when he had had enough. The point of this anecdote is that this kind of encouragement is self-paced by the child, which is usually much safer. I hope it also illustrates the fact that a little imagination goes a long way. There is always some part of any environment that can be exploited. Furthermore, the youngster is exercising/training outside a structured situation. So when he entered into competition in a little inter-school cross-country league at the age of 13, he already had some idea of what it would be like, and he joined, and what is more important stayed, in the sport quite willingly. This early period lasted until he was 12 years of age and naturally included the annual school sports and other school games.

At 12 he became a member of the local club and was joining light training in a group with other boys. He ran in a few handicap sprints for boys from which it was quite apparent that while he had some natural speed he lacked any real strength. The winter season of that year, when he was 13 years old, saw him participating for the first time in a few short legs of road relays and a couple of cross-country races. The idea was that he would profit *next* year from a winter season of cross-country racing to generally improve his strength and stamina, and to get a small foretaste of this type of running would be useful experience.

In the following summer season he raced over a very mixed bag of distances, from 100 metres to 2 miles, for which there was no special training. At this stage of development any attempt at specialising is to be avoided. Just to add extra interest, and by way of variety and experimentation, he started seeing how many points he could score in the 'Five Star' award scheme. (The attraction of this type of award is that it helps to avoid specialisation too early by making runners tackle a field event, while the big, strong, would-be field eventers have to try running.) In fact, for the next two years the racing on cross-country, road and track was as much part of the general light training as the rest of the running.

By now, not only was his naturally competitive spirit truly aroused, but in the summer of 1971, when he was still only 14 years old, he could try to win some boys' titles which I described as 'letting the dog see the rabbit', and which I have already explained as being so necessary for young people's self-esteem. Thus, in the winter of 1970–1, mainly in the Sheffield Schools League, for a period lasting from the middle of September to the beginning of February he was running cross-country races almost weekly. These short races (between 2 and 3 miles, 3–5km) were now very much part of the training and preparation for his first significant season, which was to be on the track. I repeat that this racing was treated strictly as training runs and was never an end in itself. Emphasis was put on the training nature of the runs to avoid the risk of devaluing racing by racing too often. Nevertheless, from the point of view of encouragement and self-esteem, it was a good winter, with some positive indications for the coming summer. On the way to the track season he picked up the Sheffield City, Yorkshire Schools and the Yorkshire County cross-country Championship for Boys. (The first rabbits had been seen – and caught.)

As so often, the best-laid plans can go wrong, and a period of hospitalisation in the middle of June (for dental surgery, not injury, and a secondary infection) spoilt the season, but even so he won the Yorkshire Schools Championship at 1500 metres. The ground work having been laid, his 15th year was a very selective one. By that I mean that the intensity of the training, rather than the quantity, was being stepped up and the number of races drastically cut. Cross-country racing was more than halved, and, while conceding a year in his age group, he was being placed in races with junior athletes in the next age group. The main emphasis in this year was aiming for a good reduction in his personal best times by way of Invitation Races, graded to a high standard, such as those provided over the years by The British Milers Club. Please note that the first increase in the intensity of individual sessions was balanced with a reduction in the mileage.

In an organised sport, its structure and administrators cannot be ignored. One is developing endurance in young athletes so that they may win races. They are trying to win races, presumably in the furtherance of a running career. This means that sooner or later they will have to catch the eye of selectors. Since selectors never have and never will please everybody, one of the ways to gain selection is to come up with a definitive performance which no one can ignore. The earliest age at which this has any significance is at 16 with either an Intermediate English Schools title or a AAA Youth Championship. Although not many of the winners go on to achieve great heights, these events are worth taking seriously, (a) because they are large enough to provide the first experience of the hothouse atmosphere of big competition and big games; and (b) because this will be the first real opportunity of testing the previous winter's stamina build-up, which will have been the earliest that harder endurance training should have been undertaken. The next significant year will be the last year as a Junior athlete, and even this year and the fallow year in between are not yet the time for really hard endurance training.

At the very high level that top athletics has reached today, endurance must not be seen merely as the ability to run for a long distance. It must be seen as the ability to sustain the highest possible speed associated with the event for as long as possible. I seldom use the word endurance alone; when I do, I always mean speed endurance. This is the most demanding element in running and requires sufficient all-round strength and maturity to be achieved and maintained. The pursuit of this demanding and necessary element in training should be left to mature athletes and mere size is not a sufficient indicator on its own.

I maintain that if the coach 'tunes-in' to the athlete, that athlete will prescribe his own training. To this extent, I feel that the break-down between aerobic and anaerobic training suggested by the aerobic/anaerobic content of the race is a good guide. Once the sound early base of general aerobic fitness has been laid down (and for the first year this will not include any speed endurance), the training over the year should follow this guide. Obviously, some sessions will be totally one or the other, and according to the time of year some period will be heavily weighted in either direction, but each full year's training should follow the aerobic/anaerobic breakdown of the event. (See Appendix 3, page 47.)

To test this theory, I went back to the training diaries for when Sebastian was 16 and 18 years old respectively, and broke down the training for those two years into the aerobic/anaerobic content. The results in both cases matched the theoretical division almost exactly. I submit that one random year might be accidental, but that two separated key years represent more than a coincidence (see Appendices 4 and 5, pages 48/49, 50/51. The training schedules that created these figures were not compiled with that theoretical proposition in mind, they were arrived at by my trying to bring the athlete along in balance to achieve the necessary winning condition. They are also offered in support of my contention that high mileages are neither wise nor necessary to achieve stamina in a young athlete, particularly if a lasting career is to be desired.

In addition, Appendix 6 (page 52) shows the sessions for the fortnight preceding the English Schools 3000 metres title, and the 1500 metres AAA Youth title, and Appendix 7 (page 53) shows the build-up periods before the NCAA 1500 metres, NCAA 3000 metres and the European 1500 metres Junior Championships.

Endurance

This concludes a statement of my attitude to the problem of endurance training for young athletes. It would be fair now to say, 'We have a good idea of what you do not like, but what would you do and when would you do it?'

In my approach I do not differentiate between girls and boys simply because there is a slightly different physiological time scale. This difference would have some bearing on learning ballet or gymnastics, but not on endurance training for running, which should be started much later and so slowly that the age difference becomes smoothed out. Performances will differ with sex as should the loadings, but not the over-all direction of the programme.

Excellent summaries of the sequence of anatomical and physiological changes in the growing child are given in two papers that were printed in *Athletics Coach*. The first is Frank Dick's, read at the Midland Coaching Conference, 1977, and the other is Gordon Adams' 'Altro Mundo' lecture, 1980. These I recommend to those who would like some physiological breakdown of the various stages of development.

Let me now re-state my definition of endurance in running. Endurance is about *speed* endurance, because competition is about getting there first – not merely arriving. So here is my plan.

Stage 1

From the time the child is fairly steady on its feet until the age of seven or eight years, encourage it to be as active and mobile as possible in its play (not, of course, frenetic and uncontrollable). When the young child does this it will break all the physiological rules about not being exposed to intensive short recovery and anaerobic work at the pre-puberty stage. Children do not know about this, so they are happy doing their own thing.

Simple observation shows, as many parents can testify, that a child will frequently stop absolutely breathless, then dash about again like quicksilver, having recovered very quickly, then as suddenly fall asleep like a healthy puppy, leaving you exhausted from just watching. Like Seb's early 'gated road running', they are their own safety against overwork, because they are self-paced. Young uncomplicated animals do not try to destroy themselves. This phase will taper off between seven to 11 years.

Stage II   11–13 years

Ensure that the child participates at school in a broad spectrum of games, with a bias to those games with longer periods of activity. Unfortunately rugby and soccer, with 45 minutes each way for the older lads, are contact sports with unpleasant injuries; even the slighter ones cause trouble for runners, but at least these sports will help runners to keep on their feet in some 800 metre races! During this time, any running ability should be discernible and the youngster encouraged to run.

At this stage, steady running should be encouraged, not just because it is physiologically better or safer, but because in the large amount of running that most children do in their games it will be the missing element. Remember, always keep a balance between what can be called speed work and steady running. If puberty has any significance for girls, it is a time when there may be sudden increases in weight and lethargy, so a lot of encouragement may be necessary to keep them moving unless they are already dedicated sports girls.

Stage III　13–15 years

Into every week's training, even though the emphasis is on steady distance, have at least a couple of sessions of faster work. Throughout a running career, remember that, if running is about being speedier than someone else, never get too far away from speed. Keep the fast twitch fibres twitching rapidly (Appendix 8, page 00). Young male adolescents need supervision to prevent them from going through an early macho phase and overtraining.

Stage IV　From 15 onwards there is just one steady progression of balanced training.

After a few cross-country races from October–January which demand a little extra speed, the training is mainly steady distance until March when a full mix of running is commenced. From now on this is the regular pattern of training; only the intensity, or the speed if you like, changes and the sessions are broadly the same.

This year is also the first serious preparation year, because of the Intermediate Schools and AAA Youth titles. This programme is maintained until about 19–20 years when serious circuit and weight training can be introduced. The training from 15 years onwards is what I like to call five tier or multi tier training (Appendix 9, page 55). Appendix 10 shows sample weeks of Seb Coe's training when 16.

For me, the best early endurance training is seeing that the young person acquires the necessary stoic application never to miss a training day and never to be deterred by bad weather. Any urging should not be towards high mileages, but towards helping not to miss a session, or fail to finish one, except through injury.

Earlier, I stressed that endurance is really speed endurance. Speed endurance is a product of speed and stamina, and without either one of these the runner is not equipped for endurance. But what guide can we have to striking the right balance throughout the training of young athletes?

I suggest charting their progress in a very simple way (Appendix 12, page 58).

Using a points system to evaluate performances, I used a Five Star Award chart, connecting up points, say three, representing speed and distance. When a child first starts running, any performance at any distance is much the same until some special emphasis in the training is applied, when the original near-straight line is distorted in the direction of the emphasis.

The ideal is the horizontal straight line, not always obtainable in the ultimate specialisation, but giving a good guide to balanced training on the way up. It is interesting to compare Appendix 12 with Appendix 13 which uses the IAAF scoring tables to evaluate Sebastian's world records over 800m, 1000m, 1500m and 1 mile.

Not much early work was done on the track and it is still not over-used. Fartlek is too uncontrolled for young athletes. Although it means speed play and the name is attractive to our conception of free-wheeling young runners not under pressure, it will not produce speed endurance unaided. (A version of controlled fartlek that I have used is shown in Appendix 14.) On a good grassy slope or hill, find a course of 600–800 metres, similar to the one shown, where you can see the young athlete at all times. Using a whistle, signal the runner to sprint hard until the next blast on the whistle, when he drops back to a slow recuperative run. This way the duration and intensity of the run is completely under the coach's control. This ensures that the young athlete does neither too much nor too little. It also has the advantage of simulating to some degree the racing situation, where the runner has to respond to the pace changes of others which are absent from ordinary fartlek.

In conclusion, I must state that I firmly place quality before quantity and, while I strongly deprecate over-training, I have always placed the stress on intensity as the ingredient that produces the greatest stimulus and results. This only serves to underline that the sessions have to be very carefully measured and assessed. It is just as easy to overdo this type of training as it is to resort to heavy mileage.

Appendix 1

The reference points in a career plan (boy)

AGE

Up to 12 years   All the child's general sporting activities should be encouraged, but with the accent on play and enjoyment. Athletics should be specially encouraged from the 12th birthday.

13 years   Interschool and other competitions, cross-country in winter and track in summer (80–400m). Training on alternate days throughout the year; also an occasional 800m race.
Winter: total distance 100km/month; one long run (8km) each weekend.
Summer: sprint training; not too hard speed endurance type of training; no interval work.

14 years   Train for boys age-group championships. Train 4 days each week all the year (30km/week).
Summer: harder speed endurance runs up to 1600m. Occasional sets of 6 × 200m and 'down the clock' sessions (200 × −20−100m).

15 years   Increase previous year's work by 33% (40km/week). Include more interval training.

16 years   Final year as a youth.
Winter: 50km/week.
Summer: Start speed repetitions over 200, 300, 400m. Introduce short run hill sprinting, fartlek and 4–6 × 800m.

17 years   As for 16 years. A consolidating year, 55–60km/week. Easy circuit training. Consider event specialisation. Start emphasising mental preparation for serious Junior competition.

18 years   An important under-20 year. Must attract selectors' attention when 18–19 years. Should now be competing successfully with most good Seniors. Must achieve Junior International status, especially for big overseas meeting experience.

19 years   As for 18 years. Consolidate.

20 years   The aim is Senior International. Get invitations to the big permit meetings – the 'spectaculars'.
NOTE: Check estimates of World performances.

Sebastian Coe – Major Titles and Events up to Olympic Games (Los Angeles) 1984

Age	Meeting	Place	Event	Class	
14	Yorkshire County Championship (= State)	1st	1500m		Boy
16	Northern Counties Championship (= Area)	1st	1500m		Youth
	UK Championship	1st	1500m		Youth
	English Schools Championship	1st	3000m		Youth
18	UK Championship	1st	1500m		Junior
	European Championship	3rd	1500m		Junior
20	UK Championship (Indoors)	1st	800m	(CBP)	Senior
	European Championship (Indoors)	1st	800m	(UK & CWR)	
21	Ivo Van Damme Memorial (Brussels)	1st	800m	(UKR)	
	European Championship	3rd	800m		
	Coca-Cola	1st	800m	(UKR)	
22	UK Championship (Indoors)	1st	3000m		
	UK Championship (Indoors)	2nd	400m		
	Europa Cup (Turin)	1st	800m		
	Bislett Games (Oslo)	1st	800m	(WR)	
	Weltklasse (Zurich)	1st	1500m	(WR)	
	Golden Mile (Oslo)	1st	1 mile	(WR)	
23	Bislett Games (Oslo)	1st	1000m	(WR)	
	Olympic Games (Moscow)	2nd	800m		
	Olympic Games (Moscow)	1st	1500m		
24	UK v. GDR (Indoors)	1st	800m	(WB)	
	Florence	1st	800m	(WR)	
	Oslo	1st	1000m	(WR)	
	Weltklasse (Zurich)	1st	1 mile	(WR)	
	Golden Mile (Brussels)	1st	1 mile	(WR)	
	World Cup (Rome)	1st	800m		
25	European Championship	2nd	800m		
	4 × 800m Relay	(Fastest leg)		(WR)	
26	UK v. USA (Indoors)	1st	800m	(WB)	
	Oslo	1st	1000m	(WB)	
27	Olympic Games (Los Angeles)	2nd	800m		
	Olympic Games (Los Angeles)	1st	1500m	(OR)	

Abbreviations: **CBP**= Championship's Best Performance
CWR= Commonwealth Record
OR= Olympic Record
UKR= United Kingdom Record
WB= World Best
WR= World Record

Appendix 2

Amateur Athletic Association Division of Administrative Areas

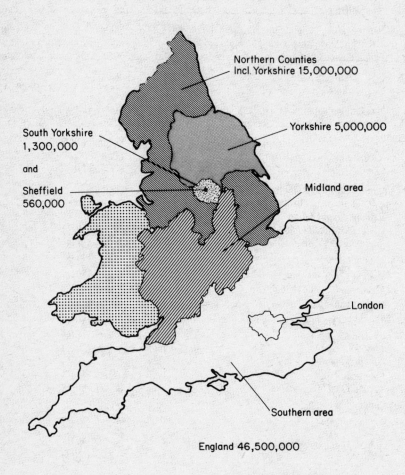

Northern Counties
Incl. Yorkshire 15,000,000

Yorkshire 5,000,000

South Yorkshire
1,300,000

and

Sheffield
560,000

Midland area

London

Southern area

England 46,500,000

Appendix 3

Distance (metres)	100	200	400	800	1000	1500	5000	10 000
Anaerobic %	95	90	75	55	50	35	10	5
Aerobic %	5	10	25	45	50	65	90	95

Appendix 4

Sebastian Coe age 16 years (1973). Analysis of the year in which he won two major youth titles

	Week no	Training days	Miles	km	% aerobic	% anaerobic	
	5	5	11	18	100	0	
	6*	7	15	24	50	50	Raced X–C
	7	6	24	29	75	25	
	8	6	35	56	82	18	
	9	7	47	75	87	13	
	10*	6	21	34	55	45	4 races
	11	5	27	43	49	51	Raced Indoors 800m
	12	3	25	40	80	20	
	13*	6	34	55	57	43	Raced X–C
	14	6	30	48	66	34	
	15	6	14	22	33	67	
	16	5	26	42	23	77	
Apr.	17	7	36	58	54	46	Raced 100m and 800m (START OF TRACK SEASON)
May	18	6	20	32	75	25	Raced 800m – 1500m
	19	7	23	37	38	62	Raced 800m (1–56.0)
	20	6	21	34	28	72	
	21	6	24	38	50	50	Raced 3000m (City Selection)
	22	6	24	39	77	23	
	23	7	39	63	36	64	Raced 3000m (Yorks Schools)
	24	6	9	14	0	100	Raced 1500m (NCAA Championship)
	25	6	29	46	73	27	
	26	6	23	37	82	18	9 races

Week	Days					Notes
27	5	28	45	59	41	English Schools 3000m easy
28	7	28	45	64	36	
29	7	21	34	50	50	
30	7	29	41	46	54	CBP (42 sec/300m)
31	4	17	27	35	65	Raced 1500m AAA Youth Championship 3.55 easy
32	7	24	39	79	21	
33	3	7	11	0	100	Raced 3000m (Seniors)
34	5	26	46	100	0	
35	5	11	17	91	9	
36	7	20	32	50	50	
37	4	8	13	0	100	Raced 1500m (15 Sept. END OF TRACK SEASON)
38	4	15	24	75	25	
39	5	13	21	88	12	Raced X–C
40	5	20	32	100	0	
41	6	21	35	100	0	Raced X–C
42	5	23	37	100	0	Raced X–C
43	6	13	21	77	23	
44	5	7	11	55	45	
45	5	17	27	17	83	Raced X–C
46	4	16	26	100	0	Raced X–C
47	6	14	22	50	50	Raced X–C
48	6	26	42	81	19	
49	4	14	22	62	38	
50	1	2	3	0	100	
51	5	27	43	100	0	Raced Road
52	5	21	35	81	19	Raced X–C
		1025	1646	64%	36%	
		21.3	34.3			

Sept.

8 races

48 wks 264 days
336 days = 79%
Average 5.5 days/wk

TOTAL 21 races

Appendix 5

Sebastian Coe age 18 years (1975)

Week no	Training days	Miles	km	% aerobic	% anaerobic		
Week	1		31	50	–	–	3 races
ending	2		21	34	–	–	
19 Oct.	3		27	43	–	–	
	4		0	0	–	–	
	5		31	50	–	–	
	6		28	45	–	–	
	7		30	48	–	–	
	8		29	47	–	–	
	9		29	47	–	–	
	10		30	48	–	–	
	11		36	58	–	–	
	12	7	41	66	50	50	
	13	6	16	26	70	30	
	14	7	47	76	82	18	Race X–C 7km
	15	6	34	55	50	50	
	16	7	33	53	55	45	
	17	Injury 4	26	42	55	45	
	18	Injury 5	23	37	100	0	Race X–C 7km
	19	6	41	66	51	49	
	20	7	39	63	45	55	
	21	6	28	45	64	36	
	22	7	42	68	50	50	
22 Mar.	23	6	31	50	61	39	Race Indoor 3000m

9 races

Day	Date						Race
24		7	47	76	53	47	
25	12 Apr.	6	36	58	91	9	
26		7	31	50	58	42	Race 1500m
27		6	28	45	78	22	
28		7	29	47	50	50	
29		6	38	61	100	0	Race 1500m
30		6	19	31	75	25	
31		Injury	0	0	–	–	
32		Injury	0	0	–	–	
33		5	16	26	60	40	Race 1500m
34		7	33	53	55	45	Race 800m
35		7	39	63	54	46	
36		6	25	40	56	44	Race 1500m NCAA
37		7	31	50	50	50	Race 3000m NCAA
38		7	37	60	40	60	
39		7	39	63	69	31	
40		6	36	58	61	39	Race 1500m u/20 AAA Championship
41		7	25	40	60	40	
42		6	29	47	60	40	
43		7	33	53	55	45	Race 1500m
44		6	37	60	57	43	
45	24 Aug.	7	22	35	89	11	Race 1500 u/20 European (3–45.2) 3rd
46		5	22	35	78	22	
47		5	37	60	100	0	
48		6	29	29	88	11	
49		7	38	61	81	19	
50		2	10	10	90	10	
229 days 273 = 84%		39 wks 229 / 5.9	1459 / 29.2	2343 / 46.9	Ave. 66%	34%	TOTAL 12 races

Appendix 6

Sebastian Coe   Age 16 years

The following are the 14-day periods which preceded
(a) The English Schools Championships (3000m)
(b) The AAA Youth Championships (1500m) in 1973

(a) *3000m (7 July 1973)*	(b) *1500m (4 Aug. 1973)* *3 min 56 sec (CBP)* *(last 300m – 42 sec)*
DAY	
1 3km steady warm-up (10 × 100), (6 × 200), (2 × 300), (1 × 400)	School Races 800m 1500m
2 10km Cross Country	15km on raod first 7.5km fast, second 7.5km medium
3 7 × 800m on road (average 2m–15s)	(4 × 400), (4 × 150)
4 (1 × 300), (2 × 200), (4 × 100)	3 × (10 × 200) with 5 min recovery
5 (4 × 400) 56, 55, 57, 60	7 × 800 (average 2 min–15 sec)
6 REST DAY	(2 × 150), (6 × 100), (2 × 200), (8 × 80)
7 a.m. 10km cross country. p.m. (5 × 200) *40km*	(2 × 200), (4 × 400), (4 × 200) *48km*
8 (20 × 200) 45 sec recovery	14km cross country
9 a.m. 4km fast (4 × 800), (1 × 400) p.m. (6 × 800)	REST DAY
10 a.m. (30 × 100m) up 10° hill p.m. 1000, 400, 300 (4 × 200)	(7 × 800)
11 a.m. 10km, p.m. (2 × 400), (2 × 200)	(10 × 400)
12 a.m. 8km p.m. (15 × 200m)	a.m. – 8km p.m. (5 × 200), (2 × 300), (3 × 100)
13 REST DAY	(30 × 100m) up 10° hill
14 *Race 3000m (1st)*	1500m heats
15	*1500m* FINAL (1st)

Appendix 7

Sebastian Coe   Age 18 years (1975)

'Build-up' periods to NCAA 1500m and 3000m Championships and European Junior Championship 1500m [Athens]

---

7 June	1	11km	
	2	Raced 800m	
	3	*a.m.* 8km, *p.m.* 30 × 100m 10°	
	4	7km	
	5	7 × 800m	
	6	11km	
	7	*a.m.* 400, 300, 200, 150m, *p.m.* 5km	
	8	4 × 1200m	
15 June	9	10 × 150m	9 days = 75km

	10	30 × 100m 10°, *p.m.* 65km	
	11	7 × 400m	
	12	11km	
	13	*a.m.* 6.5km, *p.m.* 10 × 100m	
	14	5km	
21 June	15	Raced NCAA, Heat and Final 1500m 3 min 50 sec	5 days = 37km

---

	16	REST	
	17	*a.m.* 6.5km, *p.m.* 200, 400, 300, 200m	
	18	*a.m.* 7km, *p.m.* 20 × 200m	
	19	100, 300, 2 × 400m	
	20	*a.m.* 8km, *p.m.* 8km	
	21	8km easy	
28 June	22	Raced NCAA 3000m (8 min 14.2 sec)	6 days = 45km

	1	*a.m.* weights (cond.), *p.m.* 14km	
	2	*a.m.* 6.5km, *p.m.* 20 × 200 (28 sec)	
	3	*a.m.* 6.5km, *p.m.* 4 × 400, 1 × 1600m	
	4	4 × 150 @ 18 sec, 3 × 300 @ 41 sec, 1 × 400m	
	5	*a.m.* 6.5km, *p.m.* 10 × 400 @ 60 sec	
	6	Rest (weights cond.)	
	7	7 × 800 (2 min 10 sec)	
	8	200, 400, 200, 300, 4 × 100m	
	9	10km	
	10	6.5km	
	11	6.5km, *p.m.* strides and accelerations	
	12	Raced Heat 1500m	
	13	Raced Final (Athens) 3 min 45 sec	11 days = 53km

Appendix 8

All Groups trained 100km/week for 26 weeks. Distance Group continued with the same training for 14 weeks. Interval Group reduced to 50km/week but 50% of training was intensive intervals

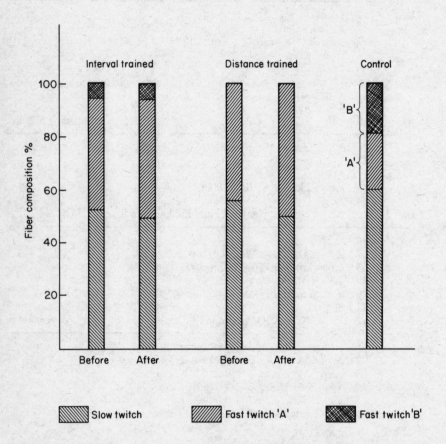

The above graph shows that when training takes place with only steady distance and without any faster running as is provided by some interval work it appears that some of the fast twitch fibres (speed fibres) lose their function.

Appendix 9

Five Tier Training
(With acknowledgements to Frank Horwill)

4–5 levels of training over 10–14 days

1	Sunday	– OR 4 × 1600m 3 × 2000m	5000m pace
2	Monday	– Fartlek	
3	Tuesday	– 8 × 800m	3000m pace
4	Wednesday	– Road	
5	Thursday	– 16 × 200m	1500m/1 mile pace
6	Friday	– Rest if race If not racing – fartlek	
7	Saturday	– Race or time trial	
8	Sunday	– 4 × 400m	800m pace
9	Monday	– Road run	
10	Tuesday	– 1 × 300m, 2 × 200m, 4 × 100m, 8 × 60m – 400m pace	
11	Wednesday	– Fartlek	
12	Thursday	– Race or choose pace for the next race e.g. (800m pace for 1500m race) (400m pace for 800m) (1500m pace for 5000m)	

Appendix 10

February 4–10		** March 4–10*
Sun.	10 × 400m with 2½ min recovery	3½ miles 8 × 400m – jog recovery
Mon.	10 × 100m (1 in 6) jog ⬚ recovery	REST
Tues.	27 min steady run	8 × 400m jog recovery
Wed.	40 min in gym + 3½ mile run off	4 miles X–C running
Thurs.	40 min in gym + 3½ mile run off	4 miles X–C running
Fri	3 hrs badminton	2 hrs badminton
Sat.	2 miles + 15 × 200m jog recovery (24km (15m)	*a.m.* 2 × (8 × 300m), *p.m.* 200 – 300 – 400 (34km) (21m)

* March 25–31	
Sun.	*a.m.* 4 × 200 (fast) 5 min recovery, *p.m.* 4½m
Mon.	6 × 800m
Tues.	6 miles X–C running
Wed.	4 × 800m 2 min recovery
Thurs.	*a.m.* 8 × 400m, *p.m.* 20 × 80m
Fri.	REST
Sat.	Raced 3½m (*a.m.*), *p.m.* 14 × 200m jog recovery (54km) (34m)

The weeks following had similar mixes with mileage balanced against intensity. The weeks marked thus * are those similarly marked on Appendix 4.

Session marked ⬚ is detailed on Appendix 11.

Appendix 11

Start programme with:	1 set of 10 @ 20–21 sec
Then proceed to:	2 sets of 10 @ 20–21 sec 5 min
	3 sets of 10 @ 20–21 sec between sets
	1 set of 20 @ 20–21 sec –
	1 set of 20 + 1 set 10
	1 set of 20 + 2 sets 10 5 min
When fit aim for	1 set of 20 + 1 set 20 between sets
2 × 10 @ 17–18 sec	1 set of 30 –
Then 1 set 20 @ 17 sec	1 set of 30 + 1 set 10 5 min
with the odd 15 sec run	1 set of 40 between sets

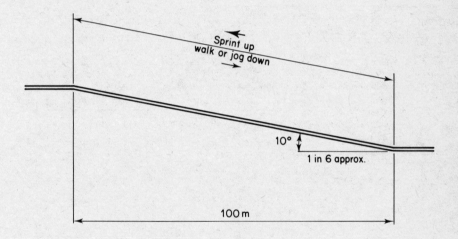

Appendix 12

From Walls' Five Star Award Scheme

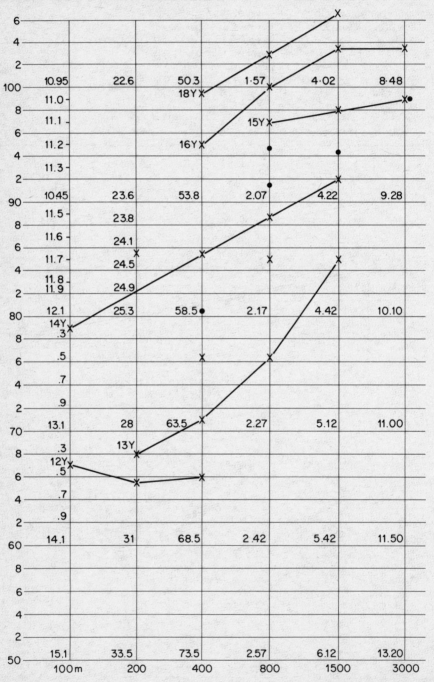

Appendix 13

From IAAF Scoring Table

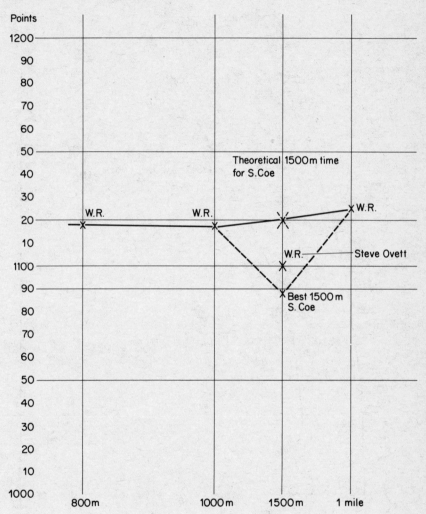

Appendix 14

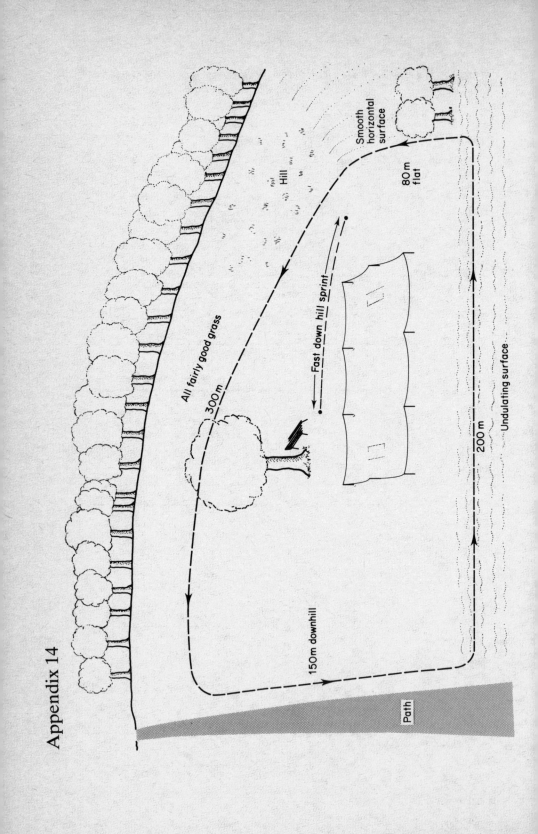

All fairly good grass

300 m

Hill

Smooth horizontal surface

80 m flat

Fast down hill sprint

150 m downhill

200 m

Undulating surface

Path

Skills

5

Technique and the Young Performer

Tom McNab

It was Mark Twain who wrote about a subject of which less and less was known the more research was done on it, till eventually, the volume of research having become overwhelming, no one knew anything about it at all. This was the way I felt in 1963 when I took over as AAA National Coach.

The leader of British athletics coaching at that time was undoubtedly the late, great Geoffrey Dyson, who will as the century closes be seen as the father of British coaching and one of the giants of British sport. Dyson led in the mechanical analysis of athletics techniques and in this laid the foundations of coaching as a science. But although he himself had a fine sense of theory relative to practice, many of his followers did not, and a British physical education profession eager for respectability seized upon Dyson's mechanics and produced various mutations of the great man's work for their bewildered students. I know, for I was one, and I remember listening agog to lectures on athletics which made me wonder how I had ever managed to run, jump, or throw.

In 1963, when I was first appointed, I attended a long jump course at Loughborough conducted by one of my senior colleagues. This was a course for our best coaches and athletes and I looked forward to the first theoretical session. As was the custom in those days, on went the 16mm Specto-Analyser, but what appeared was a loop of a cat falling from its back on to its front. Then followed the most complex analysis of all the axes of rotation round which the cat had spun. By the end of the session the cat was not the only thing that was spinning. I thought that's it, it's clear to me that not only do I know very little about long jump, but what I *do* know is wrong!

One point of this story is that, even at the highest level, it is possible to kill what would have been done naturally, which for long jumpers was simply to run fast and jump high – in fact, to analyse an event out of existence. The danger, too, in this period was that coaches did not spend enough time simply observing and extracting the essentials of what performers actually did, but instead plucked from slow-motion film interesting and esoteric detail. This showed itself particularly in high jump, where we ignored the speedy, attacking approach-runs of the great Russian jumpers because Dysonian mechanics stressed the parallelogram of forces which put no stress on horizontal speed.

The second point of the story, and it is one to which I will return, is that technique, and particularly early technical training, should concern itself only with the very essence of the event – all detail should be left to a later time.

In 1966 I produced my first book, *Modern Schools Athletics*. At the time it was looked upon, as was my general approach, as heretical, because I suggested that class athletics was too technical. At that level, the main priority should be on children finding out how far they could jump and throw, how fast they could run, and all the technique they required was that which was needed to keep within the rules.

This is what I said in a question and answer session within the book, talking of high jump.

The tendency in the past has often been to concentrate on technical inessentials. The first two girls in the 1964 Olympics both used 'scissors' or modified 'scissors' techniques, so in fact both girls used techniques which are frowned on even at class-level in most schools. Yet Mason-Brown did a pure scissors, with no lay-out at all. It was just straight up and down and she later did 1.83 metres in this way. Obviously a clearance technique is important, but the *main* technique which is common to all high jumping is a sound take-off. That is of primary importance regardless of what jumping technique is used. Up till now the tendency has been to teach the secondary factor first and forget about the primary one.

Later, when we were talking about technique, John Anderson had this to say:

What a teacher wants to know is how to get the best performance out of a group of children. It is as simple as that. He could not care less what a technically-good javelin throw looks like. He is not interested. He is interested in Bobby Brown here and how he can make him into a better thrower than he is at present. If this means that we can say do (a), (b), (c) and (d) and this will produce a class of enthusiastic youngsters getting better all the time, then he will do (a), (b), (c) and (d) happily. The average schoolteacher is not at all interested in the mechanics of the movements and neither should he be.

Let us now look at the whole area of technique. First I want to look at the age at which technical training can profitably take place, then to look at methodology, and finally the specific approaches for a young athlete.

Possibly the best book (or rather, series of books) on skill-acquisition are the INNER GAME series by the American, Tim Gallwey. Gallwey is no academic theoretician and indeed his work is unique in having no bibliography, but he has constructed a very effective way of attacking the most complex of physical skills.

Let's look at *The Inner Game of Tennis*. Gallwey starts with five statements that are frequently made by the exasperated beginner.

> When I'm practising, I play very well, but when I get into a match, I fall apart.

> I know exactly what I'm doing wrong on my forehand, I just can't seem to break the habit.

> When I'm really trying hard to do the stroke the way it says to in the book, I fluff the shot every time. When I concentrate on one thing I'm supposed to be doing, I forget something else.

> Every time I get near match point against a good player, I get so nervous I lose my concentration.

> I'm my own worst enemy; I usually beat myself.

Now Gallwey's belief is that there is too much stress with adults on the left, the analytical, side of the brain, in contrast to the right, the instinctive side, and that this dominance of the left side produces the sort of tense, choked type of destructive self-analysis in the first example. Gallwey attacks the problem by diverting the area of concentration, making *feeling* the important factor. This is something to which I will return later.

> In the game of tennis there are two important things to know. The first is where the ball is. The second is where the racket head is. From the time anyone begins to learn tennis, he is told the importance of watching the ball. It's very simple: you come to know where the ball is by looking at it. You don't have to think, 'Oh, here comes the ball; it's clearing the net by about one foot and coming pretty fast. It should bounce near the base line, and I'd better hit it on the rise.' No, you simply watch the ball and let the proper response take place.

> In the same way, you don't have to think about where your racket head *should* be, but you should realise the importance of being aware of where the racket head *is* at all times. You can't look at it to know where it is because you're watching the ball. You must *feel* it. Feeling it gives you the knowledge of where it is. Knowing where it *should be* isn't feeling where it is. Knowing what your racket *didn't do* isn't feeling where it is. *Feeling* where it is is *knowing* where it is.

The golfer Vivien Saunders, in probably the best British book on the acquisition of a physical skill, *The Golfing Mind*, puts it in another way. Appendix 1 (pages 72–74 has Vivien's words in full, as I feel that they are of great importance. I would, however, like to pluck from her statements two sentences: 'The child's approach to anything he sets out to learn shows a simplicity and delightful naïveté which is sadly lost in the adult. The child just *copies* what he sees.'

The quotations from Gallwey and Saunders tackle technique from apparently different perspectives, but both, in their books, reach the same conclusion; they emphasise the need for simplicity, for 'feel', for the minimum of analysis, but in Saunder's work the direct approach of the child is relevant not only to the coaching of the young performer (and indeed to the adult) but to the first question of the best period in which technique can be profitably introduced.

When to begin

Timing clearly varies from sport to sport, with gymnastics starting early at four or five; swimming only a little later at seven or eight; soccer at nine or ten; athletics at ten to 12. Now the problem here is what we mean by 'starting'. Clearly, gymnastics at the age of four is essentially a series of exploratory physical challenges a long way from the adult sport; swimming at seven is possibly closer to the adult sport and has the basic elements of stroke-production, albeit without the demands of butterfly swimming; soccer, using grids, is a scaled-down version of the full game; the athletics of pre-secondary school is essentially experiential rather than technical, and events such as the throws, triple jump and pole vault are unlikely to be tackled at all. So when we talk about technical training for young people, it is clear that each sport produces a different idea of what that means, some being able to get quite close to adult technical requirements and to an adult programme, and others (weightlifting is a good example) not even tackled at all until the pupil is into the mid-teens.

But all the evidence (albeit of an empirical nature) is that a wide base of general physical experience (and here gymnastics has a major role to play) is the essential platform for success in specific sports. This may not be merely a matter of anatomy, of opening up a greater number of neuromuscular pathways, but also of creating a physically confident child.

Consider the capacities of children in throwing, catching, standing jump, sprinting and muscular strength (Appendix 2, pages 74–78). Much of what we see here has dictated the age at which serious technical training has begun. Similarly, the diagram (Appendix 3, page 79) of the psychological peaks and troughs that young people experience may give some idea of the volatility of the human material with which we often have to deal.

The big problem in my sport has always been one of exposing children to athletics techniques too early. Thus, I still see tiny children of eight or nine leaping 2ft 6in hurdles (which for some of them is a personal best high jump), or kids of ten desperately trying to get a 7lb shot beyond their left foot, or to hurl a junior javelin 10 metres.

One of the problems here may not be the child himself, but rather that this pre-teens group are usually given to the least technically knowledgeable coaches. So perhaps the basic elements of some of these events *can* be effectively taught to ages nine to 12. There is little practical evidence to say that they can, but it will take only one brilliant teacher or coach to prove otherwise. The two questions here are: Are we losing out in some sports by failing to introduce children to the techniques early enough? Conversely, by introducing certain skills *too* early, are we creating later technical problems? This is certainly an area for research, one in which coaches must play the major role.

What techniques?

The next question relates to both Vivien Saunders' and Tim Gallwey's work and also relates back to one of the points I made in my introduction, when I said that in my early years as an athlete and coach an over-mechanical approach often led coaches to concentrate on the esoterica of technique. But what this approach also led to was the imposition of whole adult techniques upon young people. Thus, a long jump for a plump little boy, scraping his backside on the edge of the pit at 3 metres, had to include a hitch-kick, and everybody in shot had to hop across the circle using the O'Brien technique, or perform the straddle over the crossbar in high jump. Coaches assumed that these adult techniques were the only way to jump or throw, and failed to extract from them the essential technical core. Thus we had one physical education college lecturer who had his students practise jumping over dustbins laid on their sides so that the students could spin them backwards, simulating a hitch-kick. The numbers of survivors of this method have never been estimated, but many must still be missing in action.

Consider this simple model, the 'Must Know', 'Should Know', 'Could Know' diagram (Figure 5.1). In long jump, for a 15-year-old beginner:

> *Must Know* means an approach-run in the 13–15 strides range, hitting the board accurately and landing with heels in line, and knowing the basic rules.
> *Should Know* means holding speed into the take-off board, a vertical trunk and some attempt at lift.
> *Could Know* means some sort of flight-technique, such as the hitch-kick or the hang, and a longer, more structured, approach-run.

Figure 5.1

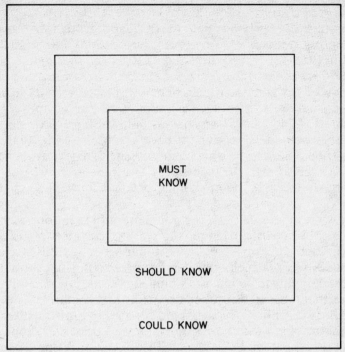

The problem all of us face is that we know too much and are often unable to extract from all this knowledge that which is the absolute essence. Take trampolining. I'm sure that Bert Scales would agree that the absolute technical core of the sport is the ability to 'spot' in balance, for without that everything that follows is impossible. But too often we want to rush on before the foundations have been built.

Imitation

Now we must look at the quality which young people have in abundance, the ability to imitate. Both Gallwey and Saunders make this point strongly. So find someone who is a good basic technical model. Let your young protégé regularly see this athlete and groove in a mental picture of a sound technique. Because we coaches are too old to do it ourselves we progressively lean more heavily on verbal descriptions rather than the best visual aid of all, another athlete doing it well. This does not, of course, rule out video or film as an imitative medium, but my experience of using both within a session is that they simply hold things up. Indeed, it was interesting to note, when I recently attended a trampolining session with Bert Scales and Sue Shottong, that, although he videoed the entire session, Sue only saw video at the end of the session.

Learning

The learning process is the one area which appears to have shown little real progress, but only if we are to rely on the literature. When I was at college in 1955–8, *Gestalt* psychology was all the rage, but the practical implications were rarely explored. As in most activities, it has been the coaches who have led the researchers. Let's look at the basic proposition that simple activities, such as running, favour a whole approach, and more complex activities, such as pole vaulting, favour a whole-part-whole method. We can go further, for those activities that coaches such as John Atkinson face may require that the parts (large enough to be considered as skills in themselves) are practised separately, pre-fabricated so to speak, before being placed within what is essentially a complex, flowing multi-skill.

Now what we are seeing is the pragmatism (and in John Atkinson's case it is often a matter of simple survival) which precedes the creation of psychological theories, and here it may seem that this is in conflict with the simplicity which I have earlier preached. No; central to even the most complex techniques is simplicity, even if the technique is so complex that it has to be broken down into sub-routines.

Luckily, as an athletics coach, I did not have to confront the complex technical problems faced by people like Bert Scales and John Atkinson; yet in some ways it was an equally difficult problem, dealing with relatively natural techniques such as sprinting. I have on film the progress of a girl I coached from 1969 to 1974, Andrea Lynch, who held the British 100 metres record for many years, won the European indoor 60 metres title, and who held the World indoor record for 50 yards.

I took film of her throughout the whole period of training. My first film shows Andrea in 1969 age 17, weight eight stone four pounds, height five foot three, then running 12.3 seconds for 100 metres. At this point there is low knee pick-up, lack of full leg-extension, and, more importantly, a cross-arm action. My second film shows her a couple of years later in 1971, by which time she had won a silver medal at the European Junior Championships in 100 metres and had run 11.8 seconds. The arm action is now direct and there is an over-all increase in range.

My next piece of film shows her in 1972 in Munich at the age of 22, when she reached the semi-finals of the Olympic hundred metres; she was then running 11.4 seconds. The whole action is now smoother, rangier.

My final film shows her in 1974, when she ran 11.16 seconds, a British record which stood for eight years and a time which has not been run this year (1985) by any British athlete. This film, taken in the same back-straight of Crystal Palace as the first, shows her at her very best, rangy and fluid, but the height and weight are still the same. Now what had happened, in the technical sense, to Andrea Lynch? The majority of our work was done, not on conditioning, but on drills, extension-drills, high knee pick-up drills, cadence-drills, arm and shoulder drills, in which each aspect of technique was focused on, polished, then replaced within the skill. In the early years, when she was 17–18, I was concerned with only the grosser aspect of technique, and particularly arms and shoulders, but as Andrea developed in sensitivity the finer aspects of technique were developed. Here I would make the following point: in 'natural' skills like sprint-running, technique is itself a form of conditioning, possibly because the fluent flow of the correct neuromuscular impulses changes the nature of the muscle itself.

Competitive transfer

Now let's look at what I call 'competitive transfer'. There are always two dangers with young people relative to competition. One is that too much stress is placed upon them by coach or parent and a technique that hs been painstakingly developed in training breaks down in competition simply because of needless pressure. The other lies in separating technique from competition, in simply imagining that the coach's job is over when he produces what appears to be a good technique and to leave it to the adrenalin of competition to produce the necessary performance.

The first problem can be met simply by changing the ambience of the training-situation; for the young person, training must be closer to play. The work-content may be high, but it must never be forgotten that these are adolescents, with other pressures upon them, however mature and physically-gifted they may appear to be.

The second problem, of allowing a separation to develop between technical training and competitive performance, is an important one. Let's take hurdling as an example. Hurdling is a rhythm-skill, and although much time has to be spent in a single lane, with no other hurdlers in adjoining lanes, it is essential that:

(a) time is spent with others in adjoining lanes in a 'non-competitive' situation;
(b) there are sessions in which a high proportion of time is spent in a competitive situation.

Here the coach must be careful. If a major technical change is in progress, he must decide when it is profitable to put it under pressure in either of the two situations. If the pressure is put on too early, then the athlete will tend to revert to the previous level of technique which has, after all, hundreds of hours of practice behind it. Practice, as Nick

Stuart used to say, doesn't make perfect, practice makes permanent. It is also essential, and here I refer again to hurdling, that the hurdler's competitive training-efforts are done with someone close in ability to themselves. Training with a 13.6 hurdler, if you are running 15.6 seconds, is of little value to you or the other hurdler! However, two hurdlers both running the 15.4–15.7 range can be of immense value to each other and, using handicaps, can provide the better hurdler with the necessary experience of holding form with people ahead of him.

This use of handicaps has been used effectively in Scotland in sprint-training, where the professional tradition of handicap athletics has a history of almost two centuries. Much of the success of Alan Wells, and more recently the European Junior champion, Elliott Bunney, is owed to the practice of handicap races in training, races which force the sprinter to concentrate on his own four feet of space, despite the 'display' of runners ahead of him.

Here I would enter a note of caution. This fusion of the technical and competitive must be achieved in an atmosphere in which the young athlete is judged, not by winning and losing, but by his performance relative to himself. Youngsters are often acutely sensitive about defeat, so the aim must always be to compete in an atmosphere of self-improvement. This method can, of course, apply also to adults, but is particularly relevant to young people.

Sensory vocabulary

The use of sub-routines is vital to develop what is an essential element of technical training in youth. This is a *sensory feel*, a physical vocabulary which coach and athlete can later share at a more subtle level in athletic maturity. The coaches' aim, starting at grass roots levels of awareness, is to guide the athlete towards a sensitivity to his own movements. This is obvious in such activities as diving and trampolining, but probably less so in running and hurdling, though there it is equally important. This 'feel', this sensory awareness, relates not only to body or limb-positioning, but to limb-velocity and the balance of relaxation and tension during movement. Once the athlete starts to 'read' his or her own body, he/she finds the acquisition of skill much less onerous. Equally important, he/she often comes back to the coach with his/her *own* vocabulary, own expression of a movement, which can enrich both athlete and coach.

Summary

So, to summarise:

1 The coach must, with the young performer, deal with absolute basics, the pillars of future performance.
2 The complexity of the skill dictates the method. The coach must not be afraid to go back frequently to sub-routines.
3 Imitation is a vital element in the technical training of the young.
4 The link between technique and competition must always be retained, though the stress must always be on personal improvement rather than on winning and losing.
5 There is a need to develop a basic sensory vocabulary through which the young athlete learns to understand his own movements.
6 Breadth of activity, i.e. other events and other sports, should be retained for as long as possible, as must the over-all element of play.

Coaching the young performer is probably the most rewarding experience any coach can have, for the coach can see, like a sculptor working from a virtually shapeless block of granite, something fine, something noble, gradually emerge. The dancer Martha Graham said that technique is freedom. More recently, the actor Simon Callow said that a good performance is 'a feeling of power, simply energy flowing uninterruptedly and unforced through your body and mind. You are above the performance – it is performing *you*.' That's it, that's where we're trying to go.

Appendix 1

From Vivien Saunders, The Golfing Mind *(pages 26–7)*

Teaching a child

Teaching a young child to play golf is a relatively straightforward and pleasurable task for most professionals. Teaching an adult, by contrast, is often frustrating and unrewarding. And yet, with some explanation to the adult pupil, the problems need not arise. *The adult needs first to be taught to learn like a child.*

During his formative years, the child is faced with a never-ending stream of new tasks to conquer. He attempts each new action over and over again, frequently failing miserably and yet at the same time being undaunted by or unafraid of such failure. The child's apparent lack of fear of failing means that he simply repeats the actions over and over again and his immense learning ability plays its part without any inhibition. The small child learning to walk is an excellent example of freedom in learning. Although his body is developing physically day by day to cope with the skill more ably, he repeatedly stumbles and falls, picks himself up and tries again. Clearly his thought processes at that age are not highly developed enough for him to analyse what he is trying to do. He makes progress simply through trial and error until his body acquires natural balance and permits him to walk unaided.

In a very similar way, the child of eight or nine years can learn to play golf, or ski, or play most other sports, with far less difficulty than an adult pupil. The difference in the pattern of behaviour between the child and the adult in learning to play golf is very noticeable. The young child will immediately imitate with reasonable ease the movements he sees his teacher perform. The results with the ball are at first almost certainly quite appalling, but the young child simply repeats the movements over and over again without making any real adjustment to his performance. He merely copies what he sees and is quite uninhibited by his initial failure. During these early years when learning ability is heightened, the child seems to be confident that if he repeats something often enough it will begin to work quite effortlessly. After all, at this age, almost everything he has previously attempted results in success. He probably has not really experienced any lasting form of failure and therefore learns in a totally uninhibited way. His golf swing is developed by learning from watching his teacher and by copying. If he fails at first – which almost certainly he will – he continues with the same actions, knowing that success is almost certainly round the corner. He does not analyse his movements; he does not analyse his successes or failures in a particularly complex way. He is content to imitate and persevere with this imitation until results improve.

The child's approach to anything he sets out to learn shows a simplicity and delightful naïvety which is sadly lost in the adult. The

A child can look at a visual example, picture the movements in his mind, and copy the movements very simply. The adult, by contrast, usually looks at the example, describes it to himself in words, uses these words as a set of instructions to his body, and produces his own interpretation of the actions

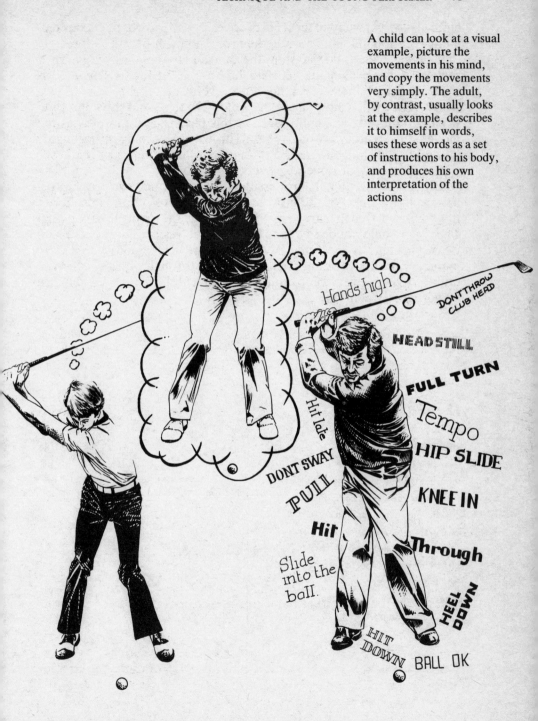

Hands high

DON'T THROW CLUB HEAD

HEAD STILL

FULL TURN

Tempo

HIP SLIDE

Hit late

DONT SWAY

PULL

KNEE IN

Hit

Through

Slide into the ball.

HIT DOWN

HEEL DOWN

BALL OK

child just *copies* what he sees. He may need gentle words of encouragement occasionally, but as a rule the professional or parents appreciate
that all they have to do is to show the child and the child will copy. They
realise that the child has certain limitations as far as language is
concerned and therefore tend not to conceptualise problems into
words. They will simply say to the child, 'Do this', and show the child
what is required. The child looks at this pattern and reproduces the
movements as accurately as he can. This way of learning is thoroughly
natural to the child and, to a certain extent, the younger he is and the
simpler his view of novel experiences, the better he will learn. The
young child will watch the professional or parent and develop a kind of
picture in his mind of the movements involved, slotting himself into
this picture so that in his own mind he *becomes* the model he is copying.
The child would not be saying to himself, 'Ah yes, he's doing X, Y and
Z with his legs or X, Y and Z with his arms.' He would have a vivid
picture of the body turning back and turning through with a swish in the
middle. This he would copy quite naturally, with virtually no reliance
on verbal instructions.

Appendix 2

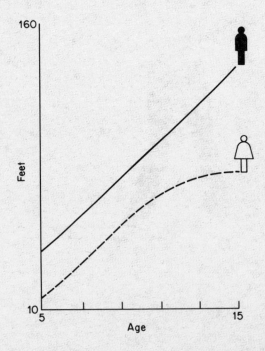

THROWING

Increase in throwing distance is
mainly marked by development of
an overarm throw. This coincides
with changes in feet position to
allow greater body rotation. A
right-handed child uses a weight
shift from rear left foot to leading
right foot on delivery. In an
adolescent, the shift is from rear
right foot to leading left.

CATCHING A BALL

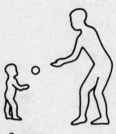

	2 years
General strategy	Almost nil
Hand movements	Static
Timing and co-ordination	Almost nil
Eye gaze	On thrower
Stance	Rigid

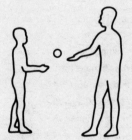

5 years
Half formed

Intentional and appropriate,
  but excessive
Effective but slow

On thrower, ball, and hands

Jerky

15 years
Complete

Directed, smooth,
  and effective
Co-ordinated,
  and unhurried
On ball

Adaptive

STANDING JUMP

This shows development of the standing broad jump - taking off and landing on both feet. (The running jump confuses the situation by adding in running abilities.) Achievement in boys continues at an almost steady rate throughout childhood and adolescence.

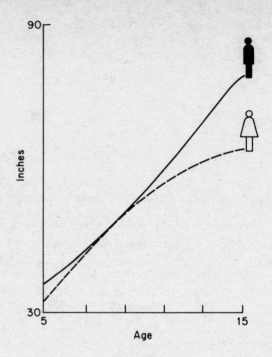

SPRINTING

A simplified run begins by about 18 months but true running (with a moment of no body support) does not appear till the age of 3. Adult running pattern is established by about 5 or 6. Thereafter speed of running is largely determined by body size, which increases the length and the strength (and so frequency) of stride

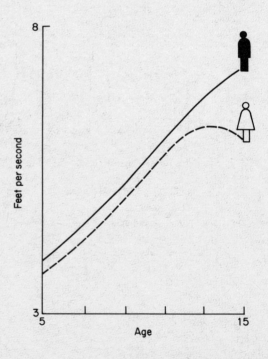

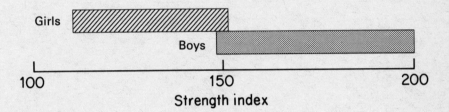

Strength index

STRENGTH INDEX
These strength scores summarize grip, pull, and push.
The strongest child is almost twice as strong as the
weakest. Most boys are stronger than most girls –
but there is considerable variation within each
group

78

MUSCULAR STRENGTH

Here we show how different aspects of strength develop with age. The main determinant of strength is body size. This is not surprising, since muscle is 40% of body weight. But body weight only accounts for 30 to 35% of strength variation, and height for only another 10%. Age in itself (independent of growth) also shows some effect – perhaps because of developments in the centers of motor control. But strength also varies with constitutional factors such as somato type*: mesomorphs are stronger for size than ectomorphs, and ectomorphs than endomorphs.

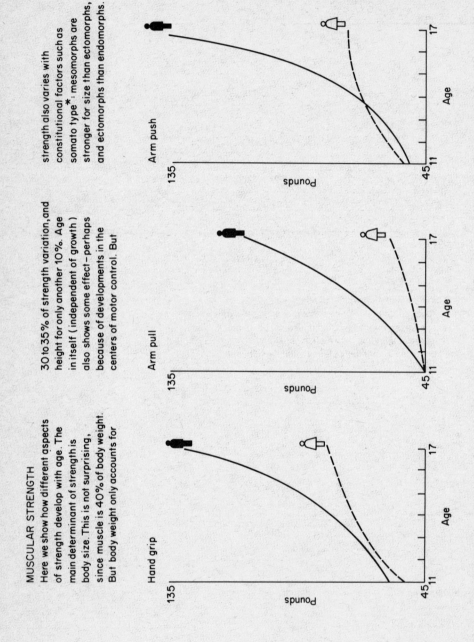

Hand grip

Pounds
135

45
11   Age   17

Arm pull

Pounds
135

45
11   Age   17

Arm push

Pounds
135

45
11   Age   17

Appendix 3

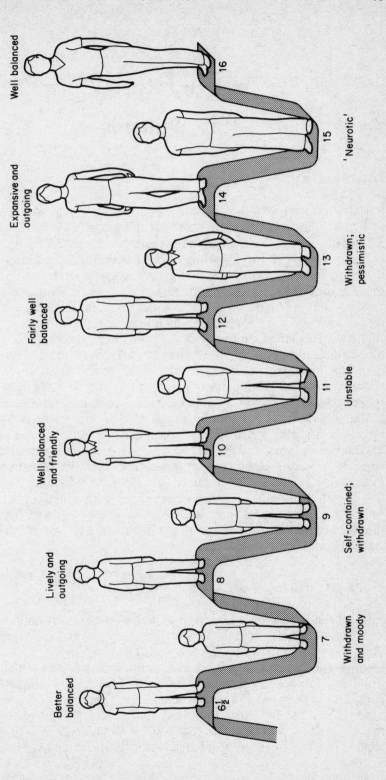

6

Mini-Rugby

Ray Williams

Introduction

Perhaps it would be helpful for those people who have little knowledge
of Rugby Union Football to state that the game originated in Rugby
School during the first half of the nineteenth century, although it was
not until 1863 with the founding of the Football Association that the
handling and non-handling games were recognised as separate sports.
Prior to that time they were both part of the generic term 'football'.

The game is played on a world-wide basis and in the British Isles
there are four Unions, each of which is over 100 years old. Between
them they form the Committee of the Four Home Unions which acts as
a co-ordinating body for the British Isles. Each of the Unions, England, Scotland, Ireland and Wales, has a Schools Union as part of its
constituent body. It is a game which is widely played, has a very strong
spectator following, and is run on strictly amateur lines. Each of the
Home Unions has substantial properties in the form of National
Grounds, and the Welsh Rugby Union has only recently completed a
15-year development of the historic Cardiff Arms Park which has cost
some £10 million. All that money, apart from £160,000 from the Sports
Council for Wales, has been raised through Rugby football itself.

The situation can be summed up by stating that Rugby Union
football is a substantial sport in the British Isles, played by very large
numbers of adults and schoolboys, with a dedicated, loyal and enthusiastic band of spectators.

Background

Each of the Four Home Unions is an autonomous body and conducts
its business and affairs in the way which it is believed is appropriate for
the Union concerned. In 1970, the Welsh Rugby Union (WRU) called
a conference of all those Rugby organisations in Wales which made
provision for players under 19 years of age. The purpose was to
consider the organisation and structure of the game for young players,
especially in the light of a rapidly-changing educational system. The
result of that conference was that a special Under-19 Working Party
was established by the Welsh Rugby Union, whose terms of reference

were to 'examine the state of Under-19 Rugby in Wales and make recommendations for the future'.

One of the first tasks which the Under-19 Working Party undertook was to conduct a survey of Rugby football in Welsh schools. The survey showed that only something like 25% of the junior schools in Wales (i.e. with pupils under 11 years of age) played Rugby football. In fact, there were 423 junior schools affiliated to the Welsh Schools Rugby Union and playing the fifteen-a-side game. It was therefore felt that the junior school age range was one where there could be the greatest expansion in the playing of the game.

It was also known that there were people involved in the education of young children who did not think that Rugby football, certainly the fifteen-a-side game, was a suitable game for very young players. Furthermore, the rural schools in Wales had so few children that it would be impossible for them to form Rugby teams. It was at this stage that the WRU Coaching Advisory Committee began to look at the possibility of launching a new game especially designed for young players, in the hope that it would prove to be more acceptable to primary schools.

There had developed in Britain over the years a tradition whereby education was the great provider of sport for schoolboys and schoolgirls, and the governing bodies of sport had very little work to do in introducing young people to sports and games because so much of it was done through the school educational system. There were signs however, that this pattern was beginning to change and the WRU took the view that if education could not provide, then Rugby football had to provide. The embracing of this particular philosophy meant that the new game which was visualised would not only develop in the schools, but also be organised and encouraged within the existing club structure.

This then was the background against which the new game, to be called Mini-Rugby, was launched in 1971.

The Game

It would not be appropriate to delve too much into the technicalities of Mini-Rugby, except to say that it is a nine-a-side game which has been devised and adapted to suit the abilities of young players. The fifteen-a-side game is too complicated for beginners, the range of skills required for the full game, together with the laws involved, make too many demands on those who are new to the game. The result is nearly always depressing to watch. Thirty players chasing the ball and little involvement because so few players touch the ball; consequently there are few opportunities for players to acquire and develop the fundamentals of the game.

The Mini-Rugby game is a modified game. It has reduced numbers and less requirement in terms of skill and law. It is not intended in any way to replace the full fifteen-a-side game. It could not possibly do this, but it is an excellent lead-up to the big game. As there are standards and rules laid down for Mini-Rugby, it means that, as well as being an introductory game, it can also be played competitively. This is a very great advantage. Most introductory games get forgotten in the haste to progress to playing the real thing, and the result is that the skills and principles which can be developed through a modified game are often neglected.

There are those, of course, and there are many it would seem in the educational world, who state that competition is inappropriate for young children, but the fact remains that man is a competitive animal and a glance at the average primary school playground will more than justify this observation. What is often wrong is the way in which competition is used, especially by those involved with young children, teachers, coaches and very often parents, but more of this later. In Mini-Rugby the emphasis in the game is on handling, running and contact. These are the main elements of Rugby Union football and those who see the mini game played can have no doubt as to what kind of game it is. There is another quite important factor, too, that small schools are not denied the opportunity of playing Rugby because they do not have a sufficient number of players.

The Response

Perhaps the response to Mini-Rugby can best be described in the way in which the British economy is described – *mixed*! Mini-Rugby to many, to the clubs in particular and those in England specifically, felt that Mini-Rugby was akin to manna from heaven! There were other individuals and organisations, notably the Welsh Schools Rugby Union, who felt that the development of Mini-Rugby was a gross interference in their own affairs, that the concept was ill conceived, unnecessary and unwanted. The fact remains that Mini-Rugby grew at a staggering rate and many clubs in England in particular, had on Sunday mornings literally hundreds of young boys playing the game. It stretched the resources of clubs to the limit, but at least it also had a more lucrative element. All the players were very young, they all came in the charge of their parents, and while the coaching and playing took place, the parents at least were bolstering the club finances by having a pre-lunch drink at the bar.

Despite initial opposition from the Welsh Schools Rugby Union, the game continued to flourish and prosper in Wales, and a lot of promotional publicity was gained for the game by playing Mini-Rugby matches immediately before major games at the Cardiff Arms Park.

Perhaps the most significant step taken in Wales at that time was the development of the Mini-Rugby Festival – in essence a bringing together of many teams so that they could enjoy a festival of Rugby.

The WRU then launched, with support from the *South Wales Echo*, a Cardiff-based evening newspaper, the concept of a National Mini-Rugby Festival. It was organised by the WRU with support from the Junior Group of the Welsh Schools Rugby Union. The original philosophy of the Festival was that it was not a knock-out competition, there were no prizes for winners, in fact all children who participated received a badge stating that they had taken part in the National Mini-Rugby Festival.

In the early days, competition was for children under 11 years of age. It was organised initially at district level throughout Wales and the most successful teams, that is to say those that scored the greatest number of points in their respective festivals, came to Cardiff to play in the National Mini-Rugby Festival which was held on the Cardiff Arms Park. Play began in the morning and continued until 6 o'clock in the evening. There were 16 teams and each team played in a pool of four, so that every boy had an opportunity of playing in three matches during the course of the day. The team that scored the greatest number of points moved to a semi-final play-off. Again, as a reward the two teams with the greatest number of points played a match immediately prior to the Schweppes Cup Final at the Cardiff Arms Park on the last Saturday in April.

In subsequent years, the Welsh Schools Rugby Union undertook the organisation of the Festival. They reduced the age range to Under 10. This proved to be a very productive rule because it encouraged many more schools to participate until, at the present time, some 200 teams compete in the National Mini-Rugby Festival. It is now less of a Festival and much more of a competition in that winning matches has become the prime aim and there are trophies and so on for the winners. The organisers have, however, still recognised the concept of participation by awarding badges to all those who take part.

The Festival is very strictly controlled and extremely well organised. Spectators are not allowed anywhere near the playing areas and therefore one does not have the unseemly sight of people rushing up and down the touchline, exhorting young children to dubious acts.

Reflections

There is no doubt that the introduction of Mini-Rugby was well worth all the effort, because it is a game which has been modified with young children especially in mind. It provides all the basic elements of Rugby Union football without ever overloading the young player in terms of skill, physical requirements, or knowledge of the laws of the game. These views can be supported by the fact that Mini-Rugby, or versions of it, is now played in most of the Rugby-playing countries throughout the world.

The concept of the Mini-Rugby Festival is a good one. Unfortunately, however, at times those involved in these Festivals become overzealous and overcommitted in their approach. In this respect, one is not talking about the players because time and again they have shown that they can handle any amount of competition. One is referring specifically to teachers, coaches and, more often than not, parents, because they put pressure on young children to succeed, sometimes in situations where it is almost impossible. However, the fact that people sometimes behave improperly is never a reason for throwing aside something which has a very valuable contribution to make, not only to the development of the game, but also in establishing standards for young children.

Mini-Rugby is much more than developing techniques, skills and principles of play because, expert though people may be at these things, if their personal attitudes towards the game are wrong, then their success will only be temporary.

Rugby football has survived for well over 100 years and become one of the world's greatest amateur sports, as much by the spirit it creates as by the skill with which it is played. In this modern age it is often thought clever to sneer at terms like the 'spirit of the game' and 'ethics', but Rugby football, in company with other sports, has demonstrated on many occasions that these qualities are not entirely lost. Of course, there have been instances when the halo has slipped temporarily, but these have only emphasised what a precious heritage the game possesses. It is the responsibility of those who play and coach the game to preserve and enrich it. They must ensure by their actions, both on and off the field, that they do nothing to discredit the game.

One of the features of Rugby football is that it is a game of physical contact and it is inevitable that hard knocks will be given and taken. It is vital that these take place within the context of the game. Any player taking part in this kind of physical contest knows that there is an injury risk, even though the ethics and the laws may be strictly observed. He should never be subjected to risks which are outside both ethics and law.

In essence, players must respect the game and those who take part in it. They must especially respect the authority of the referee. His judgement and decision must be final, accepted without hesitation and certainly without question.

Presumably people play the game because they enjoy it. That is probably the best reason, but they should remember that there is no disgrace in wanting to be successful. There is no dishonour in wanting to win. All players should pursue excellence. Each according to his ability will achieve varying degrees of success. All cannot be Internationals, but all can display high standards of behaviour and sportsmanship. Defeat must be accepted with good grace and victory with humility, and Mini-Rugby is the ideal vehicle by which these attributes can be developed.

Needs of the Young Athlete

7

The Athletic Child and Boarding Education

Paddy Garratt

Millfield School is a fee-paying co-educational boarding school which is also a charitable trust. It is situated in the heart of Somerset, where it has grown to become an integral part of the town of Street, two miles from Glastonbury, six and a half miles from Wells.

During my eighteen years at Millfield I have watched it grow from a well-known rugby and cricket playing traditional type of independent school (probably best known as being the highest fee-paying school in Britain, or the place where the rich and famous send their children) to a 1150-pupil academic and sporting establishment unrivalled in its facilities for all-round development of its pupils' academic, sporting and social ambitions.

While there are some children of the rich and famous still at Millfield, there are numbers from various levels of society who receive bursaries offered to academically and/or musically gifted children, together with holders of 'All-Rounders' bursaries granted to young people with a reasonable amount of talent, both sporting and academic.

Because of the publicity which Millfield's sporting success receives, it tends to attract an above-average level of talent, but in no circumstances does the school recruit by direct approach. I have had no brief to do this, nor have I ever wished to do so. I want swimmers to come to the school because of what it has achieved and because they need it, not because we want to build the best team. The type of swimmer we are attracting is not only above average as a swimmer but also above average academically, one who is looking for a place where the two interests go hand in hand. I have no doubt that many people suspect us of recruiting, and my answer is, if I were able to recruit I would have the best team in Great Britain, not the second best.

My personal philosophy on winning is clearly defined and so is the school's: we like winning, and we want to win because it is a very enjoyable feeling to win, but we do not want to win at all costs.

I see my job as organising conditions within my given circumstances to provide the chance for any swimmer to achieve full potential at that period of his or her life, at the same time completing secondary schooling and emerging still enjoying swimming and wanting to carry on competing for as long as possible, whether it be at a British university or college, or an American further education establishment.

Swimming is considered a child's sport and will continue to be thought of in this way as long as we have a massive drop-out rate around the ages of 15 or 16 in the majority of clubs. At least at Millfield, and indeed also at Kelly College, Tavistock, Devon, we are keeping young people in the sport until they are 18 or 19 years of age, but, most important of all, we are keeping them at a high performance level during the public examination years.

It is my belief that the level of British sport could be lifted to the level of the East Germans and the Soviets by utilising the facilities of our many boarding schools or organising professional coaching and offering bursaries of the type available at Millfield and Kelly College over a range of sports. However, for swimming the old problem would still remain – where can the swimmer go in order to continue in the sport after leaving school, apart from the USA? That is another subject altogether.

So what are the advantages of boarding education and what problems do we have to face in the day-to-day running of a swimming team under these conditions?

Many coaches, I am sure, would say that to have an 'orphanage' situation, where young people are out of the grasp of parents for much of the year, would be ideal. To a certain extent it is, as we all know that parents can over-react at times and their judgement can be clouded by emotions which often cause friction among the three parties: coach, swimmer, parent. On the other hand, at a boarding school the coach must be prepared to step into the role of parent and help pupils through the problems of growing up by exercising a great deal of patience and understanding. Of course, the coach's 'family' is then not one, two, or even three children, but (as in my case) as many as 45 to 50. Of course, support from house parents, group tutors, counsellors and teaching staff, together with a sports-minded school doctor and the availability of a child psychologist, is essential in helping to cope with the problems which do arise from day to day.

We have to come face to face with the highs and lows of young people going into, during and coming out of puberty. Boys are very complex, but girls seem to me to be even more so. The boy's change from childhood to adulthood seems to be more gradual and is spread over a greater period of time, whereas the girl's change (whether it be complete or not) seems much more rapid and dramatic. Maybe this is because there are more obvious signs in the female, particularly with regard to anatomical development, the development or enlarging of the breasts and the increase in body fat causing a change in shape which can be very marked in many cases. In a controlled (boarding) situation, it is possible for the coach to help the female swimmer through this stage by keeping an eye on food intake and by keeping the workload up to a level sufficient to keep the body fat between 12% and 15%.

Working below this percentage can and does retard the development of females because the hormone balance is affected. If the fat percentage rises to over 15% (which could happen when a holiday is taken, or if an illness interferes with training as in the case of Nadia Comaneci), the hormone balance will change, allowing the completion of puberty in a very short time. We have all seen the transition from 'tomboy' to young lady, the change of personality from tough, aggressive, competitive, to gentle, passive, and less competitive. This could well have given rise to the statement which a certain young lady made to me: 'I seem to have lost my guts.' Did she mean that she did not feel competitive any more? I think so.

The little doll-like gymnasts are a good example of the body fat issue. Like swimming, gymnastics is all about shifting the lowest possible weight (without affecting the health) at the greatest possible speed by utilising the best possible technique.

The extreme of the theory of low fat level is borne out by the problems of anorexia nervosa sufferers. If sufficient food is not eaten, body fat diminishes and the menstrual cycle stops – apparently the exact opposite to the situation when the body fat level is over a certain percentage. The coach has at least some control over the situation and can help girls in their training plan, but of course holidays take them beyond control. They can, and do in some cases, arrive back at school overweight and, of course, with all the weight in the wrong places.

With boys, it is just a matter of building their workload and making sure they do not become overtired which can happen very easily, particularly when they are going through a period of rapid growth. (This also applies to the girls, of course.) Generally, if boys have talent and ability they will naturally swim faster as they grow stronger, provided a well-planned programme of work is carried out on a regular basis.

Being in such close proximity to my charges helps me to keep a pretty firm grip on things. For instance, I see them first thing in the morning (6.30 am) for training, when they can discuss any problem which they may have, such as being overtired (or on seeing them I may think that they look very tired and will act accordingly). Some will not rest themselves, and some will try to swim through ear, nose and throat troubles, even with heavy colds. I am able to send them straight to the surgery as soon as they get to school. I also eat breakfast with them each morning before they go into school; any problems which I may want to discuss, or they may want to talk about, can be sorted out early in the day and action taken. I see them again at midday during land training (and eat lunch with them afterwards) and finally at the afternoon or evening training session before they go back to their houses at the end of the day. I may add that I am also available at break-time during the morning when they can come and see me privately in my office if they so wish.

This situation alone must surely be the greatest advantage of boarding education, as it make for a very close athlete/coach relationship and allows medical problems to be sorted out very quickly apart from all the other benefits.

For training the fact that everything is in such close proximity and all aspects can be catered for on the campus – water work, technique/video, weights and flexibility, as well as medical and psychological aspects such as physiotherapy and counselling – is of immense value. Because the athlete's diet can be watched from day to day, to some extent I can advise on intake of protein and carbohydrates during certain training periods, but, most important of all, I can encourage pupils to eat a well-balanced diet, so important in the building of young bodies at such a vital time in their lives.

From an academic point of view, provided the instruction is of a very high standard (and we at Millfield are in no doubt that it is) and provided there is a good and close relationship and understanding between the teaching staff and sports coaches, the young athletes can continue their education without any problems, if they are prepared to organise their days and keep up with the homework. It is really easier to do this at boarding school than at day school, as the school and swimming day is finished by 6.30 pm and there is a set prep time of one and a half to two hours every evening after the evening meal. Interviews often reveal stories about young swimmers who have to eat breakfast in the car on the way to school after starting training in the morning at 5.30 am, and who do not get home in the evening from training till 10 pm or later, with a couple of round trips of, in some cases, 50 miles or so – all this being done on a packed or 'fast food' lunch. It is little wonder that the drop-out rate in swimming is so high!

In many cases the competitive side of the swimming programme can have a very positive effect on academic work, as the competitive atmosphere tends to spill over into the classroom. I have seen many Millfield youngsters who in normal circumstances would not consider taking O-levels (particularly if they make International standard) who, because of the competitive spirit amongst their peers have gone on to pass A-levels with good grades. The very nature of their way of life after a year or so of self-organisation and self-discipline leads them to aim for the highest achievement possible, both sporting and academic.

Of course, in any society there are those who are unable to cope and we do have from time to time pupils who reach only a very moderate level, both sporting and academic. These very occasional and untypical pupils will leave to go on to some form of further training and either give up or swim at club level only. Against this, we have pupils who have represented their country at youth level, but who have not developed to senior International level because of academic priorities. They have gone on to university and have then made the senior International grade at a later stage.

I am naturally very aware that I play an instrumental part in the shaping of these young people's future lives and find it rather stressful at times – especially when having to make what I know are key decisions. However, I like to think that I will, when presented with a conflict of interests, most often err on the side of the academic considerations.

One of the greatest advantages for athletes at boarding schools is that their aims become much higher than when working at normal club level. A young swimmer coming into Millfield will be mixing very closely with National, International, World and Olympic level team members, whom they will see as just ordinary people like themselves, and they can identify with them. We have had at times as many as twelve international swimmers in the squad at various levels from Schools International to Olympians, so it is not difficult for pupils to see that progress through the levels for them is possible. As a consequence they are often dissatisfied with County standard.

In any situation of this kind there have to be some disadvantages. Occasionally, home sickness can be a very real problem. For girls it seems to attack straight away during the first two weeks or so of the first term, but boys seem to feel it much more in the second term, just when the girls are settling down. I have come to the conclusion that boys enjoy the freedom of being away from parents in the early days, but when this is accepted and the novelty wears off (and they find that in some cases the house, prefect and school discipline – and indeed the discipline of the swimming programme – is greater than at home), then home sickness hits them. The girls miss the love found at home, and they miss their pets and former school friends straight away, but they soon make new friends and respond very quickly to the security of organisation and discipline, though there are, as ever, exceptions to the rule among both sexes.

For some girls, infatuation with the opposite sex can interfere with their training; at times this has been a problem, but I do not think that I have ever found this to be the case with boys. Perhaps the girls subconsciously seek the love they are missing from home in boyfriends, but, having said this, I can honestly say I am sure that the majority of girl swimmers have not allowed their association with boys to stand in their way while at Millfield.

Incentives, in this day of world travel and an abundance of consumer goods which are available to most youngsters in the strata of society from which we draw, are very difficult to come by. My team is sponsored by Speedo, and the whole team is supplied with half-price track suits, free swimsuits, caps and goggles. What would be the point of using as an incentive a weekend trip to the Continent when some of the team spend 10 weeks in the summer in their own homes in places like California, Trinidad, and so on? We do at times take trips to the

USA and Canada with the whole team – a major undertaking and one which obviously cannot be organised every year.

Comparative wealth, school trips abroad, package holidays, parents based overseas leave us with fundamental incentives such as improvements in times, steady progress, a happy and enjoyable atmosphere during the training programme and good coach/pupil relationships (not always easy at 6.30 in the morning). Naturally, the setting of reachable and progressive goals is of paramount importance if the athletes are going to be able to relate to the demands made upon them. So these are the incentives we must rely on. They are the key to keeping young people interested in their sport.

How often do we hear the comment that what the British require in order to become a great sporting nation is a balance between the American and Eastern block programmes? I feel that we have part of the answer in the many boarding schools throughout Britain. All our sports people should have the chance to develop their athletic ability together with their academic studies. I am sure that it would not be an impossible task for the government to get together with the national sporting bodies to develop systems throughout Great Britain with this object in mind and make use of the outstanding facilities which many boarding schools have. In the early stages, bursaries could be given to the more talented athletes and full-time trained coaches could be placed in these schools. I realise that this would be a vast undertaking, but it is not impossible if done in controlled stages. Millfield have produced a professional scheme for swimming, tennis, cricket, golf and riding, Kelly College for swimming, and the Football Association has a simular set-up for young soccer players.

This, or something on these lines, is surely the answer to the early development of young British athletes, but then what? Where do they go from there? We have no effective organisations in British colleges and universities, except the traditional courses such as those at Loughborough, recognised chiefly for track and field. So where? To the USA?

8

The Role of the Parent in Youth Sport

Stephen Rowley

Introduction

The subject of the parent's role is particularly pertinent to contemporary youth sport, since the child's involvement in, and enjoyment of, his or her sporting activity goes beyond the responsibility of the coach. In many cases the support and interest of one or both parents is crucial to the child's participation. Recently, however, concern has been expressed about the adverse effect the overzealous or intrusive adult has on children's competitive sport, a concern which suggests that parents are overstepping their role or function. There is now considerable anecdotal evidence for the existence of the so-called 'pushy parents' who drive their children on to performance success, set unrealistic objectives and force them to participate. Although empirical evidence is slight, two studies in the mid 1970s suggested that when parents do participate in youth sport there is a danger that they follow ambitions of their own and that they place an excessive emphasis on winning (Orlick and Botterill, 1975; Sherif and Rattray, 1976). The contemporary view of the parent is perhaps illustrated in the following story.

A junior football coach called one of his players off the field. 'Let me explain some of the game's principles of sportsmanship, John,' he said. 'We don't believe in temper tantrums, screaming at the referee, and being a poor loser. Do you understand that?' 'Yes,' replied John. 'Well then,' asked the coach, 'do you think you can explain that to your father so that he will behave?'

The sentiments expressed in this example clearly portray the parent's behaviour as extreme or even maladaptive. The question is whether this is an accurate picture of parental behaviour and, if so, how can it be prevented? Many coaches will have had their own experience of parents, good, bad and indifferent. I think all would agree that parents do have an important role to play in children's sport. However, perhaps there needs to be some attempt to define their contribution and to educate them in their role (I will return to this point in the conclusion). If this is not done, there is a danger that the popular view of the parent as outlined in the story will persist, and not only their support and interest but parents' function as role models will be lost, for they will be alienated from the sports environment in an attempt to protect the child. There is also the additional problem that parents may be scapegoated for the shortcomings of the coach, so that any decrease in performance or complaint from the child is immediately blamed on the parent.

Therefore I propose, first, to describe what we do know about parental participation by briefly reviewing the major findings of previous research; secondly, to supplement the salient points with some very general findings from the 'Training of Young Athletes Study' currently in progress at the Institute of Child Health, University of London; and thirdly, to draw some tentative conclusions which may be taken further by other workers in the field on either a practical or a theoretical basis.

Previous Research

Based upon the findings of previous studies, two major factors within the child's family environment appear to be directly related to the attraction to, or avoidance of, sports participation: the significant role models which are available to the child, and the extent of family reinforcement for the child's participation in sports activities. Parents, therefore, appear to have a dual role in youth sport which can be generally defined under the headings of 'socialisation' and 'support'.

The socialisation function of the parents includes their role in encouraging involvement in sport and the introduction of the child to the values and attitudes associated with sports participation. Work by Orlick in 1972 and Greendorfer in 1977 suggests that initial involvement is usually a function of the parents' own sports participation, although it has been suggested by Lewko and Greendorfer (1982) that within the family it is the father who has the most significant role in determining both the extent and appropriateness of a child's sports participation, regardless of the child's sex. It must be pointed out, however, that the role of demographic variables such as socio-economic class, age and ethnicity of the parents have also been found to influence a child's involvement, or non-involvement, in sport. As regards the supporting role, this includes changes in meal times, transportation to and from the training or competition facility, and supplying financial assistance to the extent that it may affect the availability of money for other domestic needs. Peter Coe, coach of that athletic luminary Seb Coe, recently described the extent of this supporting role. He commented that: 'The impact on the family [of Seb's sports participation] was quite marked. Mealtimes became staggered; the regular wash-day cycle hugely increased; holidays were ruined because they came during the track season; and absences from home were frequent.'

It is important to realise therefore that, apart from supporting the child's sports participation, the parents have also to maintain normal household routines and responsibility to other children.

Training of Young Athletes Study

Because of the integral role parents play in determining the extent of sports participation, certainly initially, and the concern expressed over the effects on the young child of the intrusive parent, during the Young Athletes Study I was particularly interested in determining both the extent and effect of parental involvement. Consequently, I tape-recorded interviews with over 40 parents with children participating in several different sports. It must be noted at this stage that these interviews were part of a feasibility study and as such they provide a general overview of parents' contributions. Moreover, the comments pertain to the parents of children who were involved in high levels of training and competition, rather than participation in sport on either a recreational or casual basis. We hope that the Sports Council will fund a major project into the effects of intensive training on young athletes in which an analysis of the role of the parent will form a significant part. The following are some brief descriptions of the parents' perceptions of their role in their child's sport.

Motivation

In general the parents were instrumental in initiating their child's sports involvement. However, the reasons given for doing so differed. These responses can be roughly classified into four categories. These are:

1　Comments by others.
2　Parent-motivated – no skill factor present.
3　Parent-motivated – skill factor present.
4　Child self-motivated.

1　Comments by others
An example of the first category was the parent who described how, when on holiday, a fellow holiday-maker had commented favourably on his son's hand/eye coordination. On return the eight-year-old was enrolled in a tennis club and has subsequently played competitively for four years. Another example was the comments of a next-door neighbour on the physique of a young girl who was pushing a swing in the garden. On his advice the mother took the girl to a local swimming club. She learnt to swim and now trains four nights a week.

2 Parent-motivated – no skill factor present

The most striking example of the second category was given by the father of a young tennis player who commented, 'I didn't see talent as such . . . I wanted her to be good.' As a consequence he drew a chalk circle on the front room carpet, stood his four-year-old daughter inside with a 'customised' tennis racquet, and hand-fed balls to her until she could return them consistently. The whole process was described as taking weeks and months of patience. The girl went on to achieve considerable success at an early age. However, to prove that this success wasn't a fluke he then repeated the above process with his second daughter.

3 Parent-motivated – skill factor present

Only one parent fell into the third category. A father thought his son had a good eye for the ball so he was taught to play tennis.

4 Child self-motivated

In the fourth category, child-motivated, it was mainly the adolescent athletes who had initiated their own sports involvement, although they usually had the subsequent support or encouragement of one or both parents. Alternatively, sport was seen as a 'whole-family' activity and the child took up sport to be in line with other family members. This was particularly the case with the sibling who wanted to be like a brother or sister.

As with the findings of previous research, it seemed to be the case that either one or both parents had been or still were actively involved in some kind of sporting activity. One family described sport as 'a family business', the mother and father commenting that they couldn't imagine a child of theirs who wasn't involved in sport to some extent. However, some children upset their parents by changing to a sport their mother or father didn't approve of.

The attitudinal component of the parental socialisation process concentrated upon facilitating aggressive behaviour. A mother said of her daughter (9.5 years), 'The aggression's got to be there – if you don't hate the man next to you, you're not going to get anywhere.' Similarly, a father commented that you had to nurture a sort of aggression. Part of my interest here is to determine whether this parental emphasis on the development and display of aggression increases the likelihood of the child behaving aggressively in other non-sporting situations or developing conduct disorders or other behaviour problems.

Supporting Roles

Once 'talent' had been identified, the child was then enrolled in a club. Very few parents coached their own children, although most supervised additional training sessions. In order to further his child's sporting career, one father wrote to 'Jim'll Fix It', a children's television programme, and arranged for his son to play against Billy Jean King. However, in terms of supporting roles, the parents' responses could be divided into three areas: (1) Emotional; (2) Financial and (3) Provisionary.

1 Emotional Role

The emotional role described by the parents centred mainly on support before, during and after performance. Behaviours described included discussion of tactics, analysis of defeats and victories and, as one father said, 'watching out for cheats'. Some parents and children seemed unable to separate themselves once within the training and perform-ance situations. One child described how she always looked at the expression on her father's face to see if she was playing well. In some instances this kind of dependence led to an emotional over-involvement. (The child's use of the pronoun 'we' provides an interest-ing marker of parental overinvolvement. Consequently, a swimmer commented, 'It is my fault we lost'; and another stated, 'If we come last I feel ashamed.') Where the young athlete had become self-motivated, however, the parents then felt that it was their responsibility to evaluate the scale of future sports involvement, and decide how much they should push, persuade, or support the young athletes' fantasies or sporting objectives. A consequence of this was that some adolescents reported that their parents only saw them as athletes and not as individuals in their own right. The impact of this positive labelling process prompted one successful 16-year-old footballer to remark that his parents' continual interest was a considerable source of stress as they constantly reminded him of his sporting aspirations.

2 Financial Role

Many parents gave considerable financial support to their children's sporting activities, although none complained about cost. Sports dif-fered, however, as to how much money was required, with tennis demanding the most financial investment. Figures quoted for keeping a child on the tennis circuit varied from between £30 to £80 per week. This included money spent on coaching, transport and equipment.

3 Provisionary Role

The main function of the parents was to take the child to and from the training or performance facility. Because of the commitment of the parents' time, in many cases this necessitated staggering meal-times to cater for all the family members. However, there appeared to be a clear division of labour within the family as to who took responsibility for these provisionary supporting roles. Although it was the father who usually initiated sports participation, it was left to the mother to provide the supporting role and therefore enable the child to continue. This included taking the child to training, waiting, coming home, and arranging a number of different meal times – a situation which was described as having implications for marital disharmony, as arguments arose over the frequent absences of the wife in a number of the families interviewed.

The extent of any of these parental supporting roles is dependent on two factors: the child's particular sporting activity and the degree of training commitment. Many of the parents, particularly those of young swimmers and tennis players, had at the outset little idea of the extent of the commitment necessary to enable a young athlete to train and compete regularly in these sports. Many complained of having no time to see friends, weekdays being taken up with training, weekends with competition. This involvement also had severe effects on other aspects of family life, and in particular on any siblings who, for nothing more than logistical reasons were also taken training. This situation led to its own kind of domestic problems, with some athletes feeling guilty over the level of parental interest in them, others feeling that the sibling resented his/her success. Because of this type of disruption of family life, some parents expressed a secret desire that their child would give up sport so that they could become a 'normal' family once again.

Conclusion

It is evident from the above, albeit brief, review that the parent provides a number of important functions in youth sport. When questioned, however, many were unclear as to the exact nature of their role – a position not helped by frequent parental criticism of the coach who was often accused of not communicating fully with parents about their child's progress. Similarly, in keeping with research in developmental psychology, the role of the child in eliciting various parental behaviours has been ignored. It is obvious that a great deal of what parents do is determined by their children's prior actions. In keeping with this thesis Smith and Smoll (1983) have recently proposed the athlete triangle as a model for facilitating the interaction between the parent, coach and athlete. All contribute to the success and enjoyment of youth sport programmes. Parents naturally identify with their children to some degree and want them to be successful. However, whether or not this involvement becomes maladaptive seems to depend very much on the level of communications and understanding between the athlete, parent and coach. Parents must be taught, therefore, not to see their children's sports participation solely in terms of winning and losing; they can also help children to develop a sense of autonomy and independence from their participation in sports activities by allowing them to think for themselves. Some sporting organisations are now endeavouring to maximise this contribution by preparing guides for the parent. He or she is as much in need of guidance and recognition, particularly in the early stages, as the young child.

We must endeavour, therefore, to educate and involve parents so that they, like their children, can enjoy youth sport. Alienating them from the sporting environment would deny many parents a considerable source of pride and vicarious enjoyment, and deprive youth sport of an important resource, necessary if children's sport is to flourish.

References

GREENDORFER, S. (1977) 'The role of socialising agents in female sports involvement.' *Research Quarterly*, 48: 304–10.

LEWKO, J. and GREENDORFER, S. (1982) 'Family influence and sex differences in children's socialisation into sport: a review.' In R. MAGILL, M. ASH and F. L. SMOLL (eds) *Children in Sport*. Champaign, IL: Human Kinetics.

ORLICK, T. (1972) *Family Sport Environment and Early Sports Participation*. Paper presented at the Fourth Canadian Psychomotor Learning and Sports Psychology Symposium, Waterloo, Ontario.

ORLICK, T. and BOTTERILL, C. (1975) *Every Kid Can Win*. Chicago, IL: Nelson-Hall.

SHERIF, C. and RATTRAY, G. (1976) 'Psychological development and activity in middle childhood: 5–12 years.' In J. G. ALBINSON and G. M. ANDREW (eds) *The Child in Sport and Physical Activity*. Baltimore, MD: University Park Press.

SMITH, R. E. and SMOLL, F. L. (1983) 'Approaches to stress reduction in sports medicine: health care for young athletes.' *American Academy of Paediatrics*: 210–17.

Physiology

9

Some Aspects of the Exercise Physiology of Children

N. C. Craig Sharp

As exercise and sport become more popular, many coaches are being asked to coach younger and younger performers. I have, for example, been associated with the England Under-10 Boys' Squash Squad, and there are many other instances of youth sport, apart from the traditional early-recruiting sports of swimming and gymnastics. Children differ from adults in some of their responses to hard physical activity. Children are not simply 'little adults' physiologically, and here I shall discuss important areas of difference, both qualitative and quantitative.

Size

Children do not grow at an even rate. In particular, there is an 'adolescent growth spurt' which carries them through puberty, and is a time of very marked growth with up to 6in (15cm) over two years being not uncommon. The spurt occurs about two years earlier in girls than in boys. It commonly begins between the ages of 10 to 12 years in girls, and 12 to 14 years in boys, and stretches over about two years for each. Thus there is a stage when many girls will be bigger, heavier and possibly stronger than boys of the same age. Also, children of the same sex and age may be at very different stages in their growth, and this has implications for age-group sport. Some early-maturing athletes may become demoralised when their slower-growing peers catch up, and some later-maturing youngsters may give up the unequal struggle and drop out of sport altogether.

Bones

Before the growth spurt, boys and girls are much the same in skeletal terms. After their respective spurts, however, the girls end up with a broader pelvis and hips, and the boys come to have relatively broader shoulders and longer arms. Their broader hips are one reason why some girls tend to throw out their heels when they run. Some girls may also develop a pronounced 'carrying angle' in their arms, which may cause some interference with girls' throwing.

Long bones grow from epiphyseal plates of cartilage near each end; anabolic steroids may interfere with the epiphyseal plates, which may also be damaged by overload stress. Various other parts of bone fuse together to form the mature bone, throughout the teens. Repetition stress may affect this process, and Grisogono (1985) has noted the frequency of heel pain in 12-year-olds, knee pain in 16-year-olds, and back pain in 20-year-olds.

Body fat

During childhood, girls have only slightly more fat than boys. For example, at the age of eight a girl may have 18% and a boy 16% body fat. During the growth spurt, the girls tend to put on fat, up to about 25% at 17, while the boys tend to lose it, going down to 12% to 14% at the same age. This difference may well help the girls in swimming (buoyancy, streamlining) and in keeping warmer under cold conditions – and, of course, it is largely responsible for the changing shape of the female adolescent, a change which may bring with it alterations in the centre of gravity in the body and in limb segments which may influence some high-skill sports, such as gymnastics, diving and trampolining.

Contrary to popular belief, fat children are often not greedy in terms of excess calorie intake. For example, Johnson *et al.* (1956) (Figure 9.1) have shown that overweight adolescent girls tend to have a much lower calorie turnover than their normal weight controls. Similarly, Rose and Mayer (1968) have shown that the percentage body fat of six-month infants is positively related to lack of activity rather than calorie intake. Lack of exercise or activity is extremely important in adolescent obesity. With sports groups, of course, one has always to bear in mind the possibility of anorexia nervosa in some female adolescents. Naturally, with my own squads I counsel that low body fat is desirable, but with the vulnerable female age-groups I indicate that a 'reasonable' level of body fat is desirable, and I tend to place that level at least around 18%. In my experience, between 16% to 18% is the threshold body fat value in the young woman below which she may well temporarily stop menstruating. Such amenorrhoea may be associated with a degree of osteoporosis, or calcium loss from bones, which may in turn be associated with stress fractures. Thus one can make out a reasonable case for the teenage to early 20s sportswoman not to get too low in body fat.

Increases in body fat occur because of increases in fat cell size, or in the number of such fat cells, or both. Fat cells appear to increase in number until early adolescence, after which increases in body fat occur mainly by increasing cell size. It may be possible to affect the development of fat cells during the growth of the child by means of diet (cutting

Figure 9.1   *Frequency distribution of 29 overweight and 23 control adolescent girls according to their daily calorie turnover. Based on interviewer-administered recall questionnaires. Schematic adaptation from Johnson et al.*

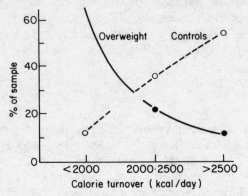

out too many sweets and 'junk food'), physical activity and exercise. Fat children occur in both sexes, and 80% of them go on to be fat adults. As mentioned, lack of exercise is a very important factor in obesity, and obese children take much less exercise even when they are active. Obese children require a higher oxygen uptake to do a given task, yet their maximal oxygen uptake is often lower than that of leaner children, so activity seems harder for them (Boileau *et al.*, 1985).

Children in general possess more of the heat-producing tissue known as 'brown fat', which diminishes as they get older. Brown fat may have a weight-regulating function, acting as a 'ponderostat', and it may be that obese children are born with relatively less of it.

Heart and lungs

Maximal adult heart rates for both sexes are about 200 per minute at 20 years old. Children's rates can go higher, up to 215 or more, but decline once physical maturity has been reached. This high rate is presumably to compensate for their relatively smaller hearts. At relatively equal exercise loads, a child's heart may well beat at 20 per minute more than an adult, but at considerably lower blood pressure.

It has been thought (e.g. Morganroth, 1975) that much isotonic exercise in childhood (swimming, running, hockey, lacrosse, squash, football) would produce large hearts with relatively unthickened walls, whereas 'strength' sports (rowing, canoeing, weight-training, gymnastics) would produce smaller hearts with relatively much thicker walls. It was wondered whether such thicker-walled hearts might not lead to higher increases in blood pressure in later life. However, Dr Len Shapiro, among others, has shown that these two heart responses do not occur as previously thought.

Children have much higher respiratory rates than adults during exercise, taking shorter and shallower breaths; for example, where an adult might take 40 breaths a minute, a child might take 60. This is not harmful, but it is wasteful of energy and body water (and, en masse, may be one cause of the 'contagious hysterias' of children – a response to the feeling induced by blowing off too much carbon dioxide). This may also lead to cramp-like contractions of hands and feet, one cure for which is to breathe in and out of a medium-sized paper bag for periods of around 10 seconds at a time. The six-year-old child may need to breathe 38 litres of air to gain one litre of oxygen during maximal exercise, whereas the 18-year-old needs only 28 litres (Figure 9.2).

Figure 9.2   *Ventilatory equivalent during maximal exercise, as related to age*

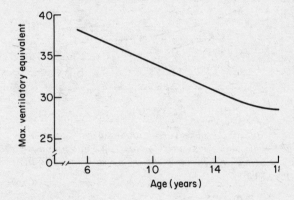

Aerobic power

This term refers to the amount of oxygen the body can use in a given time. The more oxygen that is used, the more energy is generated by muscle. Between five and 10 years of age aerobic power is much the same in both sexes. During their earlier growth spurt some girls may go ahead, but from about 14 onwards they tend not to improve on a volume-of-oxygen-per-weight basis (mainly because of the marked increase in body fat percentage), whereas boys go on improving until 18. Children are 'wasteful' of energy, probably for various biomechanical (muscle mass relative to limb levers) and biochemical (lower stores of muscle glycogen, lower concentrations of appropriate muscle enzymes) reasons. For example, the oxygen costs of walking and running in children are higher than in adults. Figure 9.3 shows that the energy cost of treadmill walking to decrease from, for example, 47ml $O_2/kg^{-1}/min^{-1}$ at six years old down to 38ml at 17 (boys at 10km/hr^{-1}: Astrand, 1952) and Figure 9.4 shows similar differences in uphill walking (Skinner *et al.*, 1971).

Figure 9.3 *Submaximal O₂ uptake and age. 67 girls and 72 boys, 14 to 18 years of age*

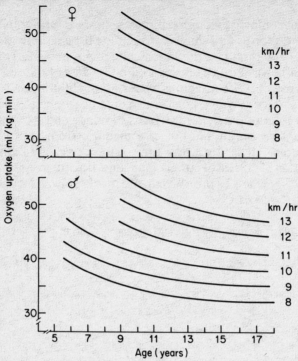

Figure 9.4 *Oxygen cost of walking at various slopes. Mean values for 6- to 15-year-old girls (n = 64) and boys (n = 83) subdivided into four age-groups. Subjects walked at 5–6 km/hr on a motor-driven treadmill. Based on data by Skinner et al.*

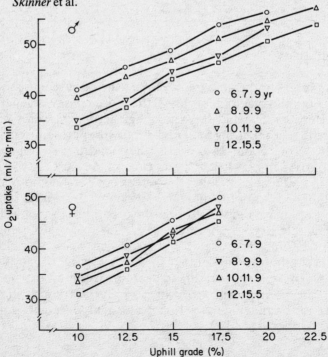

For cycling, the energy costs are much closer for younger and older children; the cycle seems to make the younger children relatively more efficient.

Thus older children are higher in 'aerobic power' than younger children, but as we will see below all children gain a higher proportion of their energy from aerobic than anaerobic sources compared to adults. Children may be said to be very aerobic creatures, being relatively poor at producing energy anaerobically.

Anaerobic power

The ability of children to perform anaerobic activities is distinctly lower than that of adolescents who in turn are lower in this ability than adults. Anaerobic activities may be taken to include those which are very intense and last up to a minute, such as the sprint swims and runs, and the jumps and throws, or those games such as netball, lacrosse, shinty, hurling, football and squash where frequent bursts of activity are required (as they are to an even greater extent in Olympic and rhythmic gymnastics, karate, akido, judo, boxing and wrestling).

Even when normalised for body-weight differences, the anaerobic energy produced by an eight-year-old is only 70% of that produced by an 11-year-old, which in turn is less than that of a 14-year-old (Kurowski, 1977), as is shown in Figure 9.5. Figure 9.6 (Bar-Or, 1983) indicates the comparison of the availability and utilisation rate of the two anaerobic energy sources, creatine-phosphate and glycogen in the muscles of pre-adolescent boys. As shown, the child's muscle has less glycogen, and a much lower rate of utilisation of the glycogen, and it

Figure 9.5 *Maximal anaerobic power and age. Chemical power expended in the Margeria step-running test of 294 9- to 16-year-old girls and boys. Mean value of age-groups represented in absolute terms (○ = girls, ● = boys) and per kilogram body weight (□ = girls, ■ = boys). Based on data by Kurowski*

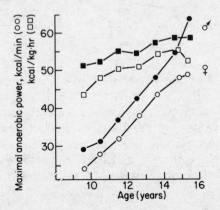

Figure 9.6   *Substrate availability and utilisation in muscles of pre-adolescent boys*

Substrate	Resting Values		Utilisation Rate During Exercise
	Concentration in Muscle mmol/kg Wet Weight	Compared with Older Individuals	
ATP	3.5–5	No change with age	Same as adults
CP	12–22	Lower in children	Same or less than adults
Glycogen	45–75	Lower in children	Much less than adults

has less creatine-phosphate, the anaerobic energy store. Eriksson (1971) among others has shown that children's muscle produces very much less lactic acid than that of the adult (Figure 9.7). Children incur less of an oxygen deficit at the beginning of exercise (Figure 9.8: Macek and Vavra, 1980) which implies that they gain their 'second wind' quicker than adults. Also, their capacity for acquiring an 'oxygen debt' (post-exercise recovery oxygen) is less than that of adults and their 'anaerobic threshold' (the point at which they eventually do go anaerobic) is much higher.

Figure 9.7   *Muscle lactate of children and adults. Comparison between 13.5- to 14.8-year-old boys and young men of muscle lactate concentration (per wet tissue) at different cycling intensities. Vertical lines represent 1 SEM. Data of Eriksson*

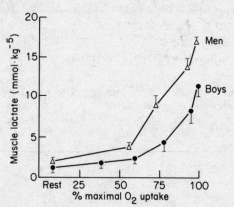

The implications of this are that children are much more aerobic than adults, so ideally their activities should be longer, rather than shorter. They are metabolically more at home running slightly longer distances (800 and 1500 metres) than 50 to 200 metres; in fact, they are well adapted to relatively long periods (with rest intervals) of moderate physical activity. Nevertheless, as Eriksson has shown with boys from 11 to 15 years, all their anaerobic parameters may be increased with training.

Figure 9.8   *Oxygen deficit of children and adults. Oxygen uptake transients of 10- to 11-year-old boys and of 20- to 22-year-old men who cycled at 90%–100% of their predetermined maximal power loads. Adapted from Macek and Vavra*

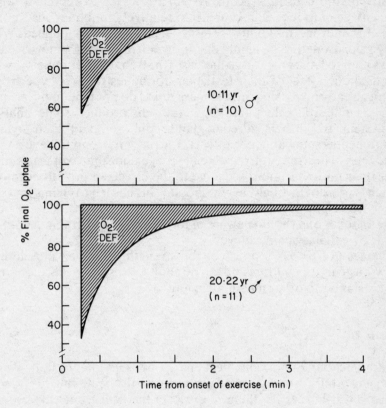

Metabolic specialists

Mature adults, of either sex, tend to fall into three activity groups: those who are good at vigorous short exercise (anaerobic); those who are good at the 'long' activities (aerobic ones, such as cycle-touring, marathons, long swims and fell-walking); and a third group who can do both but neither particularly well. In other words, adults tend to specialise, metabolically speaking. They do not have much control over this as it is to a considerable extent due to the genetic make-up of their muscle in terms of fast and slow fibre types. Young children, say up to 10 (girls) and 12 (boys), are very much less specialised in this way; the ones who can run fast can usually run far as well, but this gradually changes as they get older. The muscle cell patterns are decided from birth, but the patterns do not become fully effective until the time between puberty and full maturity.

Strength

For adults, at least part of the process of becoming stronger is the ability of the central nervous system to 'learn' to recruit a higher percentage of its individual fibres into relatively simultaneous contraction. In children, this ability seems to be much less pronounced. When they gain strength it is mainly due to hypertrophy of the muscle cells. Boys tend to have fairly large increases in strength after puberty, when the anabolic effect of their testicular hormones triggers hypertrophy on an already increasing muscle mass. Girls do not tend to have such a marked pubertal effect (although they do produce some anabolic androgens from their adrenal glands, and some of their ovarian hormone has some anabolic effect). Indeed, girls tend to have a more gradual rise in strength from a younger age and some workers believe that their muscle is more sensitive to the effects of growth hormone, which is present throughout childhood. This has led to claims that girls are more responsive to strength-training before puberty than are boys. In both sexes one should beware of too heavy weight-training until full bone growth has been achieved.

Davies (1985) has found that the strength of human muscle is 33 Newtons/cm^2 for children and young adults, irrespective of age and sex – very similar to other mammalian muscle.

Heat balance

Children expend more chemical energy per kilogram of body weight than do adults, so they produce more body heat, but for various reasons it is harder for them to disperse the heat from the skin. The sweating apparatus is developed by the age of three, but even so children sweat less than adults – in the case of boys a lot less (Figure 9.9), as women tend to sweat less than men by considerable amounts. Twelve-year-old boys may sweat 400 to 500ml per square metre of body surface per hour, compared to a man's rate of 800 to 800ml. There are actually more sweat glands in a given area of a child's skin, but they seem to produce nearly three times less sweat per gland. Also, children tend to have higher skin temperatures, which hinders the flow of heat from the body core to the periphery because the heat gradient is less. If the environmental temperature is greater than body temperature (or if exposed to too much direct sun), then children run into overheating problems for another reason – connected with their surface area.

In general, for the same shape, the smaller an object is, the bigger is its surface area relative to its weight. A young adult, 177cm tall and weighing 64kg, will have a surface area of 1.80 square metres. An eight-year-old, 128cm tall and weighing 25kg, will have a surface area

Figure 9.9 *Development of sweating rate. Forty boys 7–16 years old exercised at moderate intensity (mean rate 160–170 beats/min) on the cycle ergometer, at 29°C, 60% relative humidity. Exercise time was 15–35 min. The arrow indicates the age at which pubertal changes were first noted. Data by Araki et al.*

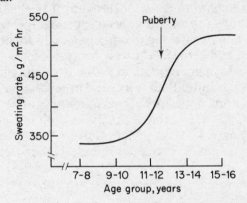

of 0.95 square metres. Thus the young child has 36% more skin surface for his weight. In too hot an environment, that can lead to a faster rate of heating. Children can 'heat acclimatise', but may take up to three times as long as adults to do so.

In too cold an environment – for example, during swimming, especially outdoors, the greater skin area of the child can lead to overcooling and hypothermia much sooner than in adults. Also, young children have less insulating fat immediately under their skins, compared to adults of both sexes. In work with age groups from eight to 19 years old, the subjects were asked to swim at a speed that represented an increase of five times their resting rate of metabolism, for 30 minutes in a pool at 20°C. The older age groups completed the swim without difficulty, but the younger children showed distress and had to be taken from the water in around 18–20 minutes, when their body temperatures were found to have dropped by 2° to 3°C. Municipal and other pools are usually maintained at 25°C or above, but many outdoor swimming situations occur at temperatures of 20°C or much lower. This provides a potential risk, especially for the very keen, lean, small-sized swimmer, who is often reluctant to leave the water. Euphoria, excitability and disorientation are warning signs of hypothermia in such situations.

Voluntary dehydration

With their ability to be physically active for very long periods of time and with their very high breathing rates (and ventilatory equivalents) – both leading to losses of body fluid – children quite easily become relatively dehydrated. This is because, although they become thirsty and drink, tests have shown that they only drink about two-thirds of what they lose – hence the term 'voluntary dehydration'. It will tend to happen gradually on long hot days, and will tend to aggravate any other heat-loss problem such as vigorous exercise. There is a recognised condition in some warmer countries known as 'thirst-fever'. The 'fever', or raised body temperature, is not due to any infection, but is simply a combination of too long overheating and too little fluid, and disappears on the child being adequately rehydrated.

Obese children are at greater risk in the heat (less in the cold!), and as they tend to sweat more than normal, can be at greater risk from dehydration. After one hour walking at 4.8km/hr^{-1} on a 5% incline in dry heat at 40°–42°C (25% relative humidity), nine- to 12-year-old boys classed as 'obese' had rectal temperatures 0.5°C higher than 'lean' controls, and heart rates 35 beats per minute higher (Haymes *et al.*, 1975).

Exercise perception

There are various simple methods whereby a level of exertion may be rated in terms of its relative degree of hardship. On this basis, exercise at equivalent levels is perceived as much easier by children than adolescents, and hardest by adults (Figure 9.10). Also, partly because of their more aerobic metabolism, there is a much faster rate of recovery in young subjects. After a maximum aerobic test in the laboratory, it may be several hours before adults can be persuaded into a further test. Yet most children want to repeat the test well within the hour, to see if they can do better! The habitual high levels of activity of children may result from their not perceiving it as particularly strenuous; adults may prefer their more sedentary style just because they do perceive exercise as particularly fatiguing.

Figure 9.10   *Exercise perception and age. Rating of perceived exertion (RPE) at a given percentage of maximal heart rate (%HR$_{max}$) in some 1300 9- to 68-year-old males who exercised at 100 watts. Schematic presentation, based on Bar-Or.*

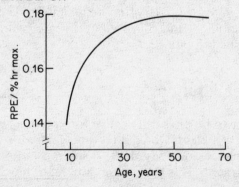

The lesson for sport is that in working with youthful squads, the coach should call for short breaks every 20 minutes or so. This is to act as a check against dehydration, overheating and simple exhaustion.

Conclusion

It is both completely natural and important that children should indulge in considerable physical activity. However, they are not simply small adults, and some of the ways in which they differ from adults are discussed above. The safest course is to let children set their own levels of activity for the most part. Problems arise when children are made to conform to an adult concept of sport, training and exercise.

References

ARAKI, T., TODA, Y., MATSUSHITA, K. and TSUJINO, A. (1979) 'Age differences in sweating during muscular exercise.' *Japanese Journal of Physical Fitness and Sports Medicine*, **28**: 239–48.

ASTRAND, P.-O. (1952) *Experimental Studies of the Physical Working Capacity in Relation to Sex and Age*. Copenhagen: Munksgaard.

BAR-OR, O. (1977) 'Age-related changes in exercise perception.' In G. BORG (ed.) *Physical Work and Effort*. Oxford and New York: Pergamon Press (255–66: reference for Figure 10).

BAR-OR, O. (1983) *Pediatric Sports Medicine*. New York: Springer-Verlag (32: reference for Figure 2).

BOILEAU, R. A., LOHMAN, T. G. and SLAUGHTER, MARY H. (1985) 'Exercise and body composition of children and youth.' *Scandinavian Journal of Sport Science*, **7**, 1: 17–27.

DAVIES, C. T. M. (1985) 'Strength and mechanical properties of muscle in children and young adults.' *Scandinavian Journal of Sport Science*, **7**, 1: 11–15.

ERIKSSON, B. O., KARLSSON, J. and SALTIN, B. (1971) 'Muscle metabolites during exercise in pubertal boys.' *Acta Paediatrica Scandinavica*, Supplement 217: 154–7.

GRISOGONO, VIVIAN (1985) 'Injury and the role of the physiotherapist.' *Coaching Focus*, 2, Autumn: 5–6. (National Coaching Foundation)

HAYMES, E. M., MCCORMICK, R. J. and BUSKIRK, E. R. (1975) 'Heat tolerance of exercising lean and heavy pubertal boys.' *Journal of Applied Physiology*, **39**: 457–61.

JOHNSON, M. L., BURKE, B. S. and MAYER, J. (1956) 'Relative importance of inactivity and overeating in the energy balance of obese high school girls.' *American Journal of Clinical Nutrition*, **4**: 37–44.

KUROWSKI, T. T. (1977) *Anaerobic Power of Children from Ages 9 through 15 Years*. MSc Thesis, Florida State University (quoted in BAR-OR, O., 1983).

MACEK, M. and VAVRA, J. (1980) 'The adjustments of oxygen uptake at the onset of exercise: a comparison between pre-pubertal boys and young adults.' *International Journal of Sports Medicine*, **1**: 75–7 (reference for Figure 6).

MORGANROTH, J., MARON, B. J., HENRY, W. L. and EPSTEIN, S. E. (1975) 'Comparative left ventricular dimensions in trained athletes.' *Annals of International Medicine*, **82**: 521–4.

ROSE, H. E. and MAYER, J. (1968) 'Activity, calorie intake, fat storage and the energy balance of infants.' *Pediatrics*, **41**: 18–29.

SHAPIRO, L. (cardiologist, National Heart Hospital, London) – personal communication, 1986.

SKINNER, J. S., BAR-OR, O. and BERGSTEINOVA, V. (1971) 'Comparison of continuous and intermittent tests for determining maximum oxygen intake in children.' *Acta Paediatrica Scandinavica*, Supplement 217: 24–8.

General Reading

An *excellent* book is:

BAR-OR, ODED (1983) *Pediatric Sports Medicine*. New York: Springer-Verlag.
Three chapters are especially relevant: Chapter 1, 'Physiological Responses of the Healthy Child' (pp. 1–65); Chapter 6, 'Nutritional Diseases' (pp. 192–226), covering anorexia nervosa and obesity very well); Chapter 9, 'Climate and the Exercising Child'.

Also worth reading selectively is the collection of articles published as:

ILMARINEN, J. and VALIMAKI, I. (eds) (1984) *Children and Sport*. New York: Springer-Verlag.

10

Increasing Joint Range of Movement in Young Athletes

Keith Russell

The range of movement about joints is limited by the shape of the articular surfaces, the resistance of connective tissue (tendon, ligament, joint capsule and muscle sheaths) and the resistance of muscle tissue. This chapter discusses the anatomical nature of these joint limitations and the responses of the connective tissue and muscles to various stretching procedures.

Connective tissue response to stretch

Connective tissue is a composite material consisting mainly of parallel arrays of the protein collagen in an interfibrillar ground substance.[1] The collagen *fibrils* form into long, ribbon-like *fibres* which have regular (periodic) waves or crimps. These fibres are densely packed in a mucopolysaccaride matrix and the entire tissue is surrounded by a loose, irregular connective tissue sheath.

Being a viscoelastic material, connective tissue is a combination of elastic solids and viscous fluids and has the properties of strain rate dependency, creep, and stress reduction. Strain rate dependency is a condition whereby a given stress will be met by a given tension (resistance) depending on the rate of stress application. That is, increases in strain rate produce increases in the tension or resistance. This quality allows tendons to accommodate safely to very rapid and powerful muscular contractions.

A constant stress on connective tissue results in a constant strain unless the stress is maintained. If maintained, there is an increase in the tissue length which is termed creep. Moderate stress for prolonged periods causes greater permanent elongation than high stress for short periods.[2]

If the same extension strain (length) is maintained there is a reduction in the amount of stress required to maintain that length. This is termed stress reduction.[3]

Adult tendons respond to stretch by first straightening the crimp or wave pattern of the collagen fibrils (0–1.5% strain). From 1.5–3% strain there is considerable increase in tension as the intra-molecular structure of the fibrils is taking the strain. This is the limit of the elastic or recoverable length. From 3% to 5% strain the increase represents slippage of adjacent molecular chains and is the plastic or non-recoverable length. Fibre rupture begins at 5% strain.[4] Young tissue, lacking the fibril cross bridging of adult tissue, has an elastic limit of 14% or greater.[5]

Cyclic stretching (repeated stretching and relaxing) of at least 10 × 6 second stretches at greater than 2% strain results in permanent tissue elongation.[6,7]

A last point about connective tissue elongation is that long tendons are less prone to rupture than short tendons of equivalent diameter due to their greater energy absorbing capability.[8]

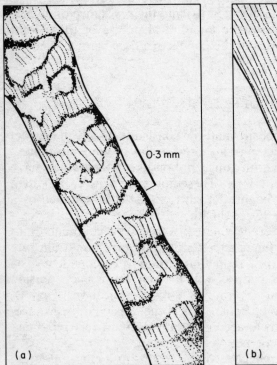 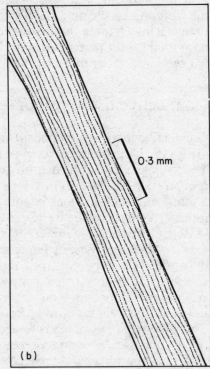

Figure 10.1(a) *A wet unstretched rat-tail tendon as seen under polarized light*
Figure 10.1(b) *The same rat-tail tendon as in (a) stretched slightly: the wave pattern has disappeared. Upon unloading this tendon will immediately revert to the condition shown in (a) provided it has not been stretched more than 4% (after Rigby et al. 1959)*

Muscle tissue response to stretch

The response of muscle tissue to stretch involves elongation of both muscle tissue and connective tissue (muscle sheath and musculo-

Figure 10.2   *The organisation of a skeletal muscle. (F), (G), (H), and (I) are cross sections of the filament at the levels indicated*

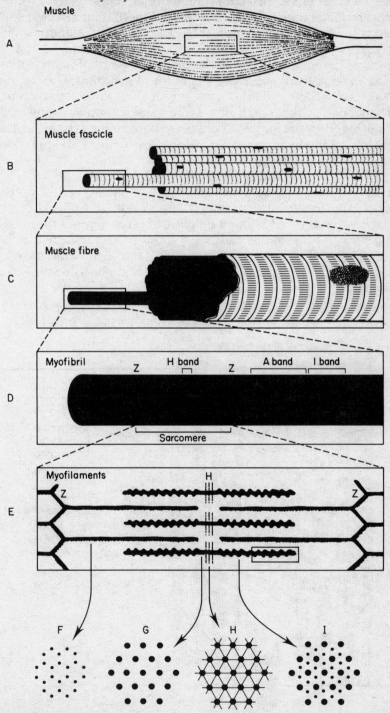

tendinous junction). In addition, there is the complication of the muscle contractions associated with the stretch reflex.

When skeletal muscle tissue is stretched there is an increase in the length of the 'I' band which represents the actin myofilaments 'sliding' over the myosin myofilaments. Since muscle tissue has an optimal amount of myofilamentous overlapping (2.8 μ in tetanic isometric tension and 5% to 10% greater length for twitch contractions)[9] they increase or decrease their resting length to maintain this optimal overlap. That is, the length of a given muscle fibre varies with the habitual length of the muscle to which the fibre belongs. If the habitual length of a muscle is increased, the length of muscle fibres must increase to maintain the optimal overlap of contractile filaments. Similarly, if the habitual length of the muscle is decreased then the muscle fibre lengths must be shortened to maintain the optimal overlap. The lengthening or shortening of muscle fibres is accomplished by the serial addition or deletion of sarcomeres at the ends of fibres.[10,11,12] The stimulus causing muscles to increase in length is prolonged stretch, which elicits an increase in protein synthesis resulting in contractile protein being added longitudinally and cross-sectionally.[13,14]

As muscles are stretched their intrafusal fibres (muscle spindles) are likewise stretched. Connected to these spindles are primary afferent

Figure 10.3 *Structure of the muscle spindle*

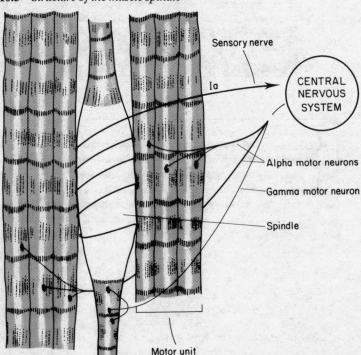

Sensory nerve

Ia

CENTRAL NERVOUS SYSTEM

Alpha motor neurons

Gamma motor neuron

Spindle

Motor unit

(Ia) neurons which, upon stretch of the spindle, send signals to the central nervous system which evoke a 'reflexive' contraction of the extrafusal fibres of that muscle just sufficient to relieve the stretch. This is termed the stretch or myotatic reflex. The Ia neurons fire impulses with a frequency directly related to the velocity of the stretch. This is termed the *phasic response*. Upon reaching a maintained length, the frequency drops to a lower level appropriate to the new length. This is termed the *tonic response*.

Another muscle response to stretching is the *habituation* or lessening of the Ia firing over time. A quick stretch elicits a strong reflex contraction which quickly habituates, while a slow stretch results in a weak reflexive contraction that is slow habituating.[15] Thus stretching a muscle elicits a reflexive contraction which resists the stretch, but which can be reduced by maintaining the stretch.

In addition to the Ia innervation of the muscle spindle there is also efferent innervation via the gamma motor neurons which innervate the contractile ends of each spindle. Innervating the spindle ends cause them to contract thus stretching the central portion of the spindle. This stretch, in turn, elicits the 'stretch reflex'. The activation of the gamma motor neurons allow the muscle spindles to be 'pre-set', thus adjusting their sensitivity independent of absolute muscle length or load. This is called setting the gamma bias and is under volitional control of the motor cortex of the brain. It is a relaxation mechanism that can be utilised in some stretching methods. (A conscious effort to relax can depress the response to the tendon tap.)[16]

Methods of increasing joint range of movement

The limits of movement about joints can be divided into two ranges. The first is the *passive range* which is the maximum range possible and which is attainable only with the aid of external forces such as gravity or a partner's assistance. The second range is the *active range* which is attained by internal muscular forces. For example, doing a splits on the floor demonstrates passive range whereas hanging on a bar and lifting the legs to a splits demonstrates active range.

Methods That Increase Passive Range

Increasing the limits of the passive range necessitates elongating both the muscle tissue and the connective tissue in the 'target area'. In addition, reducing the stretch reflex reduces the amount of resistance.

The following are methods for increasing passive range:

Method 1: – initiate stretch slowly, maintain for prolonged period of time.

Rationale: – reduces resistance of connective tissue to quick stretching (stress rate dependency);
– decreases the resistance of connective tissue due to stress reduction;
– decreases the resistance of connective tissue due to viscoelastic creep;
– reduces the reflexive contraction due to habituation of the stretch.

Method 2:   – consciously relax the target area and imagine it more flexible than it is.

Rationale: – set the gamma bias. That is, relax the contractile ends on the muscle spindles in the target area thus pre-setting the spindles in elongated position.

Method 3:   – contract (slowly to maximum and hold at least 6 seconds) the target muscles while they are being stretched (passive PNF).

Rationale: – results in a four direction stretch of the tendons.

Method 4:   – cyclically contract (slowly to maximum and hold at least 6 seconds) and relax the target muscles while they are being stretched.

Figure 10.4

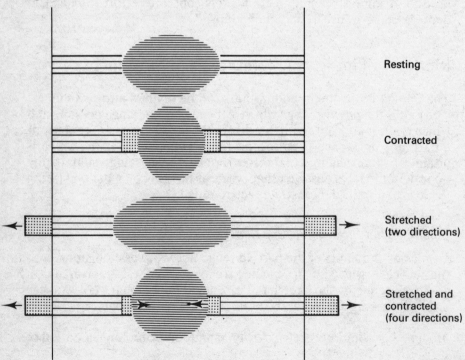

Resting

Contracted

Stretched
(two directions)

Stretched and
contracted
(four directions)

Rationale: – this does the same 'super stretching' as method 3 but also cyclically stretches the connective tissue.

Method 5:   – contract the agonist muscles while target muscles are being stretched.

Rationale: – should result in less reflexive contraction of target muscles due to reciprocal inhibition (a recent study by Moore and Hutton[19] does not support this).

Stretching plus applications of heat,[2,20] cold,[21,22] and massage[23,24] have been studied, but the results do not warrant the additional methodological complexity.

Methods That Increase Active Range

Sport movement demands the active displacement of limbs to the limits of range of movement much more than the passive displacement of limbs. Methods for developing active range should therefore predominate in sports training. Research has been equivocal on the relative efficacy of different methods of stretching on the active versus the passive ranges.[17,18,25,26,27,28] This author, through much 'field' experience, is convinced that too much time and effort is wasted in flexibility training because not enough attention is given to the strength/power aspect of active flexibility. That is, to increase active range *the resistance of the target tissues must be reduced but also the strength/power of the agonist muscles must be increased*. The following are methods for increasing active range:

Method 6:   – passive stretch plus active hold (passively stretch target area while contracting the agonists).

Rationale: – attains both goals of decreasing resistance while increasing strength through the isometric contraction of the agonists.

Method 7:   – dynamic or spring stretching – this method involves the cyclic or repetitive lifting of a limb in and out of the end range of movement. (This is commonly seen in ballet bar exercises.) This method should be done with a limited amplitude – moving only near the end range such that limb velocity is reduced.

Rationale: – develops the concentric strength/power needed to enhance active range while at the same time cyclically stretches target area.

Method 8:   – in passive range (with aid from external force), contract the target area followed by contraction of agonists (active PNF).[17,18]

Rationale: – being at end range (passive range) stretches target area; contracting target muscles gives 'super stretch'; and contracting agonists develops strength/power of agonists plus may reduce stretch reflex via reciprocal inhibition. The successive contracting of target muscles and agonist muscles induces stronger contractions from each (successive induction) thereby increasing both the stretch and the strength/power adaptation.

Method 9:   – as method 8, but alternating passive or passive cyclic stretching as the athlete rests between sets of contractions.

Rationale: – as method 8 plus benefit of cyclic stretching and recovery of muscle energy sources.

References

1 SOKOLOF, L. and BLAND, J. H. (1975) *The Musculoskeletal System*. Baltimore, MD: Williams and Wilkins.

2 WARREN, C. G., LEHMANN, J. F. and KOBLANSKI, J. N. (1976) 'Heat and stretch procedures, an evaluation using rat tail tendon.' *Archives of Physical Medicine and Rehabilitation*, **57**: 122–6.

3 FROST, H. M. (1973) *Orthopaedic Biomechanics*. Springfield, IL: Charles C. Thomas.

4 BENEDICT, J. V., WALKER, L. B. and HARRIS, E. H. (1968) 'Stress-strain characteristics and tensile strength of unembalmed human tendon.' *Journal of Biomechanics*, **1**: 53–63.

5 VIIDIK, A. (1973) 'Functional properties of collagenous tissues.' In D. A. HALL and D. S. JACKSON (eds) *International Review of Connective Tissue Research*. New York: Academic Press.

6 RIGBY, B. J. (1964) 'Effect of cyclic extension on the physical properties of tendon collagen and its possible relation to biological ageing of collagen.' *Nature* (London), **202**: 1072–4.

7 ABRAHAMS, M. (1967) 'Mechanical behavior of tendon in vitro.' *Medical and Biological Engineering*, Vol. 5, pp. 433–43.

8 WELSH, R. P., MACNAB, I. and RILEY, V. (1971) 'Biomechanical studies of rabbit tendon.' *Clinical Orthopaedics*, **81**: 171–7.

9 CLOSE, R. I. (1972) 'Dynamic properties of mammalian skeletal muscles.' *Physical Review*, **52**: 129–97.

10 GOLDSPINK, G., TABARY, C., TABARY, J. C., TARDIEU, C. and TARDIEU, G. (1974) 'Effect of denervation on the adaptation of sarcomere number and muscle extensibility to the functional length of the muscle.' *Journal of Physiology*, **236**: 733–42.

11 GOLDSPINK, D. F. (1977) 'The influence of activity on muscle size and protein turnover.' *Journal of Physiology*, **264**: 283–96.

12 TABARY, J. C., TABARY, C., TARDIEU, C., TARDIEU, G. and GOLDSPINK, G. (1972) 'Physiological and structural changes in the cat's soleus muscle

due to the immobilization at different lengths by plaster casts.' *Journal of Physiology*, **224**: 231–44.

13   FRANKENY, J. R., HOLLY, R. G. and ASHMORE, C. R. (1983) 'Effects of graded duration of stretch on normal and dystrophic skeletal muscle.' *Muscle and Nerve*, May.

14   HOLLY, R. G., BARNETT, J. G., ASHMORE, R. G., TAYLOR, R. G. and MOLE, P. A. (1980) 'Stretch induced growth in chicken wing muscles: a new model for stretch hypertrophy.' *American Journal of Physiology*, **238**: C62–71.

15   GARDNER, E. B. (1969) 'Proprioceptive reflexes and their participation in motor skills.' *Quest*, **12**: 1–25.

16   EDINGTON, D. W. and EDGERTON, V. R. (1976) *The Biology of Physical Activity*. Boston , MA: Houghton Mifflin.

17   HARTLEY-O'BRIEN, S. J. (1980) 'Six mobilization exercises for active range of hip flexion.' *Research Quarterly*, **51**: 4: 625.

18   RUSSELL, K. W. (1977) *A Comparison of Six Methods of Stretch on the Passive Range of Hip Flexion*. Unpublished Master's Thesis, University of British Columbia, Canada.

19   MOORE, M. A. and HUTTON, R. S. (1980) 'Electromygraphic investigation of muscle stretching techniques.' *Medicine and Science in Sports and Exercise*, **12**, 5: 332.

20   HENRICSON, A. S., FREDRIKSSON, K., PERSSON, I. *et al.* (1984) 'The effect of heat and stretching on the range of hip motion.' *Journal of Orthopaedic and Sports Physical Therapy*, **6**, 2: 110.

21   EBRAHIM, KHOSRON (1982) *The Effect of Cold Application and Flexibility Techniques on the Hip Extensor and their Influence on Flexibility*. Ph.D. Thesis, North Texas State University.

22   CORNELIUS, W. and JACKSON, A. (1984) 'The effects of cryotherapy and PNF on hip extension flexibility.' *Athletic Training*, Fall.

23   WIKTORSSON-MOLLER, M., OBERG, B., EKSTRAND, J. and GILLQUIST, J. (1983) 'Effects of warming up, massage and stretching on range of motion and muscle strength in the lower extremity.' *American Journal of Sports Medicine*, **11**, 4: 249.

24   CROSMAN, L. J., CHATEAUVERT, S. R. and WEISBERG, J. (1984) 'The effects of massage to the hamstring muscle group on range of motion.' *Journal of Orthopaedic and Sports Physical Therapy*, **6**, 3: 168.

25   HARDY, L. (in press) 'Improving active range of hip flexion.' *Research Quarterly*.

26   CORNELIUS, W. L. and HINSON, M. M. (1980) 'The relationship between isometric contractions of hip extensors and subsequent flexibility in males.' *Journal of Sports Medicine and Physical Fitness*, **20**: 75–80.

27   HOLT, L. E., TRAVIS, T. M. and OKITA, T. (1970) 'A comparative study of three stretching techniques.' *Perceptual and Motor Skills*, **31**: 611–16.

28   TANIGAWA, M. C. (1972) 'Mobilization on increasing length.' *Physical Therapy*, **52**: 725–35.

11

An Overview of Sports-related Lower-limb Epiphyseal Injuries

James Watkins

Introduction

Over the past decade there has been a considerable increase in the number of children and adolescents involved in organised sports (Kozar and Russel, 1983). In the USA, for example, there are at the present time an estimated twenty million participants between the ages of six and 16 years. The increase in the number of children and adolescents involved in organised sports has been paralleled by an increase in the number of injuries. In the present context injury refers to damage to part of the musculo-skeletal (M-S) system. All of the tissues of the M-S system have a certain mechanical strength, i.e. they can tolerate a certain amount of force without being injured. Injury occurs when the strength of a tissue is exceeded. Most injuries, at all ages, heal with no long-term disability. However, damage to the growing parts of bones, i.e. in the period between birth and adulthood, may have serious long-term consequences.

Growth Plates

Prior to maturity the ends of a bone, i.e. the epiphyses, are separated from the shaft of the bone by plates of cartilage. These plates of cartilage are responsible for growth in length of the bone and are called epiphyseal growth plates (Figure 11.1). In addition to epiphyseal growth plates there are also growth plates which separate the bony anchorages of certain tendons from the shafts of bones. These bony anchorages are called apophyses (*apophysis* = outgrowth) and the growth plates are called apophyseal growth plates. These growth plates are largely responsible for the growth of the bone shaft adjacent to the bony anchorages and are usually found at the attachments of very powerful muscles, for example, quadriceps, hamstrings, triceps surae (Figure 11.1). The proximal and distal epiphyseal growth plates contribute different amounts to the growth in length of a bone; for

Figure 11.1   *Epiphyseal and apophyseal growth plates of the femur*

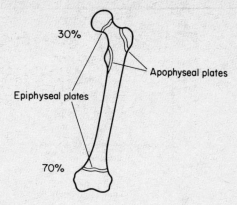

example, the proximal and distal epiphyseal plates of the femur contribute 30% and 70% respectively (Figure 11.1). It follows that injury to the distal femoral epiphysis is likely to have a more serious effect on the growth of the femur than an injury to the proximal epiphysis. At maturity, when a bone has achieved its genetically pre-determined adult length, the epiphyseal plates become ossified (transformed into bone) such that the epiphyses are fused with the shaft and no further growth in length can occur. The time at which fusion between epiphyses and shaft occurs is not the same for all bones. The time of fusion is usually between 14 and 20 years of age. Injury to epiphyseal growth plates may result in serious growth abnormalities. Whereas apophyseal growth plates do not affect growth in length of a bone they do affect the alignment and strength of the tendons which are attached to them. Consequently, damage to apophyseal growth plates can seriously affect the mechanical characteristics of certain muscles which, in turn, may seriously affect normal joint function.

Forms of loading and types of injury

Bones and, therefore, growth plates are subjected to a variety of forces (loads). There are three basic forms of force, namely compression (squashing), tension (stretching), and shear. Shear force is difficult to describe but can be visualised as the action of scissors or garden shears. These three basic forces are often combined in the form of bending and torsion (twisting) (Figure 11.2). Epiphyses, especially those forming weight-bearing joints, are most frequently subjected to compression loading and as such are sometimes referred to as 'pressure epiphyses'. Apophyses, on the other hand, are most frequently subjected to tension loading and are sometimes referred to as 'traction epiphyses'.

Figure 11.2 *Forms of loading*

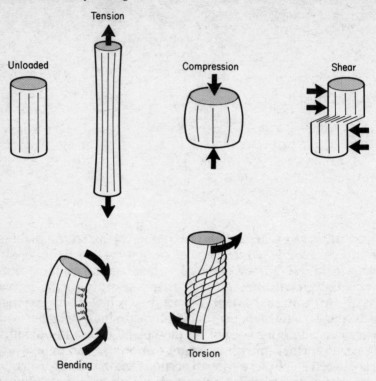

As mentioned earlier, the fundamental cause of injury is excessive loading. Such loading can be in the form of a sudden massive force which results in macrotrauma such as bone fractures or serious ligament and tendon tears. These type of injuries are referred to as acute. Excessive loading can also be in the form of repetitive loading which is not large enough to cause acute injury, but is large enough to cause microtrauma. In the absence of adequate rest the microtrauma gradually accumulates and eventually results in what is referred to as a chronic or overuse injury; for example, stress fractures in bones, tendinitis, bursitis. The growth plates tend to be the weak links in the chain of load transmission and consequently are very susceptible to both chronic (osteochondroses) and acute (fractures along or across the growth plate) injuries. Whereas most growth plate injuries heal with no long-term effects, growth abnormalities in the form of reduced bone length and asymmetric bone growth may result (Barnes, 1979).

Throughout the pre-adolescent and early adolescent periods the development of muscle and tendon strength is less advanced than that of bone. Since one of the major functions of muscles is to minimise bending and torsion load on bones, it is clear that prior to adulthood the skeleton as a whole and the growth plates in particular are very susceptible to injury. The skeleton and growth plates are most susceptible during the adolescent growth spurt when the discrepancy between the growth of the skeleton and the growth of muscle is greatest (Larson, 1973).

Effect of type of activity on the load exerted on the M-S system

Activities which involve large accelerations and decelerations, i.e. large forces in order to rapidly increase or decrease the speed of the body or body parts, subject the M-S system to the greatest load. Activities in this category include the following:

Sprinting and sprint starting;
Jumping and landing;
Throwing and bowling;
Striking: kicking, punching, spiking, tackling in soccer and rugby;
Rebounding: triple jump, vaulting.

In addition to the above sports-related activities, various forms of strength-training are potentially dangerous during the pre-adolescent period. Strength-training activities in which the resistance is provided by free weights (barbells and dumb-bells) and/or one's own body weight are potentially dangerous when performed with rapid changes in direction. For example, Figure 11.3 shows a frequently-used sit-up exercise for developing the flexor muscles of the hip and trunk. A rapid change of direction from extension to flexion (shown in Figure 11.3) will result in rapid deceleration and acceleration of the trunk and, consequently, very large forces in the hip and trunk flexor muscles. In the pre-adolescent such high forces have been found to produce both acute and chronic injuries to the apophyseal growth plates adjacent to the anterior superior and anterior inferior iliac spines which are sites of attachment of hip flexor muscles (see Figure 11.4). It is worth pointing out that the form of sit-up shown in Figure 11.3, like many other strength-training exercises, is only likely to be dangerous when per-

Figure 11.3 *Exercise for developing flexor muscles of hip and trunk*

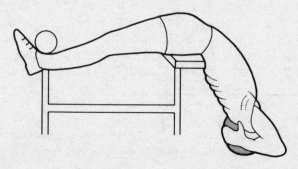

Figure 11.4 *Major pressure and traction epiphyses of the lower limb*

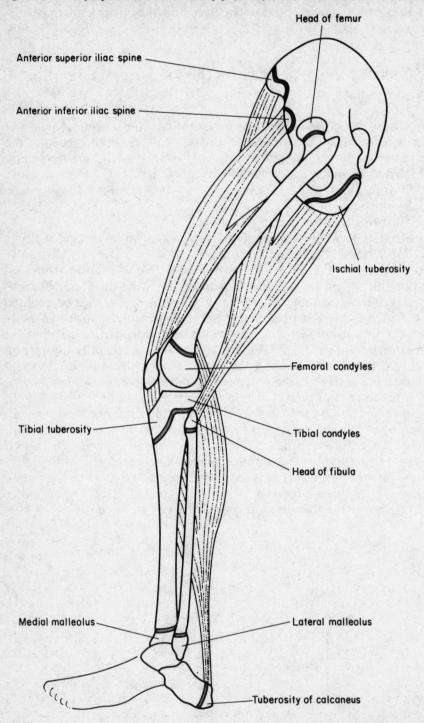

formed inappropriately, i.e. with rapid changes of direction at the start and end of each repetition.

Clearly, all sports which involve impulse-type movements and/or impact of the body with some object or another participant are potentially very dangerous due to the very large forces involved. Whereas most sports subject the body to high loads, the forces generated in impulse/impact sports are not only high, but are also produced very rapidly and it is this combination which results in acute injuries. Activities such as long-distance running, rowing and swimming frequently involve high forces, but the forces are produced over a relatively longer period compared to impulse/impact sports and as such tend to produce chronic rather than acute injuries.

Incidence of epiphyseal injury in different sports

Studies of sports-related injuries in children show that the proportion of injuries involving growth plates is between 6% and 18% of the total number of injuries (Speer and Braun, 1985). According to Larson (1973), only 5% or less of all epiphyseal injuries, i.e. injuries resulting from sports and free-play, proceed to a variation in growth. On the basis of the above figures the number of growth plate injuries resulting in growth variation is in the region of 3 to 9 per thousand. However, this estimate is likely to be a conservative one in that many injuries are not reported. Furthermore, it is only recently that very large numbers of children have been involved in intensive training programmes and the long-term effects of these programmes are not yet known.

Safeguards to the health of the child athlete

The onus is on coaches and administration to safeguard the health of young children participating in organised sports by ensuring high standards with regard to:
1   Proper medical care:
    (a) regular health appraisal;
    (b) availability of medical care during training and competition.
2   Proper physical conditioning:
    (a) development of whole body strength, muscular endurance and flexibility, and the prevention of strength and flexibility imbalances;
    (b) gradual increase in the amount of training/competition.
3   Proper coaching of technique:
    based on fundamental kinesiological and mechanical principles.
4   Appropriate equipment and facilities:
    clothing, apparatus, playing surface.

5   Good officiating and appropriate rule revisions: promotion of enjoyable and safe participation.

References

BARNES, L. (1979) 'Pre-adolescent training: how young is too young?' *Physician and Sportsmedicine*, **7**, 10: 114–19.

KOZAR, B. and RUSSEL, R. M. (1983) 'Overuse injury in the young athlete: reasons for concern.' *Physician and Sportsmedicine*, **11**, 7: 116–22.

LARSON, R. L. (1973) 'Physical acitivity and the growth and development of bone and joint structures.' In G. L. RARICK (ed.) *Physical Activity: Human Growth and Development*. New York: Academic Press.

SPEER, D. P. and BRAUN, J. K. (1985) 'The biomechanical basis of growth plate injuries.' *Physician and Sportsmedicine*, **13**, 7: 72–8.

Stress

12

The Growing Child and the Perception of Competitive Stress in Sport

Glyn C. Roberts

It is no accident that sport performance has improved so dramatically over the past few years. In my opinion, this improvement is directly attributable to application of knowledge from the sport sciences. For example, knowledge of the physiological system under exercise stress has allowed sport scientists to modify training regimens for maximum physiological benefits. Further, knowledge from nutrition, biomechanics, exercise physiology and engineering have allowed coaches to ensure that the sport performer has the energy reserves, optimal technique, the level of strength and fitness necessary and the best equipment to perform at his or her best. (All one has to do is to look what biomechanicians and engineers have done to footwear of late to note the impact of the sport sciences.) But these knowledges and understandings are not limited to élite sportspeople. More and more, as we have heard at this conference, these knowledges are being applied to children under the assumption that, if we produce better trained and skilled junior performers, we shall have better trained and skilled senior performers. Whether this is true or not is not the issue to be debated at this time. My concern is with a facet that sport scientists, coaches, and performers have long neglected – the mind!

In North America, if we poll coaches about what aspect of performing contributes most to positive outcomes, the answer invariably implicates mental factors. Both coaches and performers recognise that mental aspects are important for consistent and enhanced performance. But the mind is the one area that coaches know the least about. Indeed, some coaches resort to psychological procedures that resemble wishful thinking or voodoo rather than the application of a sport science. For example, one American football coach was revealed to bite the heads off day-old chickens as a means of motivating children. (That coach has long since been banned from coaching.) Another coach used to have a specially constructed blackboard that would disintegrate when he punched it. This was supposed to be a motivating act. Clearly, we abhor such tactics. If we wish to enhance the performance of sportsmen and women, or children, through improved psychological functioning, let us do so from a knowledge base gathered by sport psychologists over the years.

The psychology of sport performance is a much neglected sport science. But it is one that is assuming greater and greater importance as we recognise that psychological functioning has an important role to play in sport performance. In other words, we want to make our sportspeople mentally tough. That is my purpose. I want to share with you some information that focuses upon the child in the competitive sport experience. First, I want to look at the competitive sport experience especially from the point of view of the child. Secondly, I want to address the perception of stress of children in sport and those factors that make children drop out of sport. I shall discuss the achievement goals children have in sport, and how they are manifested over the age span. Lastly, I want to address some procedures we can adopt to make the competitive sport experience more sensitive to the needs of children. In particular, I want to illustrate how we can help to prevent dropping out.

Competitive Sport for Children

Should children play highly competitive sports? This, of course, is the ultimate question that has been debated over the years. The supporters of competitive sports for children argue that sports play an important role in socialisation: children are brought into contact with social order and prevailing social values, and are provided with a structure within which to act and develop skills in the interest of social order, social skills, and, just simply, getting on with other children. Thus, sport is viewed as an anticipatory model of society. Sport prepares children to live in society. That sport does contribute to personality development in that it provides a forum for the teaching of responsibility, conformity, subordination of the self to the greater good, and shaping achievement behaviour by encouraging effort and persistence, is generally accepted by many. There is good reason to believe the above to be true, but the evidence is mostly anecdotal.

Critics of sport competition for children focus on the cost in human relations because of an overemphasis on winning, the increase in aggression as a consequence of competition, and so on. But again, the evidence is mostly anecdotal. My objective in this address is to sensitise you to the psychological aspects of the child participating in sport competition. In much of what we do, we sometimes forget that we are dealing with children and not miniature adults! Children do not think in the same way as adults. Therefore, it is important that we should understand children in order to understand how they view participation in competitive sport.

One of the first aspects to understand is the importance of participation in sport programmes for children. Participation in sport has long been assumed to be of value to children (e.g. Coleman, 1961). Veroff (1969) has argued that participation in sport may be *the* domain in which children, boys in particular, determine their standing among their peers and obtain their self-esteem. This is supported by Roberts (1978) and Scanlan (1985). But it was Duda (1981) who obtained the evidence to support this analysis.

Duda (1981) assessed the achievement domain preferences of high school aged (14–18 years) boys and girls in North America. Duda separated the achievement domains into classroom and sport contexts, whether the context was competitive or not, and asked the pupils whether they would prefer to succeed or fail in these contexts. Duda found that boys preferred to succeed on the sport field rather than in the classroom. This confirms other research which has shown that sport is an important achievement context for boys (Coleman, 1961; Roberts, 1978; Veroff, 1969). Interestingly, the girls also preferred to succeed in sport contexts rather than classroom contexts! The only context girls wished to avoid in sports was the individual head-to-head competition with other girls. This finding is consistent with other research (e.g. Kleiber and Hemmer, 1981) which also found that girls prefer not to compete directly with other girls. However, it is revealing that girls consider sport contexts (especially team sports) as appropriate contexts in which to succeed against other girls.

Failure preferences were extremely interesting. Boys indicated that failing in sports was *the* most aversive context in which to experience failure. Boys would rather do poorly in the classroom than on the sporting field. Clearly, for boys, the context of sports is extremely important for their self-esteem and acceptance within the peer group. Duda (1981) found that girls were different from boys in their failure preferences. Girls preferred to fail in sport rather than in the classroom. This very interesting sex difference in failure preference underscores the differing social expectations boys and girls have and how we are socialising boys and girls toward different achievement interests. In western society today, it is almost impossible to underestimate the importance, for boys in particular, of demonstrating competence in sporting activities.

But a paradox exists! Despite viewing sport participation as a most desirable context in which to achieve, children drop out of the competitive sport experience at rapid rates after age 12. Some statistics show that 80% of all children drop out of competitive sport by 12 years of age. And the phenomenon is not peculiar to North America. Research in England and Australia has confirmed these drop-out trends. The same is true for boys and girls. Thus, dropping out of sports is a general phenomenon.

But why do children drop out of sports? Research in this area has been disappointing. Most of the research is descriptive in nature with researchers either implicating the structure of the sport experience (e.g. adults putting too much pressure on children, too much emphasis upon winning) (Orlick, 1974), or concluding that 'conflicts of interest' (e.g. I have other things to do) (Gould, Feltz, Horn and Weiss, 1981) are the primary reasons why children drop out. The majority of researchers have been concerned with identifying the sources of stress which appear to influence the decision of the child to persist or to drop out of the competitive sport experience.

The Perception of Stress

That sport produces high levels of competitive stress is well documented. For example, Hanson (1967) found that the average heart rate of children when they were at bat in baseball (similar to being at the crease in cricket) was 166 beats per minute (bpm) with the range going from 145 bpm to 204 bpm. In contrast, the average heart rate while fielding was 128 bpm. Lowe and McGrath (1971) found similar findings with children when they attempted to determine the situational determinants of perceived stress.

When looking at the perception of stress, however, work by Scanlan (e.g. 1985) and Passer (e.g. 1982) are important to consider. Over the years, both together and separately, Scanlan and Passer have determined that the following elements are implicated in the perception of competitive stress of children. First, children who are higher in competitive trait anxiety perceive great state anxiety in competitive environments. Secondly, children with low self-esteem experience greater stress than children with high self-esteem. Thirdly, children with lower expectancies of doing well experience greater competitive stress than children with high expectancies of doing well. Fourthly, children who worry about receiving evaluation from the coach or their parents experience high stress. Fifthly, children who feel great pressure to compete from parents experience high levels of stress. And sixthly, children who lose experience greater immediate stress than children who win.

Thus, the work of Scanlan (e.g. 1985), Passer (e.g. 1982) and others (e.g. Hanson, 1967) have documented quite categorically that children perceive stress in competitive sport. They have also given us insight into the variables which enhance competitive stress. But why does the child perceive competitive stress? And do children perceive stress the same way over the age span, or is there a developmental facet to the perception of stress? This is where we need to consider a much-ignored element in the perception of stress of children – the information-processing capability of the child at various ages.

The Motivational Goals of Children

The child is an information-processing organism in his or her own right. My purpose here is to discuss the information-processing capability of children and how this affects their perception of the competitive sport experience. We are interested in the beliefs, cognitions and perceptions of children and how these affect their behaviour. In simple terms, we need to know how children think!

The model presented here is derived from contemporary motivation theory and is fully explained elsewhere (Roberts, 1984). In brief, I shall argue that perceived own ability, the perception of competence we all develop through our success and failure experiences in achievement contexts, is the central mediating construct in determining the perception of competitive stress and in decisions governing dropping out or persisting in sport. Based upon Nicholls (1984), it is important to understand the goal of behaviour of children and the *subjective* meaning of achievement within the context for the child. Thus, we need to understand the achievement goal of children to account fully for their perceptions and subsequent behaviour.

A basic assumption of my argument is that the primary achievement goal of every individual is to maximise the demonstration of high ability and minimise the demonstration of low ability. Success for the individual is when ability is demonstrated. But ability is assessed in one of two ways. First, ability may be assessed through social comparison processes where individuals are concerned with their own and the abilities of others and how their own ability compares with the ability of others. Children who focus on social comparison processes generally use win/loss records as their criteria of success and failure and are, therefore, very *outcome* oriented. Secondly, ability may be assessed by one's own personal standards of excellence. These individuals are not concerned with the performance of others; rather, they focus upon their own performance and try to do as well as possible. Success and failure to these individuals is assessed by whether they exceed or fail to exceed previous levels of performance. Therefore, these individuals are *performance* oriented.

Sport Competence

The first goal is one we term sport competence. The focus of attention of the performer is on his/her own ability and how it compares to the ability of others. Children generally try hard in order to demonstrate ability unless they perceive that they are unable to demonstrate ability after which not trying hard becomes feasible. One way to demonstrate ability is to beat other children in competitive contests. Thus, winning and losing outcomes become important criteria to these children who are motivated by the demonstration of sport competence. Winning means ability is demonstrated and competitive stress is low. Losing means insufficient ability is demonstrated and competitive stress is high. Expectancy of winning or losing will also affect the perception of stress. These children are outcome oriented.

Sport Mastery

The second goal is one we term sport mastery. The performer directs his or her attention toward achieving mastery, improving, or perfecting a sport skill rather than demonstrating higher capacity than that of others. These children typically are engrossed in the activity; merely participating often meets this goal, and these children rarely perceive stress in the competitive sport experience. Those children are performance oriented.

While I have argued that the perception of ability is the most crucial variable to understanding achievement behaviour of sportsmen and women, one other variable has been implicated. This variable is social approval (Maehr and Nicholls, 1980).

Social Approval

Sometimes sports performers attempt to solicit social approval from significant others – parents, coaches, teachers, spectators. In this case, the performer is seeking social approval rather than being concerned with demonstrating either outcome-oriented ability or performance-oriented ability. Typically, performers recognise that social approval is dependent upon the demonstration of effort. To the performer, trying hard to get social approval is the goal. When the coach or parent signifies approval, the goal is met.

In review, I have argued that the perception of stress experienced by children, and adults, is based upon their achievement goal within the sport experience. Three goals have been forwarded as being crucial to understanding these perceptions of stress on the part of performers. Further, the goal held by the performer affects whether the performer is motivated to achieve or to cease participation and drop out.

Evidence for Multiple Goals

Are there multiple goals? My students and myself have completed seven studies on this issue now, and Dr Jean Whitehead from Bedford College of Higher Education, England, has completed another. Each of the studies has demonstrated that the goals do exist and do affect achievement behaviour (e.g. Ewing, 1981). Different studies also have identified other important goals, but, in general, the studies have identified the achievement goals of sport competence, sport mastery, and social approval.

The studies have also analysed the thoughts, or attributions, underlying the goal orientations, and confirmed that the demonstration of ability was the major determinant of the goal of sport competence, and to a lesser extent, the goal of sport mastery. Further, the demonstration of effort was the major determinant of social approval. Ewing (1981) also found that the goal orientations interacted with the sport experience so that those students with the higher levels of sport competence were more likely to drop out of the sport experience. The ones who remained were most likely to be social-approval-oriented individuals. Thus, there is evidence that those goals not only exist, but do operate in the competitive sport environment to affect achievement behaviour. It is now appropriate to discuss the development of these goals.

The Development of Achievement Goals

Maehr and Nicholls (1980) suggest that children may go through several stages in the understanding of achievement goals. They suggest that young children may approach the sport because they enjoy the challenge (sport mastery) and are not concerned with the outcome (sport competence). But as children become older, their goals may change. Children may want to please others and/or be rewarded for trying hard (social approval), or to demonstrate their ability to others. Existing evidence suggests that children go through stages in the development of these goals.

Ewing, Roberts, and Pemberton (Note 1) investigated the development of achievement orientations of children who were engaged in baseball or softball. The results revealed that the younger children did not have clear-cut achievement goals as hypothesised earlier. Rather, young children had facets of each of the goals. The results revealed that young children were unable to distinguish between the relative effects of the contributions of effort and ability to success and failure in sport. However, after age 11 years, ability and effort were distinguished and the achievement goals identified earlier did appear clearly. In particular, the achievement goal of sport competence only appeared after age 11. This finding is consistent with the findings of Nicholls (1978) who found that children in the classroom were also unable to distinguish between effort and ability when they were younger than age 12 years. Thus, the evidence suggests that children only develop a full understanding of the ability–effort covariation after age 11 or 12. This means that children do not assess their own competence at the activity until after that age.

It is important to note that understanding the relative effects of effort and ability to performance outcome is crucial to understanding the goal orientation of the child in sport. And age 12 seems to be an important watershed in the development of this understanding.

Children under age 12 think differently from children over age 12. The younger children focus almost solely on effort and most of them believe effort is ability. Indeed, these children believe equal effort leads to equal outcomes. These children are sport-mastery and social-approval-oriented; therefore, their typical behaviours are to try hard and please others. Just participating is enjoyable for these children. And the comments of the coach or parents are important to them. Thus, if they are criticised or praised, they are crushed or elated accordingly. Because they are unable to assess their own ability well, the comments of the coach are particularly important to them. This is why young children typically do not drop out of sports. They enjoy participation and try hard to please. These children do not focus on outcomes (winning and losing) *per se*. Rather, they try to please the coach. These children like to win, but only because winning pleases the coach. The important point is that these children do not understand what the outcome means for their own competence.

Older children, on the other hand, are able to differentiate between ability and effort and are able to assess their own ability to perform within the activity more accurately. It is only when children are able to differentiate between the causes of outcomes that they are able to judge their own capacity at the sport. When children become approximately 12 years of age, they begin to recognise, for the first time, their own ability to perform in the sport. This can be an exciting, or traumatic, discovery. In other words, the achievement goal of sport competence develops, and they assess the available information to make judgements about their ability.

The major criterion that sport competence children focus on is the outcome – in sport, winning or losing. If they, or their team, wins, they feel competent and enjoy the experience. If they, or their team, loses, they feel incompetent and do not enjoy the experience. Thus, the children's motivation to perform, and their perception of competitive stress, is closely allied to their *perceived attainment*. For those children who win and perceive themselves as competent, then little stress is perceived and they enjoy the experience. These children are not likely to drop out. For these children who lose and perceive themselves as incompetent, then great stress is perceived, as being competent in sport is important to them, boys in particular. These children do not enjoy the experience and become candidates to drop out.

Burton and Martens (1986) have data to support the above interpretations. With wrestlers who continued participating or who dropped out, they found that the wrestlers who dropped out were those whose won/loss records led them to perceive that they were low in ability. The wrestlers who persisted were higher in their perception of their own competence.

It is clear that perception of ability as it has developed in children who are aged 12 or over becomes important in the decisions children make about their involvement in competitive sports. If their perception of ability is low and they are unable to cope with the stresses of competitive sport, then they may drop out. But the perception of ability is important for other behaviours, too. Figure 12.1 helps to illustrate the total effect of the perception of ability.

Figure 12.1   *Enjoyment model for children's sport*
(modified from Csikszentimihalyi, 1977)

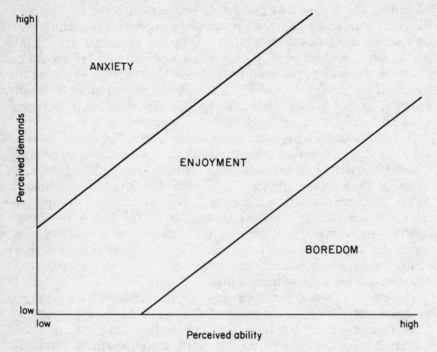

As we have discussed, the perception of ability of the child is crucial to understanding his or her perception of competitive stress. If the perceived demands of the sport experience are considered to be higher than one's ability to cope with them, then competitive stress is experienced and anxiety results. The greater the discrepancy, the greater the perceived stress and subsequent anxiety. If one's ability meets the demands of the task, then enjoyment and satisfaction are experienced. However, if the child perceives his or her ability to be *greater* than the demands of the sport experience, then the child may become bored. The behaviours of these children will change depending upon their perceptions.

We have already discussed the stressed child to some extent. These children often give up and drop out. The reasons they give for dropping out are that they do not enjoy the sport experience, but the reason they do not enjoy the sport experience is because they perceive that they have low ability and feel unable to cope. There is pressure to remain in the experience as participating is valued by the children (Duda, 1981). To reduce the perception of stress, these children often become the 'problem attitude' players. They undermine the statements of the coach, and they try to recruit other children to do the same.

For the child who perceives high ability and who does not feel challenged, then these are the children who feel somewhat bored. These are the players who become the 'show-offs' and who 'hot dog' it! The reason why is that by taking risk, or by not apparently trying hard, and still succeeding, is evidence of even higher ability. Winning by not trying hard is one way of overcoming boredom.

The child who perceives that his or her ability meets the demands will try hard and enjoy demonstrating ability, especially after age 12 years. This is the perception we try to have in all participants. These are the children who are keen and want to succeed.

Summary

Up until now I have tried to illustrate that the perception of stress is dependent upon the player's perception of his or her own competence to perform in the competitive environment. This perception certainly affects the behaviour and enjoyment of the player. The player may enjoy the experience and persist, or the player may not enjoy the experience and drop out. But what can we do about it? It is to that aspect I turn next.

Enhancing Enjoyment for Chidlren

Are children's sports *too* stressful? That is a difficult question to answer. Some children enjoy competitive stress because it allows them to demonstrate their abilities in a contest of importance to them. But other children do experience too much stress and feel anxious and ill at ease. Something should be done for these children. But we can't initiate a program of stress management for 12-year-olds! What we should do is to reduce the amount of evaluation anxiety in the environment.

The one aspect that creates the most evaluation anxiety is the importance the coach places upon winning and losing within the game. The more the coach focuses upon winning and losing for children, the more evaluative is the situation and the more stress is experienced by children. And, as we have seen, for children under 12 years of age, the criteria for success and failure that is adopted by the coach is the criteria that is adopted by the child. Thus, if the coach is outcome oriented, so is the child. This feature has implications for the perception of enjoyment of the child. Because the child does not have a sound understanding of his or her own competence, then the win/loss record of the team and the comments of the coach become the major criteria by which the child assesses his/her own competence. If the child wins, then he or she enjoys the experience. If the child loses, he or she fails to enjoy the experience. Thus, it is important that the coach should do as much as possible to de-emphasise the game outcome as the criteria of success and failure.

Emphasise Sport Mastery

Earlier, we discussed two perceptions of ability held by the child, especially after age 12. One is based upon social comparison processes and the outcome becomes the major criteria to judge the perception of ability held by the child. By emphasising the outcome, we force the child to use a sport competence goal orientation. For the child who sees him or herself not winning, then low ability assessments are made and competitive stress is experienced. The second perception of ability is sport mastery. For a child motivated by mastery, the outcome is *not* an important criteria of ability. As is obvious, what I am advocating is that we attempt to make all children mastery oriented. We want these children to stop comparing themselves to other children and focus on how they are performing in relation to their own previous perform- ance. We must shift the focus of attention of children from *outcome* goals to *performance* goals.

Performance Goals, not Outcome Goals

We have to recognise that children, despite our best intentions, are going to focus attention upon the outcome if we do not help them to change to performance goals. Children see sport on television all the time, and the very nature of the sport experience encourages these social comparison processes. So what we have to do is to encourage coaches to have children move away from asking questions such as 'Am I better than, as good as, or worse than my opponent?', and move toward asking questions such as 'Do I need to change, develop, or maintain my task or game strategy?' The coach can maintain the perception of ability through sport mastery and thereby enhance the motivation of children to remain with the experience.

To do this, we have to turn to goal setting – a psychological skill that is important to develop in children. Once it is developed, performance goal setting becomes the criteria by which children assess their own success and failure. In other words, we redefine success and failure for the child.

In the goal setting programme I advocate, we need to make the child oriented toward own performance, not how their performance compares to others. Coaches have a performance plan for each child because it is important to realise that each child is different.

A Goal-setting Programme

When you set goals, they should be:

A *Flexible* – adapt to situation. Rigid goals can lead to discouragement.
B *Challenging* – make the athlete apply effort to succeed.
C *Realistic* – not overoptimistic, or too easy. Important to realise perception of child here, too; this must be taken into account (e.g. girls overpessimistic; boys overoptimistic).
D *Personally controllable* – encourage feeling of self-determination which increases intrinsic motivation.

Goal-setting Guidelines

A *Set specific goals* – specific, explicit goals much better than general 'do best' type goals. Much research on this.
B *Set difficult, but realistic goals* – remember, difficult and realistic in eyes of child! But there is a linear relationship between goal difficulty and performance.
C *Set short-term, as well as long-term goals* – this is very important – need to recognise an athlete's limitations.
D *Set performance or technique goals* – never set outcome goals. With college swimmers, it has been found that performance goals are more effective than outcome goals.
E *Discuss goal achievement strategies with children* – we forget this. It is all very well for children to have goals, but what do they have to do to achieve them? Specific goal strategies must be defined.
F *Foster individual commitment* – research firmly established that if athlete is committed, goals are achieved. If not, there is little improvement.
G *Provide goal support* – parents as well as coaches must support goal-setting process.
H *Provide goal evaluation* – both goal and performance feedback are necessary for commitment and improved performance.

What Kinds of Goals Can We Set?

This is up to each coach and will be dictated by the sport, but, in general, the over-all mission of our programme is to encourage the child to adopt the criteria of sport mastery. We are trying to maximise the enjoyment of the child to play and to maximise the motivation of the child to continue participating.

But there are some problems in goal setting. The most common problems are:

1 Setting outcome goals, not performance goals.
2 Setting unrealistic goals both for individuals and teams. This is especially difficult when a performance decline is evident such as during the adolescent growth sport.
3 Coach evaluation is too severe.
4 Coach tries to do too much, too soon. *Start slowly*.
5 Recognising individual differences.

In the programme above, we have been discussing intervention at the cognitive level. That is, we are trying to help the children to have the right thoughts when playing. But the coach functions at the behavioural level too. Other researchers have discussed the behavioural aspects (e.g., Smith, Smoll and Curtis, 1979) in greater detail. However, in summary, the following aspects are important from a behavioural point of view.

Coach Must Be Knowledgeable About the Sport

It is essential that the coach should be knowledgeable about the sport he or she is coaching. The coach must be able to reach the fundamentals of the sport so that when children begin to assess their own competence from a social comparison perspective, they do so from a sound skill basis. Further, the coaches must understand the physiological and biomechanical limitations of children. Other people have addressed those concerns, I am focusing upon the psychological in my address today.

Other aspects the coach can affect are as follows:

1 *Modify the sport*
   Coaches can alter the sport for children in order to decrease the performance demands so that more children experience success: for example, smaller playing fields, lower baskets in basketball, and so on. Also, not keeping score, not having leagues or championships, often helps children.
2 *Modify coaching role*
   The most important aspect is to reduce the importance of the outcome as the criterion of success and failure. Children pick this up *very* quickly. The best remedy is a coaching effectiveness programme which trains coaches to deal with youngsters at their own developmental level. For example, Smith and Smoll have found improved perceptions for trained versus untrained coaches on the part of children. Also, the children liked the trained coaches more, had a better attitude, and so on. Hill found that trained teachers

reduced concern with evaluation of testing in the classroom and had gains in academic performance of two years or more with children. The same can be true in sport.

3 *Parent education*
The coach can go a long way in helping children by educating the parents to the goals of the sport programme. For example, were parents to ask a child who just came in the house from a game the question, 'Did you enjoy yourself?', rather than the question, 'Who won?', the child would pick up the difference very quickly. This is one way to reduce the perception of stress.

Conclusion

I have tried to give an overview of the thought processes of children in competitive sport, so that we can understand children better. Further, I have also tried to give the outline of a strategy to keep children within the sport experience for as long as possible and to reduce the amount of competitive stress experienced. But all of what I have discussed is predicated on the assumption that coaches want to reduce the perception of stress of children and are prepared to shift their own goals away from winning and losing toward maximising the enjoyment of the child. After all, aren't we more interested in the experiences the child is undergoing than in the game itself? Aren't we supposed to have the interests of the child at heart? So, just as the watchword of coaches to children may be something like, 'Hey, watch the ball!', my watchword to coaches is, 'Hey, watch the child!'

Reference Note

1   EWING, M., ROBERTS, G. C. and PEMBERTON, C. (1985) *A Developmental Look at Children's Goals for Participating in Sport*. Unpublished manuscript, University of Illinois.

References

BURTON, D. and MARTENS, R. (1986) 'Pinned by their own goals: An exploratory investigation into why kids drop out of wrestling.' *Journal of Sport Psychology.*

COLEMAN, J. S. (1961) 'Athletics in high school.' *The Annals of the American Academy of Political and Social Science*, November, 338–43.

CSIKSZENTIMIHALYI, M. (1977) *Beyond Boredom and Anxiety*. San Francisco, CA: Jossey-Bass.

DUDA, J. L. (1981) *A Cross-cultural Analysis of Achievement Motivation in*

Sport and the Classroom. Unpublished Ph.D. Dissertation, University of Illinois.

EWING, M. (1981) *Achievement Orientations and Sport Behaviors of Males and Females*. Unpublished Doctoral Dissertation, University of Illinois.

GOULD, D., FELTZ, D., HORN, T. and WEISS, M. (1981) 'Reasons for attrition in competitive youth swimming.' *Journal of Sport Behavior*, **5**, 155–65.

HANSON, D. L. (1967) 'Cardiac response to participation in Little League baseball competition as determined by telemetry.' *Research Quarterly*, **38**, 384–8.

KLEIBER, D. A. and HEMMER, J. (1981) 'Sex differences in the relationship of locus of control and recreational sport participation.' *Sex Roles*, **7**, 801–10.

LOWE, R. and MCGRATH, J. E. (1971) 'Stress, arousal, and performance: Some findings calling for a new theory.' Project report, AF1161–67. AFOSR.

MAEHR, M. L. and NICHOLLS, J. G. (1980) 'Culture and achievement motivation: A second look.' In N. WARREN (ed.) *Studies in Cross Cultural Psychology*. New York: Academic Press.

NICHOLLS, J. A. (1978) 'The development of the concepts of effort and ability, perception of own attainment, and the understanding that difficult tasks require more ability.' *Child Development*, **49**, 800–14.

NICHOLLS, J. A. (ed.) (1984) *The Development of Achievement Motivation*. Greenwich, CT: JAI Press.

ORLICK, T. C. (1974) 'The athletic drop-out – a high price for inefficiency.' *CAPHER Journal*, 212–14.

PASSER, M. W. (1982) 'Psychological stress in youth sports.' In R. A. MAGILL, M. J. ASH and F. L. SMOLL (eds) *Children in Sport*. Champaign, IL: Human Kinetics.

ROBERTS, G. C. (1978) 'Children's assignment of responsibility for winning and losing.' In F. SMOLL and R. SMITH (eds) *Psychological Perspectives in Youth Sports*. Washington, DC: Hemisphere.

ROBERTS, G. C. (1984) 'Achievement motivation in children's sport.' In J. G. NICHOLLS (ed.) *The Development of Achievement Motivation*. Greenwich, CT: JAI Press.

SCANLAN, T. K. (1985) 'Sources of competitive stress in youth sport athletes.' In M. WEISS and D. GOULD (eds) *Competitive Sport for Children and Youth*. Champaign, IL: Human Kinetics.

SMITH, R. E., SMOLL, F. L. and CURTIS, B. (1979) 'Coach effectiveness training: A cognitive-behavioral approach to enhancing relationship skills in youth sport coaches.' *Journal of Sport Psychology*, **1**, 59–75.

VEROFF, J. (1969) 'Social comparison and the development of achievement motivation.' In C. P. SMITH (ed.) *Achievement-related Motives in Children*. New York: Russell Sage Foundation.

13

Competition and the Growing Child – Stress or Distress?

Keith Russell

Introduction

'Stress' and 'distress' are rather ambiguous terms and need some elaboration. We know that the body responds to demands in specific ways: swinging on a bar results in calluses on the hands; exposure to heat causes sweating; prolonged stretching of muscle and tendons causes them to elongate; exposure to cold results in shivering, and so on. What these demands have in common is that they increase the need for adjustment. It is this adaptation to a demand, irrespective of what that demand is, that is the essence of *stress*.

> Stress is the non-specific response of the body to any demand made upon it.

> . . . it is immaterial whether the agent or situation we face is pleasant or unpleasant, all that counts is the intensity of the demand for readjustment or adaptation.

> It is difficult to see how such essentially different things as cold, heat, drugs, hormones, sorrow, joy could provoke an identical biochemical reaction in the body. Nevertheless, this is the case . . .

These quotations are from my fellow-Canadian Hans Selye who was probably the world's foremost authority on stress. Selye differentiates *stress* and *distress* as follows:

> Any kind of normal activity – a game of chess or even a passionate embrace – can produce considerable stress without causing harmful effects. Damaging or unpleasant stress is 'distress'.[1]

The topic of this paper – the effect of competitive sport on the growing child – will be developed from the perspective that stress is beneficial until it reaches a magnitude that elicits not only an adaptive response but goes beyond that and causes 'distress' in the form of physical or mental trauma.

Some notes on 'competition'

I am not the only person here who struggles with the duality of being both a physical educator and a coach of élite athletes. I say 'struggle' because there are disparate or incongruous philosophies between these two professions. As a physical educator I believe in the values derived from children receiving a 'balanced diet' of regular physical activity and that instruction and facilities should be made available, not only for the select few, but for the masses. But, as a former national coach and present coaches educator and mentor of young élite gymnasts, I teach that reaching international prominence in sport requires that athletes must start young and train intensely in specially-designed facilities. I will attempt to address this conference only as a coach of élite athletes, but no doubt I will occasionally slip into the more conservative mode of educator.

The focus of this paper is training young athletes and I will delimit my discussion to high performance athletes, those aspiring to national and international prominence. These athletes will inevitably be involved in competitions, which is contrary to a current trend in physical education extolling non-competitiveness. Though I endorse this trend, I also believe in the intrinsic values of competition and in the assumption that we can shape competitive experiences for young, élite athletes to be positive experiences. I do, however, feel very strongly that some of our traditional thinking about 'competition' must be altered to take much of the emphasis away from 'winning' and redirect it to 'improving' and to 'performing to capacity'. I am cognisant that competition can reduce prosocial behaviour and increase antisocial behaviour,[2] and can cause interpersonal and intergroup hostility.[3] I am aware of some very convincing arguments against vigorous, structured sport for the pre-adolescent child.[4,5,6] And I am acutely aware of the research findings that state: 'Coaches with formal training and experience tend to place more emphasis on winning and less on fun and are more self-centred, winning-is-everything types.'[7]

As a practising coach I am, however, one who witnesses and contributes to the extraordinary physical and emotional development associated with high performance sport, I recognise that: participation in organised sports aids in socialisation;[8] that the developmental period spanned by youth sport is the ideal life period for acquiring stress-coping skills;[9] that good coaching can result in enhanced self-esteem of young athletes;[10] and that the design of competitive and training situations can be altered to be predominantly co-operative in nature.

Why am I proselytising the values of competition to a group of national coaches who, by the nature of their positions, are probably better informed than I on the matter? My reason is simply to emphasise that intense competition for the growing child has some detrimental as well as some beneficial aspects. Of all groups, a group of 'coaches of coaches' must be cognisant of both. This chapter highlights, and it is hoped will promote discussion on, the different categories of physical stressors that confront the growing child in competitive sport. Both the benefits and cautions associated with these stresses in the specialised athletic training environment will be discussed.

Physical stress

Trying to find that elusive optimal level of 'stress' without reaching the level of 'distress' is one of the greatest challenges that confronts the coach of the growing athlete. This task is easier to monitor in post-pubescent athletes as there is more research data on this group and there is not the complication of accelerated pubertal growth. The coach of the pre-pubescent and especially the pubescent athlete can easily confuse the effect of training with the effect of normal growth. Accordingly, coaches of growing athletes should be knowledgeable in the subject of normal physical growth and development before designing training programmes for this specialised population of élite athletes. The material in this chapter assumes such knowledge.

The physical stresses the growing athlete is being trained to adapt to are divided in this paper as follows:

1 Stress of Resistance Loading
2 Stress of Tissue Elongation
3 Stress of Repetitive Impact
4 Stress of Acceleration and Deceleration of Limbs
5 Stress of Systemic Loading

1 Stress of resistance loading

Resistance loading can take many forms but the most common are: using body weight as resistance as in push ups and chin ups, free weights, pulleys, rubber tubing, medicine balls or springs, using ergometers such as bicycle or rowing machines, using resistance apparatus such as Universal Gym, Hydra Gym, Nautilus or Polaris systems. There is controversy in the scientific literature regarding the efficacy of resistance training to increase strength in pre-pubescent athletes. Part of the controversy stems from the fact that there is an increase in strength – 5%–10% per year – in the growing child that is independent of any kind of loading. It is a normal consequence of maturation of the nervous system and increased muscularity caused by the increase in androgen secretion. Adolescents respond similarly to adults with respect to resistance loading stress, but the data on pre-adolescent children is conflicting.[11] Mueller[12] hypothesised that children have maximum limits they cannot surpass and expectations for strength gains are represented in the ratio of the initial strength to the maximum strength. The percentage of existing strength to maximum strength was defined as the child's relative strength. Further, Mueller concluded that there could be a linear 12% increase in strength per week until 75% relative strength was reached at which time the incremental increases were reduced. Twelve weeks of training would be needed to reach the maximum or 'limiting' strength. These results are not without challenge,[13,14] but they do provide coaches of young athletes with some guidelines. Even with the conflicting research evidence as to the efficacy of resistance training for children, this author, for one, has had ample field evidence as to the gains that can occur in pre-adolescent gymnasts. Not known is whether gains are a result of increased muscle size or increased efficiency of the neuromuscular response. Given the cautions mentioned throughout this chapter, it should be possible to adapt children progressively to resistance loading and to 'stress without distress'.

Some general considerations for training muscular strength and endurance are:

- train specifically for adaptation desired (same range of movement, speed, type of contraction);
- expect similar results per unit of work for pre-adolescent boys and girls;
- expect slightly decreased results per unit of work for post-adolescent girls as compared to pre-adolescent girls;
- expect increased results per unit of work for adolescent and post-adolescent males as compared to pre-adolescent males;
- expect drops in trainability of muscular endurance at or just prior to peak height velocity in both males and females.

Resistance loading results in specific changes to various tissues. The *connective tissue* that encapsulates muscle and connects the muscle to bone responds with:

- increased density of nuclei;
- increased cross sectional area (hypertrophy).

Bone responds to resistance loading (physical stress) with:[15]

- increased density;
- gradual changes to internal architecture;
- gradual changes to external shape;
- increased density of cartilage on articular surfaces.

Muscle tissue responds to resistance leading with:[47]

- increased energy stores (CP, ATP and glycogen);
- increased glycogen depletion;
- increased maximum lactate levels.

The above adaptation to resistance loading stress represent the positive responses while the following list of overuse injuries represent the negative responses:

- swimmer's shoulder;[16]
- groin pain in soccer players;[17]
- low back pain;[18,19,20]
- plantar fasciitis[21] (inflammation of the connective tissue on the bottom of the foot);
- patellofemoral complaints.[21,22,23]

Coaches of growing athletes who are undergoing intensive training should familiarise themselves with the etiology of these overuse injuries as they represent 'distress'.

2 Stress of tissue elongation*

Connective tissue and muscle adapt to the stress of prolonged stretching by increasing their 'resting' length. This structural change is the same as the 'growth' of muscles and tendons in response to bone growth. The degree of joint mobility that coaches should develop in their young charges is dependent on their sport. In some sports, such as gymnastics and diving, there are many skills that are flexibility-dependent. In other sports there is often a mechanical advantage in being able to generate a greater force by applying it through a larger range of motion – for example, a volleyball serve, rugby punt, and so on. There is evidence that many injuries can be prevented by increasing joint range of movement[24,25,26,27] and there is also evidence that too much joint range of movement (laxity), especially in the form of joint instability (rather than hypermobility), predisposes athletes to injury.[28,29,30] Although coaches must take a sports-specific approach to this area, all should ensure that their athletes are sufficiently flexible in joints such as the hip and shoulder to prevent injuries. On the other hand, it seems intuitively clear to this author that increasing lateral flexibility in joints such as the ankle and knee will decrease their stability and should be avoided.

There does not seem to be sufficient evidence to suggest that different stretching procedures be used for the child or the adult. In the case of the adult, the additional muscle mass and the cross-bridging of the collagen fibres (connective tissue) both cause the adaptation response to be a little slower than in children! The pubescent child is a special case in that the bones grow first and the resultant stretch of the adjoining muscles and tendons is the stress that elicits their adaptive lengthening. During the rapid adolescent growth spurt the resulting

* Topic of another chapter by the same author (see pages 113–120).

'overgrowth' of bone produces an increased joint tightness and possible predisposition to injury.[31]

3 Stress of repetitive impact

The stress associated with repetitive impact can elicit adaptive changes in the physical/structural components of the growing child. (Single, trauma-inducing macro impacts will not be considered since they elicit hospitalisation rather than adaptation!) The 'impacts' or stresses associated with running, repetitive jumping, repetitive landings and so on will elicit 'positive' changes to connective tissue and the skeletal system (of course, there are muscle contractions associated with generating 'take-offs' and such, but the adaptation to those stressors was dealt with in section 1 above). The changes to the internal architecture of the bones (greater mineralisation and greater numbers of trabeculae) that occurred in response to muscle contractions will occur similarly in response to impact stresses.[15] The problem for the coach is to avoid overuse injuries as 'there is evidence that the growing bones and joints of a child are more susceptible to certain types of mechanical injury than those of the adult, both because of the presence of growth cartilage, and the process of growth itself.'[32]

Several authors indicate a recent increase in overuse injuries[33,34,35] in young athletes, paralleling abundant literature documenting the recent increase in organised pre-adolescent and adolescent sport.[37] Children are being trained for longer periods of time in fewer sports leading to more repetitions of fewer movements. This specialisation and increased practice time places considerable strain on growth cartilage (two to five times weaker than mature bone) at the growth plate, articular surfaces and some tendon-bone attachments.

> The growth plate and articular surfaces of children's bones are more susceptible to shear and impact injury, while the presence of growth cartilage at the tendon insertions increases the chance of avulsion from the bone, particularly if the child is growing rapidly and these structures are further tractioned by the growth of the bones they span.[32]

> Performing the same activity time and time again may cause one structure to rub against another (chondromalacia), repetitive traction on a ligament or tendon (plantar fasciitis, Osgood-Schlater disease), or cyclic loading of impact forces (lower extremity stress fractures).[33]

Overuse injuries are also seen in adult athletes, but they are particularly worrisome in the growing athlete because of the danger of damage to epiphyseal growth plates and the potential for disruption in the growth process. Coaches are encouraged to familiarise themselves with reviews such as Gregg and Das.[37] It is recommended that the stresses of repetitive impact are ones the coach should carefully monitor and adopt a conservative approach.

The following is a typical sampling of overuse injuries which can result from repetitive impact stresses. Coaches may want to further familiarise themselves with those that are relevant to their particular sport.
– tendinitis:[38] inflammation of tendons.
– shin splints:[33] anterior leg pain.
– Osgood-Schlater's disease[39] (an inflammation of the tibial tuberosity just below the knee due to repetitive traction).
– stress fractures.[33,37,40,41] (Bone remodels as a result of stress by way of resorption and new bone formation. If an imposed stress is excessive, then resorption will outstrip remodelling/strengthening and result in weakened bones and stress fractures.)
– slipped capital femoral epiphyses.[42]

4 Stress of acceleration/deceleration of limbs

It has been established that the continuous throwing, striking activities associated with baseball pitching and tennis serving result in dramatic increases in bone size and density.[43,44,45] Also associated with these ballistic activities are overuse injuries such as 'tennis elbow' and 'little league elbow'[46] caused by continuous micro trauma from rapid acceleration/deceleration of the limb. The coach of the pre-adolescent and adolescent child must be cautious since major muscles involved with kicking and throwing are attached to bony protruberances that are separated from the bone shafts by epiphyseal growth plates. These growth plates are vulnerable to overuse injuries in the form of epiphysitis (inflammation) or avulsion (pulling away) fractures. It must be emphasised that the stresses of throwing and kicking are beneficial and are distressful only when the frequency or intensity is too great. Close monitoring of any complaints of physical pain together with systematic conditioning should prevent any overuse injury.

5 Stress of systemic loading

The cardio-vascular and pulmonary systems of children have limited capacity for adaptation prior to puberty, and there are several differences between the child's and the adult's systemic responses to exercise.

– the resting concentration and rate of utilisation of glycogen is less in the child (therefore lower anaerobic capacity);
– the degree of acidosis in which the muscle can still contract is less in children (less resistance to fatigue);

- the anaerobic threshold (point at which lactate production exceeds its elimination) expressed as a % of maximum O_2 uptake is higher than in adults;
- the oxygen uptake transients are shorter in children (reach a new metabolic steady-state sooner).

These differences, reported by Bar-Or,[47] indicate that children have a lower anaerobic capacity than adults. They tire more quickly, but they recover sooner. Although there are differences in the way children respond to aerobic exercise, such as lower cardiac outputs but higher peripheral oxygen extraction, '. . . there do not seem to be any underlying physiologic factors that would make children less suitable than adults for prolonged continuous exercise'.[47]

The one exception to the above that Bar-Or points out is children's response to exercise in climatic extremes. Since children have a surface area per unit mass that is 36% greater than adults they are more susceptible to heat gain (convection, radiation, conduction). Children perspire less than adults thus their evaporative capacity is lower and their ability to lose heat is less. Children are at more risk when exercising at temperature extremes and acclimatisation must be more gradual and longer than for adults. As the child passes through puberty there is a gradual shift towards adult capacities for improvement. Several studies have found no changes in the maximum oxygen consumption of children following short-duration training and a few studies have reported some gains.[48] It would appear that high intensity training over a duration of at least six months is needed to make gains of up to 15% in maximum oxygen consumption and that further gains may not be possible.[49] This contrasts with the 15%–20% gains seen in adults.[50] It is interesting to note that much of the increase in children's capacity is due to stroke volume increases and that arterio-ventricular oxygen differences were minimal. This contrasts markedly from what occurs in the adult and it has been hypothesised[51] that the larger stroke volume that is attained in pre-pubertal years may result in larger adult capacities than could not normally be achieved if training were initiated later in life. Evidence from the studies of Swedish swimmers seems to lend support to this hypothesis.[52,53] Even though it seems that the seeds of cardiorespiratory fitness can be sown early in life, and that risk factors for coronary disease such as elevated triglycerides, hypertensity, obesity and low physical work capacity are all positively affected by exercise (and all can be present in childhood),[54] it still is questionable whether high intensity endurance training in the pre-pubertal child is desirable.

There is, however, growing evidence to suggest that aerobic trainability in pre-pubescents, particularly in those less than 10 years old, is lower than expected, even though their athletic performance may improve.[47]

We must look upon the data as changes that *occur with* conditioning and training but not necessarily *result from* them.[47]

There would seem, at present, no physiological reasons why children cannot do endurance training, but it does not appear that there will be an adaptation to that 'stress' that is anything like the adult adaptation.

The risks associated with repetitive impact have already been noted and the intensity of work needed to achieve significant gains may have a lasting negative effect on the child's psychological adaptation. This was clearly evident in the case of the Swedish female swimmers[33] whose maximum oxygen uptake was 20% above the national average for their age group and seven or eight years later, after retiring from competitive sport, was 10% below the national average for their age group. They still had the organic capacity that they had gained (heart and lung volume) but had decreased their maximum oxygen uptake by a mean value of almost 30% due to their lack of interest in physical pursuits.

Thus, the physiological advantage gained through intensive training as a child was being wasted as an adult due to the psychological factor of having been 'turned off' to activity by too intensive an early exposure. The implications of this study for people involved in children's sport is obvious.[31]

One must conclude that coaches should carefully consider the risk-to-benefit ratio when planning intensive endurance programmes for growing athletes.

Summary

It will be no surprise to coaches that a chapter such as this, outlining the current scientific status quo, will conclude with more questions being asked than answers being given. The nature of scientific research dictates that it must be conducted under controlled conditions and that the results must be duplicated by others before it is widely accepted. We, as practitioners, work under very different circumstances. We are all involved in training methods and 'clinical applications' well in advance of the scientific explanations of these. If we are only following what is known then we are indeed followers and not leaders. Information offered in this and similar works can help us to assess our programmes and readjust them as research untangles some of the 'unknowns'. Most importantly, we must pay heed to the potentially distressful aspects of high performance sports training of the growing child. We must continually question – are we pushing the limits of physical stress for the benefit of the child or for the benefit of ourselves?

Acknowledgement

The author acknowledges the assistance of Dr Bob Mirwald, Dr Don Bailey and Dr Bob Faulkner of the University of Saskatchewan for their assistance in gathering information and reviewing the article, and Gene Schembri for reviewing the article.

References

1   SELYE, H. (1974) *Stress without Distress*. Toronto: McLelland and Stewart.
2   JAMES, BRYAN (1977) 'Prosocial behavior.' In H. L. HAM (ed.) *Psychological Processes in Early Education*. New York: Academic Press.
3   SHERIF, M. (1956) 'Experiments in group conflict.' *Scientific American*, 2–6, November.
4   PARSON, T. (1960) 'Toward a healthy maturity.' *Journal of Health and Human Behavior*, **1**: 16.
5   LUSCHEN, G. (1967) 'The interdependence of sport and culture.' *International Review of Sports Psychology*, **16**: 27.
6   SARYRE, B. M. (1975) 'The need to ban competitive sports involving pre-adolescent kids.' *Paediatrics*, **55**: 564.
7   MARTENS, R. and GOULD, D. (1978) 'Why do adults volunteer to coach children?' In G. ROBERTS and K. NEWELL (eds) *Psychology of Motor Behavior and Sport*. Champaign, IL: Human Kinetics.
8   PIAGET, J. (1969) *The Psychology of the Child*. New York: Basic Books.
9   SMITH, R. E. and SMOLL, F. L. (1982) Chapter 13 in R. A. MAGILL, M. J. ASH and F. L. SMOLL (eds) *Children in Sport*. Champaign, IL: Human Kinetics.
10 SMITH, R. E. *et al.* (1979) 'Coach effectiveness training: a cognitive-behavioral approach to enhancing relationship skills in youth sport coaches.' *Journal of Sport Psychology*, **1**: 59.
11 KULIN, H. E. (1974) 'The physiology of adolescence in man.' *Human Biology*, **46**: 133.
12 MUELLER, E. A. (1970) 'Influence of training and of inactivity on muscle strength.' *Archives of Physical Medicine and Rehabilitation*, **51**: 449.
13 CLARK, D. H. (1973) 'Adaptations in strength and muscular endurance resulting from exercise.' In J. H. WILMORE *Exercise and Sport Sciences Review, Vol. 1*. New York: Academic Press.
14 VRIJENS, J. (1978) 'Muscle strength development in the pre- and post-pubescent ages.' *Medicine and Sport*, **11**: 152.
15 MICHELI, L. J. *et al.* (1980) 'Etiological assessment of overuse stress fractures in athletes.' *Nova Scotia Medical Bulletin*, April/June.
16 DOMINGUEZ, R. H. (1978) 'Shoulder pain in age group swimmers.' In B. ERIKSSON and B. FURBERG (eds) *Swimming Medicine, IV*. Baltimore, MD: University Park Press.

17   SMODLAKA, V. N. (1980) 'Groin pain in soccer players.' *Physician and Sportsmedicine*, **8**: 57.
18   JACKSON, D. W. and WILTSE, L. L. (1974) 'Low back pain in young athletes.' *Physician and Sportsmedicine*, **2**: 53.
19   OSEID, S. *et al.* (1974) 'Lower back problems in young female gymnasts.' *Federation Internationale d'Education Physique Bulletin*, **1**: 11.
20   AGGRAWAL, N. D. et al. (1979) 'A study of changes in the spine in weight lifters and other athletes.' *British Journal of Sports Medicine*, **13**: 58.
21   HARVEY, J. S. (1982) 'Overuse syndromes in young athletes.' *Pediatric Clinics of North America*, **29**, 6: 1369.
22   JAMES, S. L. (1979) 'Chondromalacia of the patella in the adolescent.' In J. C. KENNEDY (ed.) *The Injured Adolescent Knee*. Baltimore, MD: Williams and Wilkins.
23   PATY, J. G. and SWAFFORD, D. (1984) 'Adolescent running injuries.' *Journal of Adolescent Health Care*, **5**: 87.
24   MILLER, A. P. (1976) 'An early stretching routine for calf muscle strains.' *Medicine and Science in Sports and Exercise*, **8**: 39.
25   SCHULTZ, P. (1979) 'Flexibility: day of static stretch.' *Physician and Sportsmedicine*, **7**: 109.
26   SMODLAKA, V. N. (1980) 'Groin pain in soccer players.' *Physician and Sportsmedicine*, **8**: 57.
27   GLICK, J. M. (1980) 'Muscle strains: prevention and treatment.' *Physician and Sportsmedicine*, **7**: 73.
28   LYSERS, R. *et al.* (1984) 'The predictability of sports injuries.' *Sports Medicine*, **1**: 6.
29   EKSTRAND, J. and GILLQUIST, J. (1983) 'The avoidability of soccer injuries.' *International Journal of Sports Medicine*, **4**: 124.
30   KIRBY, R. L. *et al.* (1981) 'Flexibility and musculoskeletal symptomatology in female gymnasts and age matched controls.' *American Journal of Sports Medicine*, **9**: 160.
31   MICHELI, L. J. and LACHABRIER, L. (1984) 'The young female athlete.' In L. J. MITCHELI (ed.) *Pediatric and Adolescent Sports Medicine*. Toronto: Little, Brown.
32   MICHELI, L. J. (1984) 'Sports injuries in the young athletes: questions and controversies.' In L. J. MICHELI (ed.) *Pediatric and Adolescent Sports Medicine*. Toronto: Little, Brown.
33   HARVEY, J. S. (1982) 'Overuse syndromes in young athletes.' *Pediatric Clinics of North America*, **29**, 6: 1369.
34   CLEMENT, D. B., TAUNTON, J. E. *et al.* (1981) 'A survey of overuse running injuries.' *Physician and Sportsmedicine*, **9**: 47.
35   PATY, J. G. and SWAFFORD, D. (1984) 'Adolescent running injuries.' *Journal of Adolescent Health Care*, **5**: 87.
36   MAGILL, R. A., ASH, M. J. and SMOLL, F. L. (1982) *Children in Sport*. Champaign, IL: Human Kinetics.
37   GREGG, J. R. and DAS, M. (1982) 'Foot and ankle problems in the pre-adolescent and adolescent athlete.' *Clinics in Sport Medicine*, **1**, 1: 131.
38   TULLOS, H. S. and BENNETT, J. B. (1984) 'The shoulder in sports.' In W. D. SCOTT, B. NISONSON and J. A. NICHOLAS (eds) *Principles of Sports Medicine*. Baltimore, MD, and London: Williams and Wilkins.

39   NISONSON, B. *et al.* (1984) 'The knee.' In W. D. SCOTT *et al.* (eds) *Principles of Sports Medicine*. Baltimore, MD, and London: Williams and Wilkins.

40   MICHELI, L. J. *et al.* (1980) 'Etiological assessment of overuse stress fractures in athletes.' *Nova Scotia Medical Bulletin*, April/June.

41   WALKER, N. E. and WOLF, M. D. (1977) 'Stress fractures in young athletes.' *American Journal of Sports Medicine*, **5**: 165.

42   HOUSTON, STUART (radiologist, University of Saskatchewan) – personal communication.

43   BUSKIRK, E. R., ANDERSON, K. L. and BROZEK, J. (1956) 'Unilateral activity and bone and muscle development in the forearm. *Research Quarterly*, **27**: 127.

44   JONES, H. H. *et al.* (1977) 'Humeral hypertrophy in response to exercise.' *Journal of Bone and Joint Surgery*, **59**, 2: 204.

45   PRIEST, J. D. *et al.* (1977) 'Arm and elbow changes in expert tennis players.' *Minnesota Medicine*, **60**, 5: 399.

46   TORG, J. S. *et al.* (1972) 'The effect of competitive pitching on the shoulders and elbows of pre-adolescent baseball players.' *Paediatrics*, **49**: 267

47   BAR-OR, O. (1983) *Pediatric Sports Medicine*. New York and Berlin: Springer-Verlag.

48   Reported in GOLDBERG, B. (1984) 'Pediatric Sports Medicine.' In W. D. SCOTT, B. NISONSON and J. A. NICHOLLS (eds) *Principles of Sports Medicine*. Baltimore, MD, and London: Williams and Wilkins.

49   EKBLOM, B. (1969) 'Effect of physical training in adolescent boys.' *Journal of Applied Physiology*, **17**: 350.

50   EKBLOM, B., ASTRAND, P. O., SALTIN, B. *et al.* (1968) 'Effect of training on circulatory response to exercise.' *Journal of Applied Physiology*, **24**: 518.

51   BAILEY, D. A. (1982) 'Sport and the child: physiological considerations.' In R. A. MAGILL *et al.* (eds) *Children in Sport*. Champaign, IL: Human Kinetics.

52   ASTRAND, P. O., ENGSTROM, L., ERIKSSON, B. O. *et al.* (1963) 'Girl swimmers.' *Acta Paediatrica* (Uppsala), **147**: 1.

53   ERIKSSON, B. O., ENGSTROM, L. *et al.* (1971) 'A physiological analysis of former girl swimmers.' *Acta Paediatrica Scandinavica*, **217**: 68(c).

54   GOLDBERG, B. (1984) 'Paediatric sports medicine.' In W. D. SCOTT, B. NISONSON and J. A. NICHOLLS (eds) *Principles of Sports Medicine*. Baltimore, MD, and London: Williams and Wilkins.

14

Psychological Stress and Children in Competition

Lew Hardy

The acceptability of the psychological stress which children un-doubtedly experience during organised competition is a very emotive subject (Martens, 1978; Orlick, 1980). It is therefore important for me to make my own position clear from the outset. In this chapter no attempt will be made to discuss the political or philosophical aspects of children's involvement in organised sport. Rather, I shall start from the position that there is nothing wrong with competition *per se*, since it forms an integral part of evolution through natural selection, career success, and even on occasions the finding of a husband or wife. What *is* wrong is the way in which children's competition is sometimes used by adults to achieve their own aims, regardless of whether these aims are coincident with those of the children: for example, when emphasis is placed totally upon winning regardless of the cost to the performer, or when children are treated like circus animals and excessively conditioned using extrinsic rather than intrinsic rewards to make them 'jump through hoops'.

This chapter presents an approach to competition training which is educational in the sense that it provides the performer with the psychological means to achieve sporting excellence, should he or she so wish. The self-regulation skills which form the basis of this approach are, however, much more than sports skills. They are life skills. Should the performer choose some aim other than sporting excellence, then these life skills will help him or her to achieve that aim in just the same way. It is useful to talk about such skills under two broad headings: learning, and the maintenance of skill under stress.

Learning

In order to understand how best to teach children it is necessary first of all to understand exactly how they learn. Recent work by Lowe and associates (Lowe, 1979) suggests that when children are very young they learn in just the same way as animals; that is to say, they are conditioned by rewards as in operant conditioning, or by the pairing of stimuli as in classical conditioning. What Lowe and his associates have shown is that as children acquire verbalisation skills, round about the age of two to three years, so they also progress to higher levels of learning. More precisely, they start to process information and become experimenting problem solvers. When presented with a problem, they first of all work out the most likely solution, and then experimentally test it. If this 'solution' does not work, then they attempt the next most likely solution, and so on. This is much the same as the way adults work. Now that might seem to be quite a good thing because, if children process information and solve problems in exactly the same way as adults, then all we have to do is treat them like little adults. Unfortunately, there are two problems with this sort of approach.

First of all, it appears that verbal memory is actually separate from motor memory, so that attempts to verbalise about motor skills can lead to divided attention and interference with the acquisition of the motor skill. This is very common in adults learning 'new' skills like skiing; for example, in their self-deprecating comments, or when they stand at the top of the slope trying to reason how to ski without ever actually going down it (see Hardy and Ringland, 1984).

Secondly, children's capacity to process information is considerably less than that of adults (Gallagher and Thomas, 1980). Consequently, the amount of information which children can handle in the form of knowledge of results (KR) or feedback is considerably less than adults. KR may, therefore, simply constitute another form of interference. Following any attempt to perform a movement children need a considerable period of time before they are ready to receive information regarding that movement. They then need a further considerable period of time to process that information before being asked to

Figure 14.1 *Showing the significant differences in performance which result from different KR delay intervals.*
After Hardy (1984)

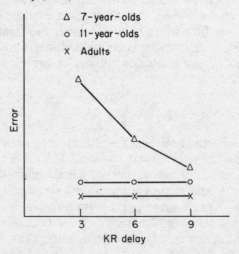

attempt the movement again. For example, Hardy (1984) has shown that even in a very simple skill children may require as long as 6 or 9 seconds after a trial before receiving KR if they are to use that information in subsequent trials to improve their performance.

Similarly, Gallagher and Thomas (1980) have shown that children may need a pause of the order 9 seconds after receiving KR, if they are to process the information contained in it to help subsequent perform- ance.

Figure 14.2 *Showing the significant differences in performance which result from different post KR delay intervals.*
After Gallagher and Thomas (1980)

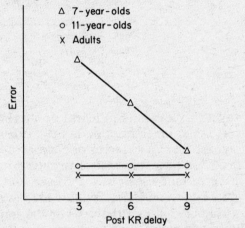

Since the task considered on these occasions was simply one of moving a linear slide a fixed distance (approximately half a metre) in a fixed time (400 milliseconds), it seems most likely that when children learn the sort of complicated skills that we ask them to learn in a sports setting, they will require considerably longer than this, first of all to store the movement and refocus their attention ready to receive KR, and then to process the information contained in the KR or feedback.

In a rather different direction, Lee and Magill (1983) have suggested that excessive KR or feedback may actually become a crutch for performers. That is to say, they become dependent upon receiving external information from a coach to such an extent that when this information is not available their performance deteriorates consider- ably. In most sports settings the coach is not in a position, during actual performance, to provide the performer with all the information which he or she needs. In this context, Ho and Shea (1978) have shown that while performers who receive intermittent KR may perform at a lower level when KR is available to other performers after every trial, when KR is withdrawn (as in competition, for example) the performers who previously received intermittent KR significantly outperform the other performers who previously received KR after every trial.

Figure 14.3   *Showing the reversal in performance which can occur in 'KR dependent'
subjects when KR is withdrawn*

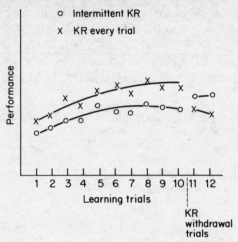

What I am saying is, let children learn, do not interfere with the
process by throwing too much information or advice at them. In my
experience as a coach and an observer of coaches, I have rarely seen
coaches who throw too little information at their performers. On the
other hand, I have certainly seen hundreds and maybe thousands of
coaches who threw far too much information at their performers.

I would like to talk about one other issue in the context of learning.
That is the way in which we store knowledge or information about
motor skills. It is generally accepted in psychology that the performer
does not store the precise description or parameters of a skill. We
simply do not have the space to handle that sort of quantity of
information. Rather, what we store is the relationship between the
parameters in some generalised form so that when faced with a
particular set of environmental conditions and desired outcomes, we
can recall the appropriate relationships and reconstruct, or generate,
the appropriate movements. This method of storage has some important implications for the way in which we practise things. In Figure 4 it
is impossible to tell the relationship between the two variables shown
in the graph, since only one data point is given. However, in Figure 5
where a large number of observations have been made at different
levels of the variable X, it is quite clear that performance in Y is
roughly proportional to performance in X. The implication of this line
of reasoning (Schmidt, 1982) is that children (and adults) need varied
practice in order to construct new relationships. For example, Moxley
(1979) has shown that children throwing shuttles at targets at different
locations (see Figure 14.6) performed significantly better when they
transferred to a new target than children throwing shuttles at a fixed
target, even though the fixed target was nearer to the transfer target

Figure 14.4   *Showing an indeterminate relationship between the variables X and Y*

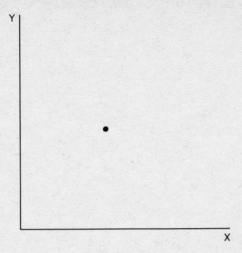

than any of the varied practice targets. At a more practical level, Fazey (1985) showed that children learning to pass a football with both feet achieved a criterion success level with both feet significantly quicker if they practised from the outset with both feet, rather than practising first with the right foot and then with the left foot, or vice versa (see Figure 14.7). There are lots of other examples of this finding in the psychological research literature.

These relationships between environmental conditions and desired outcomes are called 'schema', and it seems likely that the way in which we practise determines the precise boundaries of a given schema class (Fazey 1985). If we practise in a very varied fashion then the schemata

Figure 14.5   *Showing a clear positive linear relationship between the variables X and Y.*

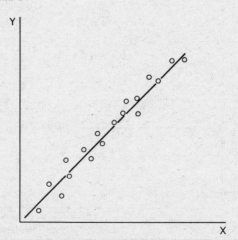

Figure 14.6 *Subjects had 5 trials at each of targets T1 to T5 or 25 trials at target T5. After Moxley (1979)*

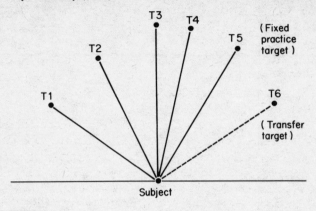

or relationship is very broad and will enable us to transfer to a vast number of different new 'skills'. Conversely, if we practise in a very fixed way the schema boundaries are very narrow and will not enable us to transfer to any different skills. Bear in mind that 'different' is used in a fairly subtle way here, since it could be argued that every time we hit a tennis ball, or kick a football, or perform a giant circle round a high bar, the skill is always different. Nothing is ever *exactly* the same twice.

Finally, there is a psychological theory called 'dual coding' which roughly speaking suggests that the information which we store regarding movements is stored in either a verbal symbolic form, or a visual

Figure 14.7 *Showing the number of trials required to reach a criterion level of performance for passing a football with both feet. After Fazey (1985)*

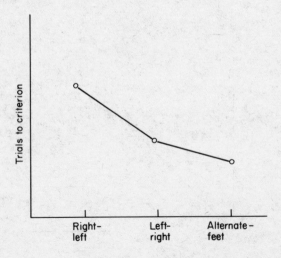

symbolic form, or a combination of both. This has some quite important implications for the way in which we practise motor skills, since it suggests that mental rehearsal of a picture or image of the skill should enhance both performance and learning of the skill. That is to say, it should have both an immediate (warm-up) and a long-term (learning) effect. These hypotheses have also been experimentally proven by Hardy and Wyatt (1985), and Feltz and Landers (1983). Of course, such mental rehearsal or imagery is in itself a skill. It is therefore little use expecting performers to produce results immediately upon the command to 'mentally rehearse'. Like physical skills, mental practice, or imagery, requires time and practice to perfect it. However, while there are big individual differences in people's ability to learn how to use imagery, most performers will notice at least some benefit from its use within approximately 50 attempts. This benefit will of course increase as imagery is used more often in a variety of situations.

Maintenance of Performance Under Stress

In competitive sport, the ability to maintain performance under stress appears to be a least as important as any physical attribute, or the ability to acquire new skills. Unfortunately, despite the publication of over 120,000 research articles on the subject, this aspect of performance remains one of the least understood of all psychological phenomena. However, some recent research thrusts do offer a glimmer of hope for the future, and it is about these that I would now like to talk.

Figure 14.8   *Showing the long-term effects of imagery on motor performance. After Feltz and Landers (1983)*

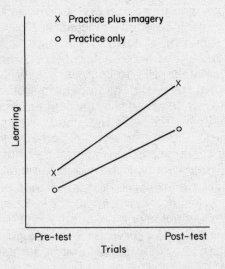

Figure 14.9   *Showing the immediate effect of imagery in reducing the warm-up decrement which is present at the start of performance.*
After Hardy and Wyatt (1985)

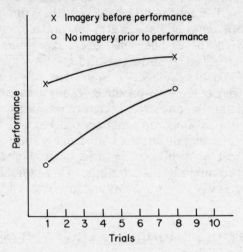

The work of Fenz and associates (Fenz, 1975) has shown that the effects of stress can be both general and specific in nature. Some people may be better endowed than others to cope with all stressors, while other people are better endowed to cope with some stressors but not others. Furthermore, for many (but not all) people mastery of a specific stressful situation can also lead to enhanced general coping. Such mastery also usually leads to enhanced self-esteem. Conversely, failure to cope with stressful situations can lead to reduced self-esteem, depression and stunted emotional development, particularly in the young. At this emotional level, people usually attempt to cope with stress first by denial and then withdrawal from the situation. In extreme cases this withdrawal can take the form of an almost trance-like state. Failure of these 'coping mechanisms' usually leads to a total collapse, or emotional breakdown. It is perhaps worth bearing this fact in mind the next time you observe a dazed expression upon the face of a performer immediately prior to competition. Whilst it is difficult to advise exactly what the best thing to do is in such circumstances, the worst things one can do are to shout at him or her to 'snap out of it', cajole, or generally put the performer under more pressure.

The behavioural response to stress is perhaps even more complex and therefore at an intellectual level more interesting.

Figure 14.10(a) shows a typical stress-performance curve.

Notice that once performance has started to deteriorate at point a, and dropped onto the lower performance curve, stress must be reduced by a considerable amount to point b before it is possible to 'jump back' on to the upper performance curve. Such a curve is called a 'catastrophe curve' and is characterised by the fact that performance is the result of

Figure 14.10(a)   *Catastrophe curve showing the relationship between stress and performance*

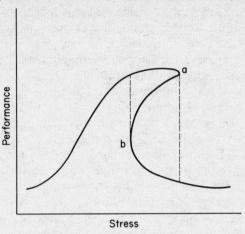

two directly-opposed forces. The competitive situation contains these two forces in the form of approach (desire to compete and succeed) and avoidance (fear of losing). These two aspects of the approach-avoidance conflict have also been described in two other ways by Hardy and Whitehead (1984), Hardy (1985), Martens *et al*. (1985).

Cognitive activation may be regarded as the availability of the cognitive processes which are necessary for performance: for example, control of perceptual focus, working memory space (for problem solving and decision making) and long-term recall (the availability of motor programmes from long-term memory stores). Cognitive anxiety caused by fear of evaluation tends to disrupt the availability or balance

Figure 14.10(b)   *Showing the three components of anxiety – self-confidence, cognitive anxiety and physiological arousal*

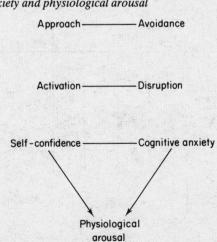

of these processes; on the other hand, self-confidence represents the performers belief, or perception that those processes which he requires are indeed available. Notice that it is therefore possible for an expert, for example, to be both cognitively anxious and self-confident at the same time. That is to say, he or she may worry about being evaluated, but may nevertheless believe that he(she) has the necessary control to succeed. Recent work in this laboratory has suggested that the time course of self-confidence and cognitive anxiety may well be different. In experts, although cognitive anxiety may be elevated for up to two or three weeks prior to the competitive event, self-confidence tends to build towards the event, whilst in novices it is suggested that self-confidence probably declines towards the event. The final influence in the triad shown in Figure 14.10(b), physiological arousal, represents the body's autonomic and physiological response to stress and anxiety. This is usually perceived by the performer as racing pulse, sweaty hands, dry mouth, butterflies in the stomach, desire to go to the toilet, and so on. Its time course is generally fast and late, that is to say, the physiological response does not usually occur until the performer arrives at the site of competition. It is thought (Ussher and Hardy, 1985) that high physiological arousal may well disrupt the fundamental motor abilities that are required to achieve fine control during skilful performance. Such disruptions to performance represent execution faults and are likely to be particularly noticeable on the day of performance. Conversely, the effects of high cognitive anxiety can often be observed several days or even weeks

Figure 14.11 *Showing the relative proportions of different cognitive processes required for a particular skill (cognitive activation pattern) and 'clouds' of anxiety depressing or disrupting this balance*

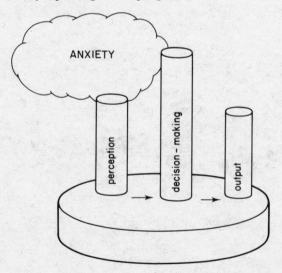

prior to an event (depending upon the importance of the event and the period of preparation which precedes it). These disruptions may take the form of an inability to pick up cues (failure of perceptual focus), failure of decision-making processes (working or short-term memory) and an inability to recall or learn solutions (failure of long-term memory).

It has recently been suggested (Eysenck, 1982; Williams, 1985) that recall from long-term memory of high association or very well-learned responses may actually be enhanced by anxiety, while recall of difficult responses, with a large load upon working memory, quite definitely deteriorates under cognitive anxiety. Although all this may well be very interesting at an academic level, the real question is: what can we do to help our performers overcome such disruptions? In mild cases, simple coaching or technical instructions may well be all that is necessary. For example, 'Have you noticed that your opponent always takes you on the outside?', as a solution to the decision-making or working memory problem of 'Which way will this opponent go past me?'; or, similarly, 'Kick later in the long swing so that you kick up the wires rather than down into the ground', as a solution to the long-term recall problem in gymnastics of performing a long swing on rings. However, these sorts of solutions are all very obvious to experienced coaches. What I want to focus on are the much more severe disruptions to a performance which occur when performers are very highly cognitively anxious, or physiologically aroused. I am an educationist, so that all the solutions which I shall present are long-term skills which the performer must learn. It is my contention that clinical solutions 'on the day' are at best an educated guess and usually a complete disaster.

Strategies to Enhance Cognitive Activation

Goals are short-term objectives and must be distinguished from long-term aims. It may well be appropriate to have a long-term aim of winning a championship medal, but such an aim does not represent a suitable goal for a performer. To be appropriate, a goal must describe what the performer has to do to achieve his aim – for example, a time of 10.9 seconds in 100 metres. Research by Locke *et al.* (1981) has shown that the performer should be actively involved in the goal-setting process, and that goals should be specific and entirely within the control of the performer. This is much easier to achieve in some sports than in others. However, with a little imagination and some knowledge of the opposition, it should be possible to state most goals in a form in which a fairly high degree of control is obtained. The research literature is quite conclusive that goals do enhance performance (Locke *et al.*, 1981), and it is thought that this enhancement occurs because goal-setting clarifies the objective or desired outcome of the forthcoming activity and therefore helps to set the system up in an appropriate way. That is to say, it improves cognitive activation and self-confidence. One of the most important phenomena in the goal-setting literature is the goal difficulty performance relationship (Erez and Zidon, 1984). Up to a certain point performance improves with increases in goal difficulty; however, after this point further increases in goal difficulty lead to very severe reductions in performance. Erez and Zidon showed that this point of inversion occurs at precisely the point where subjects cease to view the goal as being realistic and attainable. Furthermore, Hardy, Maiden and Sherry (1985) have shown that the level of goal difficulty at which goal acceptance changes from positive to negative is significantly reduced by cognitive anxiety. In fact, the cognitive anxiety associated with a major competitive event may well reduce goal acceptance levels by as much as 30%. Thus, goals that appear realistic and attainable during training may well appear totally unrealistic and unattainable as competition approaches. This problem can be reduced by discussions with performers and by setting goals for competition only during mock competition training sessions.

It is worth noting that this description of the goal difficulty performance relationship differs considerably from that of Rushall (1979), for example, who suggests that the relationship is a positive linear one. In my opinion, Rushall's interpretation presents very serious ethical as well as practical difficulties for the coach, since even if increases in goal difficulty always lead to increases in performance there will occur a point when in spite of these increases in performance the performers fail to achieve their goals. This must ultimately lead to dejection, a lowering of self-confidence and a subsequent lowering of self esteem.

Another way to improve self-confidence and cognitive activation is to perform only those skills which are overlearned. Since, as mentioned earlier, the recall of such skills may even be enhanced under

Figure 14.12   *The goal difficulty – performance relationship*

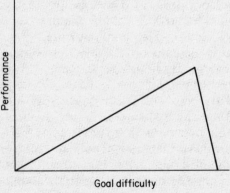
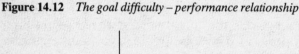

conditions of high cognitive anxiety. In this context, 'overlearned' can be taken to mean 'performed' for at least twice as long as it took the performer to learn the skill.

Stress Reduction Strategies

The previous two strategies focused upon increasing cognitive activation and therefore enhancing 'positive activation'. The following strategies focus upon reducing cognitive anxiety, and therefore reducing 'negative activation'. Some strategies will obviously be more appropriate for one sport than another, although it is sometimes difficult to specify exactly which. As a crude guideline, it is suggested that sports which require a fairly large degree of fine control will benefit more from stress reduction strategies than sports which do not require such fine control.

Relaxation training may be subdivided into physical relaxation (low muscle tension, heart rate, respiration rate, and so on) and mental relaxation (quietness of the mind). It is obviously possible to be physically relaxed but not mentally relaxed or vice versa. Two forms of physical relaxation training which are fairly popular are progressive muscular relaxation and autogenic training. Descriptions of progressive muscular relaxation training may be found in Rushall (1979), Orlick (1980), and Syer and Connolly (1984), and a tape-recorded package of progressive muscular relaxation training has been produced by Unestahl (1983). Packages for autogenic training are not at present available; however, the British Society of Autogenic Trainers does have qualified trainers situated throughout the country.

Transcendental meditation is a form of mental relaxation training which focuses upon the silent repetition of a mantra or keyword. With practice this skill becomes very passive in nature, so that rather than repeating the mantra one listens to the mantra being repeated. After initially practising such physical and mental relaxation skills in a quiet environment, the performer may progress to dissociation training where the skills are practised in a noisy or uncomfortable environment. Eventually the performer will be able to relax quickly in any environment. Such dissociation training does not require that the performer makes an effort to shut the distractions out, but rather that he or she simply allows them to pass. It is as though the distractions are not bad, they are just not relevant. Initially, of course, the performer will be distracted by such 'noise'. When these distractions occur, the performer should simply refocus his or her attention upon the relaxation and start again. Gradually, the number of distractions will become less and less, so that eventually the performer will be able to dissociate from his or her environment completely.

Distraction training is similar to dissociation training in that performers work in pairs and attempt to distract one another from the task of performing. Within the bounds of safety the coach can impose few, or no, restrictions upon what can be used to distract the performer, provided that he or she is not physically impeded. Of course, this sort of training can become quite a lot of fun, particularly for children. However, the practice is very useful, as the distractions employed gradually become more and more subtle, particularly as the children realise that the activity does have a more serious purpose to it.

A rather different approach to mental relaxation, based upon accepting the environment rather than rejecting it, is derived from Zen meditation. In Zen meditation, the subject attempts to become a part of the environment. This requires a very broad and open focus of attention which eventually leads to the performer being absorbed into the environment and totally at one with it. This is a technique which I personally use for rock climbing. In that instance, it involves sitting looking at the rock, observing its texture, strata, colour, and gradually allowing myself to become a part of the rock – not trying to work out the individual moves that I am going to have to make, just allowing myself to feel at one with it. While I would not advocate that coaches rush out and teach all their performers Zen meditation, it does lead to two forms of mental training which are quite useful.

The first of these is competition training, which is simply a very carefully and rigorously constructed mock competition training programme. For example, in gymnastics one could gradually increase the amount of competition stress in the environment by judging a performance after an unlimited warm-up, judging it after a 2 minute warm-up, or including an audience to observe the performance while it is being judged. Eventually, competition background noises could be introduced by means of a tape recording of a previous major competition. Of course, distractions could also be included in the competition training, thereby combining distraction training with competition training. In such training I usually withdraw all support from the performer. I simply call out the times for warm-ups and competition. The purpose of this is to gradually make the performer more and more independent and desensitised to the competition environment.

More severe cases of anxiety may be treated by such psychological techniques as desensitisation training, or integrated stress management training. However, these require a more advanced psychological knowledge than a coach would normally be expected to possess. Perhaps this is an area of performer preparation where sport psychologists might be expected to make a contribution in the future.

Summary

This chapter has suggested that competition *per se* is not necessarily a bad thing, and that competition training can be used to provide performers with self-regulation skills which are important to their cognitive and physical development. These skills include:

1 the ability to prepare oneself for a major sporting, or non-sporting event (notice that this has important implications for the number of major events which a young performer might be expected to take part in);
2 the ability to cope with stressful situations (it is hoped with some generalisation away from sporting situations);
3 enhanced self-confidence through the achievement of personal goals, and the realisation that self-esteem should not be performance related;
4 and – dare I suggest – the ability to enjoy fun?

References

EREZ, M. and ZIDON, I. (1984) 'Effect of goal acceptance on the relationship of goal-difficulty to performance.' *Journal of Applied Psychology*, **69**: 69–78.

EYSENCK, M. W. (1982) *Attention and Arousal: Cognition and Performance*. Berlin: Springer-Verlag.

FAZEY, J. A. (1985) *Schema theory: The development of a model for the control and learning of motor skills*. Unpublished Ph.D. Thesis, University of Wales.

FELTZ, D. L. and LANDERS, D. M. (1983) 'The effects of mental practice on motor skill learning and performance: A meta-analysis.' *Journal of Sport Psychology*, **5**: 25–27.

FENZ, W. D. (1975) 'Strategies for coping with stress.' In I. Sarason and C. C. Spielberger (eds) *Stress and Anxiety, Vol. 2*. Washington, DC: Hemisphere Publication Group.

GALLAGHER, J. D. and THOMAS, J. (1980) 'Effects of varying post-KR intervals upon children's motor performance.' *Journal of Motor Behavior*, **12**, 1: 41–56.

HARDY, L. (1984) 'Knowledge of results and attentional re-focusing in children.' Paper presented to Experimental Psychology Society meeting. University College of North Wales. Bangor.

HARDY, L. (1985) *Factors Affecting Performance*: Resource Pack 9. Leeds: National Coaching Foundation.

HARDY, L., MAIDEN, D. S. and SHERRY, K. (1985) 'Goal-setting and performance anxiety.' *Journal of Sports Sciences*.

HARDY, L. and RINGLAND, A. (1984) 'Mental training and the Inner Game.' *Human Learning*, **3**: 203–7.

HARDY, L. and WHITEHEAD, R. (1984) 'Specific modes of anxiety and arousal.' *Current Psychological Research and Reviews*, **3**: 14–24.

HARDY, L. and WYATT, S. (1985) 'Immediate effects of imagery upon skilful motor performance.' In D. G. Russell and D. Marks (eds) *Imagery 2: Proceedings of the 2nd International Imagery Conference*. Dunedin, New Zealand: Human Performance Associates.

HO, L. and SHEA, J. B. (1978) 'Effects of relative frequency of knowledge of results on retention of a motor skill.' *Perceptual and Motor Skills*, **46**: 859–66.

LEE, T. D. and MAGILL, R. A. (1983) Activity during the post-KR interval: Effects upon performance or learning?' *Research Quarterly for Exercise and Sport*, **54**: 340–5.

LOCKE, E. A., SHAW, K. N., SAARI, L. M. and LATHAM, G. P. (1981) 'Goalsetting and task performance: 1969–1980.' *Psychological Bulletin*, **90**: 125–52.

LOWE, C. F. (1979) 'Determinants of human operant behaviour.' In M. D. Zeiler and P. Harzem (eds) *Advances in Analysis of Behaviour Vol. 1: Reinforcement and the Organisation of Behaviour*. Chichester: Wiley.

MARTENS, R. (1978) *Joy and Sadness in Children's Sport*. Champaign, IL: Human Kinetics.

MARTENS, R., BURTON, D., VEALEY, R. S., BUMP, L. A. and SMITH, D. E. (1985) In press. *Competitive state anxiety inventory–2*.

MOXLEY, S. (1979) 'Schema: The variability of practice hypothesis.' *Journal of Motor Behavior*, **11**: 65–70.

ORLICK, T. (1980) *In Pursuit of Excellence*. Ottawa: Coaching Association of Canada.

RUSHALL, B. S. (1979) *Psyching in Sport*. London: Pelham Books.

SCHMIDT, R. A. (1982) *Motor Control and Learning: A Behavioural Emphasis*. Champaign, IL: Human Kinetics.

SYER, J. and CONNOLLY, C. (1984) *Sporting Body, Sporting Mind: An Athlete's Guide to Mental Training*. Cambridge: Cambridge University Press.

UNESTAHL, L. E. (1983) *Inner Mental Training* (A tape-recorded package). Orebro, Sweden: Veje Publishing.

USSHER, M. H. and HARDY, L. (1985) 'The effect of competitive anxiety on a number of cognitive and motor sub-systems.' *Journal of Sports Sciences*.

WILLIAMS, A. W. (1985) *Competitive State Anxiety and its Effect on Information Processing*. Unpublished paper, University College of North Wales.

15

The Requirements of Competitive Swimming – the Effect on Children: a coach's perspective

Nick Juba

Some years ago, at the end of a hastily cobbled articled for a swimming coaches magazine,[1] I concluded, 'I believe that we should attempt to enhance the psychological and physical welfare of our competitors in order for them to improve.' And I invited comment from the magazine's readership.

As is often the case in those sorts of situations, no response was forthcoming, but the lack of reply masked what I feel is a far more disturbing trend within British swimming. For some years I had been aware of an unusually high proportion of unhappy children in our sport, both at the top end of the scale and at club level. These swimmers were able to highlight the hours of tedious, routinised work, the anti-social training hours which isolated them from normal friendships and the strenuous commitments demanded of today's swimmer. Many were disturbed, even then, at the stagnancy of a sport where reward was consistently measured in terms of time rather than in any material form.

Some, including seasoned, established internationals, worn down by the years of on-going effort required to maintain a high degree of success, opted out in order to seek a more normal type of life. Their actions were mirrored at a lower level by dozens of less successful swimmers, youngsters burnt out by the extreme requirements of contemporary competitive swimming.

These trends, first apparent in the 1970s when training workloads took on gargantuan scales, have continued to a point where we can now ask the questions: Are we looking after our swimmers? Are they pushed beyond endurable limits? And by flogging them up and down an identical stretch of water, day in, day out, week in, week out, are we giving them long-term problems, preventing them from becoming fully-rounded adults?

The clichés 'burnt out', 'opting out' and the like are probably part of a phraseology that we have adopted from the United States, and, ironically it is our inheritance of their 'hyped-up' type of training that has brought about some of the problems. A further irony, of course, is that, after years of training monotony in Britain, many of our swimmers opt to further or end their careers across the Atlantic. Many seek a relief from the build-up of pressures accumulated over a number of arduous seasons; the majority seek 'fun' which they have heard about from their predecessors. Yet another ironical twist, of course, is that many swim faster!

In the United Kingdom, an average swimmer may train twenty hours a week and race thirty weekends a year for eight years of his or her life. At some stage such swimmers will probably reach a 'cutting-off' point beyond which they are not prepared to continue. I base this threshold on no scientific fact, but I am sure that it relates to that basic economic law of diminishing returns, where beyond the optimum point there is only a falling away. There are so many factors of an individual and group nature which determine this threshold that it is almost impossible to tie it down. It is possible, for example, that a youngster, having sacrificed his friends outside swimming for a number of years, decides that his isolation has gone on for too long and that time spent with his friends is preferable to hours of training. It could be that he would prefer, at some stage in his career, to take his girl-friend out late one evening and cut out his next day's early-morning session. Social factors such as these are a major determining factor, especially when balanced against the reality of early-morning sessions which are a particularly debilitating form of training, and each individual will have a widely differing sense of personal values.

In a wider context there is also the unique nature of swimming itself. In no other sport do you have to train so hard and so long for such a small amount of important racing time (or so scant a reward); a winter's back-breaking training may be geared towards excellence in just 15 minutes of vital racing.

I think it also helps to understand what I call the 'deprivation factor' inherent in swimming. Some years ago I spent time coaching Brian Hooper, the World Superstars champion, prior to his defence of the title. Hooper, a pole-vaulter by trade, enjoyed his swimming immensely, but spoke of the serious sensory deprivation involved by comparison with his other sporting disciplines. You can neither hear not talk while you swim. You can see next to nothing and the only taste is chlorine! In truth, to the outsider, the only social side to swimming training is a shared mutual discomfort, the joint experience of youngsters pushing themselves to the limits together.

The young swimmer setting out in his chosen sport will sooner or later almost certainly face parental and coach pressure. One national team doctor recently spoke to me about swimmers who were caught between the ambitious parent and the uninformed coach. The role of the swimming parent is certainly an interesting one. Swimmers, because they train from a relatively young age, rely heavily upon their parents for support, both physically, in the form of transporting them to and from the pool, and financially. Concurrently the parents, as a result of the peculiar nature of the average swimming timetable in this country, revolve their lives around their swimming off-spring, sacrificing a considerable amount as a consequence. For a certain span of their lives, swimming dictates the structure of their life-style.

As a result of the importance placed upon swimming within the framework of their lives – both in terms of time and financially – an unspoken pressure is immediately placed upon the swimmer. This is compounded by an ambitious parent who sees no limits to his child's capabilities. My medical colleague would call this 'parental projection'. I feel that in swimming the pressure often comes from parents who see their children as extensions of their own 'perfect' selves. Certainly many ambitious parents appear to have an element of failure in their working lives and the successful child is regarded as the potential compensation.

More surprisingly coaches, either unwittingly or even sometimes wittingly, create increased stress on the young swimmer which very often results in detrimental performances. An interesting article appeared in a national newspaper which highlighted this problem[2] and talked in terms of competitive swimming as a 'socially-approved athletic child abuse', a very different kind of child battering. Dramatic words, but the article in fact reveals quite startling evidence by two American doctors who decried the competitiveness of swimming. They studied fourteen swimmers referred to them for shoulder strain and discovered that in a normal season each youngster rotated each shoulder about one and a half million times whilst training.

In medical terms, the shoulders of all but two had bi-lateral complications, and each individual had intensive ice-pack treatment over an extended period coupled with exercises to increase the clearance under the arch. The others had to be treated surgically, having pieces of bone removed or one of the main shoulder ligaments taken out. The article also quotes a London specialist, Dr Peter Sperryn, who says, 'Devising training schedules for adolescents is a tricky business. There are times when young people are not amenable to all this pushing, not only on a psychological basis but for good physiological reasons, especially when the bones are trying to catch up with the muscles, as it were, in terms of growth.'

Sperryn continued: 'The high quantum, bullying approach to training often leads to muscular hypertrophy making the muscles too big for the space available in the anatomical box. That's when the surgeons have to go in and bore holes to make the space bigger.' His opinion was that British coaches, either through lack of zeal or because of lack of time, did not operate these punishing schedules, but evidence suggests now that as British coaches strive to match their continental equivalents, or to defeat their opponents within their own country, they are giving their swimmers much more stressful workloads and placing them in hazardous and harmful situations.

The message in all this can be spelt out clearly. Swimmers must not become sacrificial lambs to a coach's ego; the coach must not sacrifice a swimmer's well-being for his own career. I believe that too many British coaches cannot differentiate between these twin end-products.

Compounding the inherent stresses and pressures involved in competitive swimming is the stigma of a fear of failure. As in all sports, fear of failure frequently leads to poor performances (although not always so), and none of us appear equipped to teach children how to handle their fear of failure either before or after the race in which they are swimming.

With so many apparent stress factors, why should any youngster want to swim? How can we justify making children undertake gruelling work and a soul-destroying life-style without a certain amount of sport satisfaction or alternative material compensation? It is not easy to put one's finger on it. The age-old motivations of medals and trips abroad as rewards still hold true to a certain extent, but I believe that there is something else which makes youngsters want to swim. I think that it must be the unique shared sports experience that binds them together in the sport, the challenge of conquering a discipline which most of their friends could not begin to comprehend, let alone handle.

Clearly the coach's responsibility is to create an atmosphere that is conducive to bringing out the best in young swimmers. His job is not just to teach his pupil a skill and then to strive for excellence, but also to generate an enjoyable atmosphere where his swimmer can happily attempt to achieve his or her objectives. The push for success must not be made at the expense of all else. Remember the 'cutting off' point.

The multiple demands and pressures apparent in competitive swimming, and how to cope with them in relation to the growing child, provide the contemporary coach with the greatest challenge. Do enough coaches in the UK concern themselves with this? Are they sufficiently aware and sensitive to the potential problems? And are they skilful enough to bring out the best in swimmers without forcing them into a no-choice situation?

There seems to be a number of ways in which swimmers can be assisted, directing them towards goals without totally destroying them physically and mentally and damaging the fabric of their life-style. In the first instance, and on the most mundane level, it clearly pays to offer swimmers a varied, diverse programme, both to prevent the onset of boredom and as a way of continually arresting attention and motivating. Concurrently it is probably sensible to limit the long, multiple repetition, over-loading sets. Although swimmers are both resilient and tolerant to such sets, the trend is to overuse these training methods and the threshold point is soon realised.

I believe that swimmers benefit from an involvement in all the many facets of the training programme, that they enjoy continual challenging and incentive awards. Swimmers too require an in-built opportunity to relax and recover from stress situations, and there is no reason why these should not be built into the on-going programme. A period of intensive training could be followed by a week of recovery, a kind of mini-taper, which would help a swimmer to remain physically and mentally alert and refreshed. Such a week could give a swimmer a rest from early-morning sessions and involve him in a more fun-orientated, relaxing period. At this time team meetings could be held to focus on personal targets and these could be restablished or re-set as necessary.

A coach should also get involved in, or at least actively participate in, a swimmer's over-all daily timetable. He should have a major contribution to make in essential planning arrangements, including his own suggestions for the swimmer's balanced life-style.

More importantly, he should strive to create a friendly and socially-aware group around his swimming aspirations, the sort of environment which everyone wants to be part of and nobody wants to leave.

I believe that coaches too should be able to help swimmers to relax, to conquer fears and to enjoy their leisure pursuits. In a low-key week in the schedule, some self-analysis and revitalisation would always be constructive. Swimmers must be taught to relax as one of the secrets of top performance, taught how to control fear rather than ignore it and generally demonstrate the benefits of calmness. A psychotherapist is one-to-one or one-to-two situations is invaluable for isolating a problem, for ego strengthening, and for confidence building so that swimmers can assert themselves at the right times.

These positive steps can help to balance out the many negative aspects of competitive swimming in this country. Coaches, rather than dominating parents, must play a major role in this and develop their skills beyond the all too limiting boundaries of poolside hounding. They have the opportunities to influence for the better a child's development at its most crucial stage.

Certainly, in an important article on coach effectiveness training[3] (admittedly in the field of other sports) survey results demonstrated 'that training programmes designed to assist coaches, teachers, and other adults occupying leadership roles in creating a positive and supporting environment can influence children's personality development in a positive manner'. That must be the way forward for swimming in Britain.

References

1   JUBA, NICK (1982), in M. DREW and N. JUBA (eds) *Swimming Coach*, **1**, 4, December 1982 (British Swimming Coaches Association).

2   ANDREWS, DAVID (1981) 'The Pain Barrier.' *The Guardian*, 12 February
    1981: 13.
3   SMITH, R. E., SMOLL, F. L. and CURTIS, B. (eds) (1979) 'Coach Effectiveness
    Training: A Cognitive-Behavioral Approach to Enhancing Relationship
    Skills in Youth Sport Coaches.' *Journal of Sport Psychology*, 1: 59–75.

16

My Son Used to Enjoy Tennis . . .: a concerned parent's perspective

Jacqueline Smith

My chosen title is relevant to my eldest son, Jason, who started 'serious' tennis at the age of 12 having enjoyed a six-week Prudential grassroots course. A few weeks after this, he was selected for county junior coaching and, within six months of his talent receiving acknowledgement, he had become very ambitious. He spent at least 20 hours a week during school term time and double that during the holidays practising tennis. For three years he worked extremely hard at it, living for tennis, but now, aged 17, he has given up all thoughts of serious tennis and plays for maybe 50 hours a year!

The causes of this change could provide useful information for those who coach sports activities. Jason is certainly not the only one of the small talented group of 13- to 14-year-old boys, who received county and endless private coaching, to have given up the junior tennis scene. Indeed, I believe that out of ten of Jason's contemporaries only two are still playing competitively. This trend is all too common, it seems.

The discussion below, however, can only illuminate one parent's view of the reasons for such disenchantment. No doubt if psychologists had tested Jason to discern his attitude and feelings at the time, other contributory factors would have emerged. It may be true too, that, as a parent having spent a great deal of money and time on the nurturing of her son's talent, my analysis of the reasons for his dramatic decrease in motivation may well be biased. However, for what it is worth, I offer my interpretation of the reasons behind Jason's decision to drop all tennis ambitions. This is backed by what he himself says.

One of the major setbacks Jason experienced was the conflict between his private coach and his county coach. His private coach, who was also the Regional coach, encouraged Jason to develop his natural style of play which included the open stance 'Borg-like' forehand, and Jason did extremely well in a very short space of time, winning many important matches and giving ranked players a good deal of trouble in beating him. There was no doubt that his facility for serving well and his increasingly lethal forehand topspin had much to do with his success. But the senior county coach, on whose authority junior players were presented for Regional selection, made it clear to me and to Jason that if he did not change his style of forehand in particular, he would not put Jason forward for Regional consideration. He was true to his word. Jason found himself left out of any such status-enhancing opportunities. Players less able than he were offered Regional and County team chances. There is little doubt that these rebuffs affected him greatly. However, his reaction was not to give up. Rather, he determined to work even harder to 'show them' (the top county coaches) by results that they were wrong. His time spent on tennis increased even more (the school homework suffered no doubt) and being a strong lad, big for his age, he would challenge adult county players to long hard matches both indoors and outside in all weathers for many hours at a time. I was wary of the time and energy spent and tried to get Jason to cut down. He is very strong willed. There was little I could do; he kept on pushing himself.

Inevitably, a further setback came about in the form of a serious injury to Jason's shoulder which the consultant stated was undoubtedly due to *over*use rather than misuse. For three months Jason could not play tennis, and he spent a great deal of time doing the prescribed exercises and undergoing physiotherapy to combat the injury. In returning to tennis, he soon showed that he had lost little in respect of ability to play well, but somehow his dedication to the game seemed far less. Further trouble with the injury accompanied by yet another county coach demanding a change of style, and a family move to another county, gave Jason the opportunity to give it all up. However, I am convinced that if attitudes of those responsible for county coaching had been more favourably disposed towards Jason as a player, he would still be playing now. His injury proved troublesome for two years, but his disillusion and disappointments were not really related to this otherwise he would have returned to the game because his love of tennis has never diminished. On playing just recently in the 18 and under county closed tournament (a different county), Jason's tennis showed some of the brilliance it had before and his enjoyment was obvious. Asked by the county coach if he would like to pick it up again seriously, he answered, 'No fear, I don't want to go through all that performance of having to comply with official criteria for success. I am more interested in other things now.'

My view of all this as a mother is – what a loss! He may not have turned out to be a Wimbledon champion, but now we will never know just how far he might have gone, will we? The experience with Jason has taught me many things, and now that Ryan, my youngest son, is the tennis 'star' of the family, I am determined that he will not give up for any of the reasons his big brother gave up tennis.

To tell of Ryan's tennis experiences gives a much more positive view of the junior tennis coaching scene. Ryan is 11 years old. He started playing tennis when he was six because his big brother aged 12 had begun to play. Right from the start, it appeared that he has much natural talent for the game. From seven years of age he has received County coaching and from eight years of age he has received Regional coaching. He won the ten and under Regional tournament, in which the best of six counties took part, two years in succession before he was 10. Really, he was doing too well too soon, and it was perhaps opportune that at the age of nine he moved to another county which brought him into the catchment area of another Region. This Region had many more talented young players, many of whom receive six hours or more County coaching as well as the Regional input. Ryan found himself to be a little fish again and a long way down the ranking in the new Regional squad – rather a daunting experience for a child of nine. However, we have been very lucky in finding a private coach for Ryan who is also the county coach. Moreover, there is evidence of positive co-operation between the Regional coach and his own coach. This comes in the form of discussions between the two agencies and copies of written reports from the Regional coach automatically sent to Ryan's private/county coach.

For two years now Ryan has continued thoroughly to enjoy his tennis in the new environment. He loves his lessons with his private coach – a marvellous man, able to push hard yet retain the thrill and enjoyment of the game – and Ryan, through this man's approach, is becoming a very enthusiastic competitor in many tournaments. In this context, with his private coach, there are no threatening pressures on him. In the Regional context, however, he is aware of the pressures on him to do well enough to stay in the Regional squad, to show evidence of winning many matches, otherwise to be dropped; always to attend and work slavishly hard for hours at a time at the obligatory training sessions and constantly to prove oneself better than other players of lesser rank. However, Ryan does not let such pressures worry him. He has never come off the court crying, having lost, even though he has seen many of his contemporaries do this! Somehow, with much influence from his coach and from me, I think he has developed a philosophy which, I believe, if it can be retained, will ensure that he continues to play and enjoy competitive junior tennis for many years to come. As a parent, I certainly hope that the approach we have adopted is the right one. This is to do what is necessary to keep Ryan within sight of success but not to aim for the heights too soon. It is logical in our view, that no-one at the age of 12 can get to number one in the nation and hope to stay there for any length of time, or ever get there again for that matter. Better to be around number 50 and keep going up than to be near the top and slide down. The example of young world-ranked players who are now no longer on the scene is not a good one, because to have gone so far is probably sufficient success in itself. However, we don't hear of the many hundreds who drop out before reaching this ultimate level.

To do what is necessary to keep within sight of success in tennis, however, means spending a small fortune, giving up much time and energy, and suffering many ups and downs in progression. Because Ryan after four years at it is still very enthusiastic and continues to realise his potential, we as parents are prepared to support him fully. The amount of money involved is something like £2500 a year for coaching, clothing, footwear, rackets and travel – most goes on travel. But, more precious than this, is time, not only our time but Ryan's time too. An average winter week for him consists of three hours private coaching, one and a half hours County coaching, four hours Regional coaching, five hours match or tournament play. This sum of around 14 hours average per week does not include any fitness training for which extra time has to be found each week. The summer programme includes seven hours Regional training a week and many whole weeks or weekends playing tournaments. It varies, but a full week's commitment has amounted to as much as 40 hours, sometimes playing around eight sets in one day! This amount is obligatory just to stay in the running. In no way does it equate with that of boys higher in ranking than Ryan. They play for more hours, travel to more places including Edinburgh and Eastbourne, where National tournaments are held, stay in many more hotels and such like – parents of these children must have to pay out about £5000 a year (though many get sponsorship). This is some loss if their children grow tired of it all and become dropped for some reason! As I have said before, of course to have reached any heights at all is to have achieved much in one lifetime, yet what it does to the lives of the children who do make it to the top at early ages, in my view, is not worth the acclaim. I would rather my child move slowly and steadily through the ranks to reach his heights maybe at 18 or 20 years of age, and at the same time keep other things going so that when he arrives at career-choosing time he has choices to make. Ryan leads a very busy life because just ticking over in tennis means many hours' commitment, but he also plays the piano and saxophone. His social life, I am sure, will begin to develop as he gets into teenage. It will be then that his motivation and dedication to tennis is tested.

I hope Ryan sticks at it, and continues to enjoy it as much as he does now, because there is nothing more rewarding than watching one's son put into practice everything he has learned in playing a challenging match, with skill, fluency, determination, enthusiasm and enjoyment .Jason was once like that too. Perhaps Ryan will continue to have happier experiences. He hasn't yet reached the age when Jason started, so the danger time of growth and adolescence has yet to be travelled. Nurturing talent through this time must be difficult for all concerned. Perhaps more consideration of *potential* and less concentration on results would convince me and other parents that the Lawn Tennis Association is looking to successful young adults rather than 'has-been' teenagers!

Giftedness

17

Giftedness in Sport

J. E. Kane

The Nature and Criteria of Giftedness

The educational literature, while emphasising the complex nature of giftedness and the consequential difficulties in measurement, identifies three major parameters – intellectual attainment, special abilities and cognitive style (especially creativity). Controversy continues as to the relative independence of these major elements in explaining giftedness. Greatest reliance has been placed on performance in tests of general intelligence and the majority of researchers have suggested as a cut-off point IQ 130 representing about 2%–2½% of the population, though a lower IQ threshold (and a much higher percentage of the population) is suggested by recent researchers who emphasise either the importance of creativity, or who are more concerned with the identification of specific talent(s) as opposed to general giftedness. Increasingly the criteria of giftedness are encompassing more than intellectual achievement and as a result the recognition of giftedness in its many forms is increasingly difficult. Problems range from those of identifying the gifted all-rounder to those concerned with the recognition of those with exceptional talent(s) in a specific area. At the theoretical level the questions that continue to be asked include these:

> Do all forms of manifested giftedness derive from the same source, i.e. is there a 'g' factor?

> Are the gifted potentially multi-talented, i.e. are they capable of developing talents in more than one area?

> How important is cognitive style (and especially creativity) in the definition of giftedness in general and in particular talents?

> How important are non-intellectual factors, i.e. personality, motivation, interests and upbringing?

Understandably, in the absence of uncomplicated definitions and a single all-embracing measure, current procedures for identifying the gifted and talented tend to utilise a broad range of assessment methods including tests of intelligence, personality, motivation and special aptitude or talent. Such an approach seems prudent, particularly when considered against the background of our uncertain knowledge about the nature of human abilities and the overlapping nature of talents.

Components of Human Abilities

The search for the structure of human abilities has taken a slightly different course in Britain and the USA. In Britain the effective search coincided with the development of the mathematical technique called factor analysis by Spearman, whose Two-Factor Theory emphasised 'the education of relations and correlatives' and proposed 'g' (general) and 's' (specific) factors. Spearman's work was elaborated by Burt and Vernon to indicate a hierarchical arrangement of abilities (Vernon 1977).

The American psychologists, led by Thurstone, while not denying the possibility of a general factor, preferred to emphasise independent mental abilities which they considered more useful for educational or vocational guidance. Thurstone proposed a large number of primary mental abilities – for example, verbal comprehension, number ability, word fluency, perceptual flexibility and speed, inductive reasoning, and rote memory which he argued could produce a comprehensive profile of an individual's ability on the basis of his special talents. More recently Cattell (1967) has produced a sophisticated model of human ability postulating two factors, fluid (gf – biologically derived) and crystallised (gc – culturally derived) general ability, and Guilford (1969) has continued to develop his highly complex model of the intellect involving no fewer than 120 mental factors sub-divided into three dimensions which he calls operations, contents and products. Though Cattell's and Guilford's theories are speculative, they are indicative of the constant search for the understanding of the structure of human abilities and indeed they have opened up new ways of considering intelligent behaviour as, for example, in Guilford's notion of convergent and divergent thinking.

The consideration of these historic and current theories of human abilities is an essential first step to investigating the nature, the explanatory factors and then the measurement of physical/motor talent. In his earlier and seminal work on human abilities published in 1950 Vernon saw his K (Kinaesthetic) factor as incorporating psychomotor co-ordination which in turn was constituted of motor speed, aiming, dexterieis and perceptual ability, and he clearly acknowledged the possibility of a Physical Athletic Ability dimension which might subdivide into what hc called 'types of athletics and gross muscular skills'. Guilford was much more specific in proposing 'A System of Psychomotor Abilities' which reveal factors of ability concerned with the accurate utilisation of space, the dynamic use of force and balance, speed of limb movement and dexterity. However, perhaps no present-day applied psychologist has contributed more to our understanding of the factors accounting for gross motor skill than Fleishman (1964), who has systematically factor analysed, for example, manual and perceptual motor skills abilities and the components of muscular force. Even Fleishman, however, has not attempted to analyse the much more complex sports performance factors which may account for success.

The implications of present theories and speculations of the structure of human abilities for the understanding of sports giftedness are not clear. The British hierarchical explanation deriving from a factor of general ability ('g') is attractive in trying to understand performances in sports situations where success depends on decisions and judgements involving the cognitive processes, especially perceptions and kinaesthetic judgements. On the other hand, the American theorists, especially Guilford and Fleishman, have set down comprehensive 'models' of the wide variety of abilities represented in athletic and sporting performance. However, Fleishman's work is limited to relatively simple psychomotor tasks and Guilford's schema seems to be too elaborate to have much practical application, and indeed it has been found to be unhelpful in, for example, characteristing gifted mathematicians (Hills, 1955).

Overlapping Nature of Talents

Observation, teachers' reports and substantial empirical evidence suggest the existence of a diversity of talent among the gifted which in turn would seem to support the notion of a general (or 'g') source of ability. A number of studies attest to the versatility of the gifted in producing high level performasnce in a number of areas, and the point is often made that a moderately high level of general intelligence is a necessary requisite of such versatility (Vernon *et al.*, 1977). In other words, while among the gifted there are those of very high intelligence who demonstrate general academic ability, there are also many who are talented in one or usually more areas of performance and who are not of such high intelligence though they are usually well above average, say of IQ 120. While intelligence correlates highly with certain academic talents such as mathematics and science, it correlates less highly with mechanical-constructional, visual-artistic, musical-dramatic talents and athletic talents. Nevertheless it seems that for successful achievement in any area of talent an above-average level of intelligence is necessary, and it may be (as Terman and others have hinted) that it is the high intelligence which accounts for the high achievement of the gifted across a number of talents. Giftedness then tends not to be limited to a single area of endeavour, though the gifted person may be publicly recognised for a particular talent or specialty.

Longitudinal data on gifted children reveals that they have many options for pursuing excellence, and indeed the problem for many rests in choosing from the alternatives available to them, (Parkyn, 1948). They are characterised by both teachers and parents as multi-talented and extremely versatile in performances of quality over a wide range of endeavours (Martinson, 1973; Torrance, 1962). Terman's studies, too, analysed the childhood biographies of the overlapping of talents among the gifted to include the areas of art, letters, invention, philosophy, mathematics, politics and many other fields. The Report to the USA Congress (1972) summarised the evidence as follows:

'Of all human groups, the gifted and talented are the least likely to form stereotypes. Their traits, interests, capacities and alternatives present limitless possibilities for expression, and the chief impression one draws from studying groups at either the child or adult level is of their almost unlimited versatility, their multiple talents and the countless patterns of effective expression at their command.'

It seems likely therefore that those demonstrating high achievement in sport or athletics are likely to have at least a moderately high level of measured intelligence and be capable of high performance in other spheres both athletic and non-athletic. The kind of sporting and athletic talents most likely to be part of a range of versatile performance by an individual are those requiring cognitive and perceptual judgement and decisions.

Personal and Social Correlates of Giftedness

There still persists in some quarters the notion that the gifted child endowed so fully in one direction must by some kind of law of compensation be maladapted in others. Nothing could be further from the truth. More recent studies have confirmed Terman's (1925) findings that gifted children are neither retarded nor maladjusted in physique, personality, health, or popularity. They tend in fact to be above-average on all physical and behavioural traits, and in particular they are characterised by an abundance of energy, sociability, cheerfulness and an intimidating range of leisure time activities, Parkyn (1948) in New Zealand and Burt (1962), and Lovell and Shields (1967) in England replicated and confirmed much of Terman's work on the mental, physical, personality, social and moral ratings of gifted children, concurring in the conclusion that these children are richly and comprehensively endowed with desirable qualities to support their intellectual gifts. The more recent of these studies report teacher ratings of the gifted indicating that they are emotionally stable, persevering, trustworthy, interested, prudent and have a sense of humour to a greater extent than their age peers.

One of the best earlier summaries of work in the USA on the psychological and social characteristics of gifted children came from the findings of Catherine Cox Miles (1954). From her study of 100 child geniuses she was able to list the following persistent traits that distinguished these children from their age peers: independence of thought, perceptiveness, understanding, conscientiousness, strength of influence on others, persistence, devotion to distant goals and desire to excel. Other related studies in the US have shown samples of gifted children to be substantially in advance of their peers in concern for others in socialisation, psychological maturity (Nichols and Davies, 1964) and in imaginativeness, originality, independence, self-concept and in idealism (Gallagher, 1966). Indeed Martinson (1973) found that gifted seventh graders (i.e. 13-year-olds) rated higher than successful business executives on scales of responsibility, dependability, tact and realism!

It would seem from this brief survey of the appropriate literature that the gifted are not only likely to be multi-talented, but also blessed with the most admirable dispositions. It would seem to be a case of 'to him who hath more shall be given'. However, Terman and Oden issued a caution in their 1959 report against generalising, and they emphasised the wide variations among the gifted. The caution is surely as pertinent today. They wrote:

> The reader is cautioned, however, to bear in mind the limitations of composite portraiture. Gifted children do not fall into a single pattern but into an infinite variety of patterns. One can find within the group individual examples of almost every type of personality defect, social maladjustment, behaviour problem and physical handicap; the only difference is that among gifted children the incidence of these deviations is, in varying degrees, lower than the general population.

Identifying the Gifted and Talented

On the face of it the identification of general and specific talents in sports performance would seem to be a relatively easy matter. Identifying the academically gifted is, however, a complex and uncertain process relying on a mixture of intelligence testing and teacher and parent observations. In a recent HMI survey involving seven middle schools the report reads:

> Heads and assistant teachers manifested great uncertainty about

what constituted giftedness and great reluctance to identify any of their pupils as possessing it. Out of more than 1,300 pupils currently in the schools, only four were named by heads, and those with a certain diffidence. (HMI Series No. 4, 1977)

Even with the best psychological testing procedures currently available the identification of the academically gifted and talented is not entirely satisfactory. This is particularly so in the area of aptitude testing where tests of specific talent or vocational ability have low validities with subsequent achievement. The exceptions are in the assessment of mechanical aptitude and musical talent where tests have been shown to be particularly useful.

The assessment of the general ability 'g' factor and the special aptitudes that underpin particular talents in sport has not so far attracted much attention from the researchers. Tests of general motor ability have been proposed, as indeed have some specific sports aptitude tests, (cf. Matthews, 1978), but little routine use is made of either because of their low predictive value, especially for the young. The observations of parents and teachers are no less useful in the identification of sporting talents than in other areas of giftedness. However these observations often lack objectivity and tend to exaggerate and indulge wishful thinking even to the point of providing additional coaching for quite young children. This process often leads to a temporary acceleration, but just as often leads quickly to frustration where the child has neither the sustaining high level ability, interest nor motivation to progress further.

Nevertheless the child who is manifestly achieving the sporting activities at a level well beyond his contemporaries is easy to spot by parents or teachers or coaches. What is not so obvious is whether the manifest achievement is more or less an index of exceptional ability or a temporary acceleration due to advantages of opportunity and adult support or coaching, or even relatively early physical maturation. While precocious achievement of children in sporting activities makes it relatively easy to select squads for special additional training, there is no evidence to indicate how successful are these essentially subjective methods for identifying those most likely to succeed at the highest levels of competitive performance.

The chances of the gifted and talented being nurtured and recognised are clearly greatest where opportunities for participation at school and elsewhere are readily available. The school physical education programme would seem to represent the best developmental influence and opportunity for the emergence of talent where it exists, but many programmes, being geared to the 'average' pupil, or incorporating a wide range of sports activities, fail to identify the gifted performers. The emergence of the gifted and talented may in such circumstances depend on the extracurricular opportunities within the school or outside it where expert teachers and coaches of sports skills are available. Such opportunities are common in many countries and have become increasingly available in Britain, mostly as result of the enterprise of local education authority advisers in establishing special centres or classes for the enrichment and acceleration of the gifted.

Social pressures, prestige and self-satisfaction are powerful motivators which for the talented may lead to problems concerning the balance and style of their way of life. There may well be educational psychological difficulties awaiting these young people who undertake the demanding schedules of training that face aspiring athletes. Parents, teachers and coaches would be irresponsible if they ignored the possible dangers inherent in encouraging all those who display the appropriate talents to enter the highly committing regimen of high-level training with expectations of rewards and success. Only a very carefully monitored and comprehensive longitudinal investigation of the educational, psychological and social adjustment concomitants of intensive training and competitive performance would provide the evidence on which teachers and others could base reasoned judgements. Unfortunately, and surprisingly, little or no evidence of this kind exists.

However, a recently completed study at Millfield School in England attempted to throw some light on the problems of the sports gifted. The school is a unique academic institute for secondary children at which the gifted in sport are encouraged to develop both their sporting and non-sporting talent in a well-equipped and supportive atmosphere. In the study 112 sports-gifted adolescent boys and control group were compared at two points in time with respect to their standing on measures of personality, social adjustment, anxiety, self-concept and academic attitude. The main purpose of the study was to investigate the effects of the pressures to which it was thought the sports-gifted boys would be exposed and vulnerable. The result showed that, in general, both in their first year at the school and two years later, the sports-gifted boys compared favourably with the controls in personal, psychosocial and educational development. In particular:

1 Although the sports-gifted group were more extroverted this disposition was not associated with 'prima donna' behaviour nor with other negative behavioural styles.
2 Although heightened anxiety directly related to anticipated sports performance was identifiable among the sports-gifted group, no residual general anxiety was found to typify the group. Indeed, evidence was presented to support the notion that the gifted group had developed coping skills to adapt to generalised pressures coming from the combination of training, competition and educational tasks. It was also suggested that the gifted group were helped in this

process of adaptation by *carefully structured school routines* when and where they existed.

3 The sports-gifted group manifested higher social adjustment than the controls.

4 The sports-gifted group, despite their substantial training commitment, were in no way inferior in academic achievement to the controls, and at least one sub-group (swimmers) scored significantly higher than controls at the later testing.

5 The additional help and guidance supplied by expert coaches and educators was regarded as being crucial to the adaptation and development of the sports gifted.

Personal Dispositions

While high level performance is to some extent explainable in terms of a complex organisation of innate and/or developed abilities and skills, the ultimate factors accounting for achievement are likely to be the unique personal and behavioural dispositions which the individual brings to the actual performance. These dispositions incorporating the individual's interest, motivations and personality are likely to be particularly influential in shaping performance in competitive sports where, for example, motivation to achieve and ability to handle stress are widely regarded as prerequisites for success. That is not to say that the *way* in which such dispositions operate are fully understood. This area of psychology – essentially personality psychology – has its share of major controversies concerning, for example, the relative permanence of personality traits and states, the effects of cognitive and perceptual styles on performance outcomes, the nature and force of intrinsic motivation, and the importance of 'personal constructs' and previous experience in the 'set' which the individual brings to a situation. All of these are issues of significance in the understanding of high-level sport performance. They are also issues central to an appreciation of what is currently being described as the 'interaction model' of personality according to which the cognitive interpretations and perceptions of the person in a given situation are paramount. Put differently, this model emphasises the interaction between the individual's relatively permanent traits of personality and his construct of the situation. The main point to be made here is that the unique dispositions which an individual brings to the learning or performance situation in sport are important factors in determining motivation, perception and ultimate achievement.

Sports Giftedness – Pertinent Research

Reference has been made to the meagre amount of published research on the topic of sports giftedness. The purpose of this section is to attempt a review of those studies which appear to be particularly relevant for the present exercise. Our literature search cannot claim to be exhaustive, but we did try to take account of researches published abroad in languages other than English. Our attentions were directed particularly to Russian, German and French sources, where we were told there was likely to be a great deal of pertinent information. Although we gave a great deal of time to searching for original texts and to preparing translations, we were certainly not rewarded with an abundance of material. However, the evidence which was collected gives some useful indication as to research trends and possibilities for a fuller understanding of sports giftedness.

This section considers the relevant research on the nature and criteria of sports giftedness under the following headings:

1 The genetic/experiential basis of sports giftedness.
2 Cognitive ability and sport.
3 Personal dispositions.
4 Identifying and selecting the gifted.

The Genetic/Experiential Basis of Sports Giftedness

The extent to which giftedness is dependent on innate factors or environmental experience has been disputed for a long time by researchers and the topic continues to interest overseas writers working in the field of sport. Several West German sources refer to this nature/nurture problem – for example, Kirsch (1969): 'The factor which Bernhard calls 'giftedness' is largely dependent on inherited characteristics'; and Peterson (1970): 'In the field of physical education and sport, too much value has hitherto been placed on the significance of endogenous maturation processes, in relation to the development of motor talent.'

Clearly, in relation to morphological traits (height, constitution) the influence of heredity is irrefutable. Indeed the work of both Klissouras (1976) in Canada and Ulbrich (1971) in East Germany, related to the concordance of motor capacity and physiological indicators, suggests that stamina at least is a talent which is predominantly an hereditary characteristic. Klissouras (1976) cites the case of identical twins who retained a low maximum oxygen uptake, despite active involvement in sports. One twin continued to be active for some years and recorded a figure of 49ml/min/kg compared to the other twin's 35ml/min/kg, yet still below 50ml/min/kg: the average for an untrained student of the same age.

Genealogical studies have also been utilised as a means of establishing the influence of genetic factors on sports giftedness. Grebe (1956) concluded that approximately 50% of children of outstanding German athletes are likely to show marked sporting ability, given the right opportunities. Some correlation was also discovered in the USA by Cratty (1960), between the abilities of fathers and their children at the same age in several exercises: 0.49 for 100 yards and 0.80 for standing long jump.

Perhaps the most rigorous research strategy for investigating the influence of genetics on all aspects of human ability is that of twin studies, although there are methodological shortcomings associated with this type of research. The Italian researcher Gedda (1960) in a study of 351 sets of twins found that identical twins showed significantly more concordance than fraternal twins with regard to participation in sport (94% to 15%); the sport itself (83% to 31%); the subsequent position or event (87% to 66%); and actual success (70% to 22%). Similar data is presented by Fleischmann (1971), following research in West Germany.

On the other hand, the significance of environmental factors in the development of sports talent is supported by studies of intellectual development, which demonstrate the adverse effects of delayed environmental stimuli. The importance of early learning experience as a prerequisite and determinant of future intellectual progress has been demonstrated by psychologists from several countries – for example, Aebli (1969); Bruner (1971); and Piaget (1950). Aebli uses the concept of 'objective-structural prerequisites' in this respect and Peterson (1970) summarises thus:

In other words: success or failure of later stages of learning are determined less by innate potential and level of maturity and rather more by the scope and quality of previous experience.

Perhaps in sport and physical education too much emphasis has traditionally been placed on the natural endowment of talent, thereby obscuring the importance of experiential factors.

The indications are, therefore, that it is not clear at the moment quite how, and to what extent, heredity and the environment accounts for sporting talent. However, one can point to genetic limitations on certain physiological factors such as endurance and the probability of some genetic predisposition for certain abilities. Alternatively, the importance of early learning experience (i.e. before eight years old) as a decisive factor in shaping future skill levels underlines the necessity of a systematised movement education from the beginning of the school programme to give both the backward and the able opportunity to progress. In this respect, Sharpe (1979) has shown that an enriched and accelerated movement experience can facilitate cognitive development in young children.

Cognitive Ability and Sport

Although general and specific intelligence factors have been central to educational explanations of giftedness, the association between these factors and giftedness in sport has proved difficult to identify. The studies of Ismail (1965) and Ismail and Gruber (1967) have indicated that among children in the USA and Britain, intelligence quotient and attainment correlate with aspects of motor ability such as co-ordination and equilibrium. Cratty (1972) too has shown similar operational relationships and has referred in particular to the value of games activities for promoting general verbal and numerical abilities among the young and the retarded. However, Geron (1976) failed to reproduce Ismail's findings among Israeli children and concluded that there is a general lack of definitive analysis of the intellectual components of sporting activity and the relationship of these components with cognitive abilities in general.

Geron further discovered that this profile appears quite clearly among children showing talent for gymnastics and recommended that this 'gymnast's profile' be considered as a useful criterion for early selection.

The way in which general cognitive intelligence is involved in the decisions and tactics which are constant operational requirements in many competitive sports has been the subject of fascinating and fundamental research in the Soviet Union and at least one related study from Hungary has been published by Mahlo (1975).

The specific orientation of cognitive abilities in sporting activity has received more detailed attention from the Soviet researcher Rodionov (1973). The adaptability of the sportsman's psychological processes and particularly those of the central nervous system represent the central theme of Rodionov's work. He suggests (in line with Mahlo) that the basic abilities required for successful performance in sport are:

(i)   Rapid orientation during competition.
(ii) Fast and accurate processing of information.
(iii) Rapid decision making.
(iv) Fast reactions to stimuli that may occur (obstacles, etc.).

More precisely, Rodionov indicates the importance of an athlete's 'operative' or 'tactical' thinking, and in this respect he acknowledges the work of Puni (1970) who has pointed out that competitive situations demand from the sportsman an extremely well-developed and orientated cognitive ability. This developed ability is necessary in order to observe analytically his opponent's moves and ploys, to anticipate his further action and to introduce appropriate counter-plans and tactics. The sophisticated sportsman will additionally need to 'read' and interpret quickly the environmental 'field' and general game situations.

Rodionov's investigations into the characteristics of operative think-ings of sportsmen were based on simulated laboratory games, which were developed and adapted in the Soviet Union (see Ruskin, 1970, for further details). Rodionov indicates that the experimental games 'assess the sportsman's ability in relation to the critical factors of perception of the stuation and decision-making, and is analogous to tactical thinking in sport'. However, using these laboratory games Rodionov tested, in one series of experiments, seven groups.

The same tests were used by Rodionov in a further investigation of Soviet boxers (n = 56) and again operative thinking scores correlated significantly with ratings given by experts during a competition. Addi-tionally, a test of operative memory developed by the Ukrainian Institute of Psychology of the Academy of Sciences was administered to the boxers in this investigation which tested the speed and accuracy with which the subjects could work through a list of numbers, succes-sively adding to an ever-increasing total which had to be held in the memory. The results of this test (Table 1) showed that boxing appears to make significant demands on operative memory, and the compari-son of mean arithmetical indices of testing indicates the advantage of masters of sport (A), candidate masters (B) and first category sports-men (C) over novices (D).

Rodionov concluded that the main advantage of the better sports-man lay in his speed of perceiving and effecting a solution, and that this ability is noticeable as a differentiating factor at an early age of specialisation.

There are sufficient indications from these few studies of cognitive involvement in sports that this aspect of sports performance is of crucial importance in understanding the processes involved in the sportsman's analysis, perception and decision-making during the course of a competitive game. These cognitive abilities may be specific and may be more or less innate, but only further rigorous research will tell. The seminal work of Rodionov is certainly worth pursuing, and in general it seems worthwhile and possible to encourage a sharpening of the procedure by which we may assess the cognitive abilities that are required for operation and tactical success in sport.

Personal Dispositions

In general, the personality of the individual and particularly the behavioural 'state' in which he finds himself just before a critical competition will, to an important extent, affect his performance. A number of authors in the area of applied psychology have indicated the present possibilities of gaining important psychological insights which may be important in the selection, training and performance of talented athletes (for example, Vanek and Cratty, 1970; Rushall and Siedentop, 1972; Ponsonby and Yaffe, 1976; and Kane, 1976). Descriptive profiles have tended to describe athletes as more or less stable, tough-minded, achievement-oriented extraverts and, although there is a great deal of personality variance *between* different sports groups (for example, soccer players versus gymnasts), a number of studies have demonstrated the similarity of profile of outstanding performers *within* a particular sport. Even if personality assessment is limited to the two major dimensions, extraversion and anxiety, there is a great deal of practical as well as theoretical and predictive use to which such data may be put in the context of sports performance. Elsewhere Kane (1978) has outlined theoretical and practical possibilities, based on Eysenkian theory, which would have relevance to both training and performance of athletes, particularly in activities where the perceptual processes such as vigilance, selective attention and recall are of importance. Although the detailed personality study of gifted young athletes has not received much attention, Groll, Mader and Redl speculated at the 1975 Vienna Conference on talent seeking and development that:

> . . . early recognition and subsequent follow-up of the development of the psychological personality characteristics of a young maturing person, would be of considerable assistance in talent-searching and the promotion of sport.

These researchers went on to suggest that the most likely personality characteristics needed by young athletes to sustain them in training and high-level competition would include marked persistence and striving for dominance; a highly-developed urge to achieve; a high measure of stability; sure self-confidence; and a high measure of vitality (vital energy). Of the greatest importance, however, is the individual's liability to stress. The extent to which an athlete perceives a situation to be stressful and subsequently the way he can control his anxiety and arousal levels are likely to shape his performance crucially.

A number of studies have emphasised the importance of assessing and understanding both the athlete's anxiety *trait* (i.e. his anxiety predisposition) and his anxiety *state* (i.e. his response to stress.) It is surprising, therefore, that these important indices have not been systematically monitored among talented young athletes in order to anticipate stress problems. An exception is a long-term study of stress reported from the Soviet Union. The researchers, Gaitzarska, Siris and Gorozhanin[1] investigated the incidence of 'weak' and 'strong' nervous systems among speed and endurance athletes. The authors followed the Teplov (1972) postulates that success in various kinds of activities is a function of the sensitivity of the individual's nervous system. After screening more than 600 athletes (aged 10–29 years) from different sports and with differing levels of ability, the authors produced evidence to show that sensitivity of the nervous system was a factor which discriminated between endurance athletes and speed athletes and concluded that this factor should be used as a predictive tool in the selection of gifted athletes.

In a wider context, high-level performance reflects the performer's sustained general motivation. While it is not possible here to argue in detail the effect of motivation on performance, there seems little doubt that in the last analysis it is the individual motivation that is being assessed in the arduous pursuit of excellence. The concept of motivation is not tidy and simple, but centres on the strength and persistence of an individual's drive to achieve his perceived needs. Traditional notions of motivation have been applied to the athletics arena of performance without much success, but it may be that the new force in present-day psychology which emphasises more the intrinsic personal satisfaction, fulfilment and self-actualisation of behaviour (and less the extrinsic motives of success) may be more relevant. Czikszentmihalyi (1975), following this line of approach, investigated the inner experiences concerned with joy and pleasure in play and games and in a variety of life-styles and described a common form of experience *flow* and suggested that it gave rise to feelings of exhilaration, of creative accomplishment and of heightened functioning. The gifted and talented people who attain or aspire to attain the highest levels of achievement in sport will need to be sustained by the most appropriate psychological support system. It is more than likely that there are many possessing the skill and physical attributes necessary for high-level achievement who are psychologically unsuited and ill-equipped to handle the problems of competitive involvement. *Even those gifted young athletes with strong initial motivation and personality will need a psychological education and training programme paralleling their physical development programme if they are to realise their ability.*

Identifying and Selecting the Gifted

The early selection of children who are gifted in sport, so that they may receive the benefits of accelerated and enriched developmental programmes, has been pursued in many countries. The Soviet researchers Zatsiorsky, Bulgakova, Raginov and Sergienko (1969) have indicated that the basic requirement in the development of a consistent and dependable system of selection is to determine the ideal qualities necessary for success in particular sports:

The main prerequisite for successful selection is a thorough knowledge of the components making up the athlete activity in question, so that a preliminary analysis of the constituent skills and movement characteristics can be made.

The search for these basic motor abilities, which are the fundamental components of skilled performance, and the construction of tests to evaluate an individual's capabilities on these dimensions, have been generally recognised as essential for accurate prediction. So far, however, the research has produced no definite predictors, even though understanding of the fundamental physical (e.g. strength, mobility, endurance) factors in sports performance is reasonably well advanced. The more refined predictors of specific skills and the even more refined predictors of competitive behaviour seem to be still a long way off. Nevertheless there are examples of forward-looking researches and procedures, in particular Fleishman's (1964) work in America on perceptual-motor abilities and Kirsch's (1969) West German research on basic sporting abilities.

As a result of his experiences Kirsch (1969) advocates a comprehensive screening process for the identification of the gifted in sport, consisting of a combined battery of tests to evaluate the child's potential in all aspects of the activity in question. These tests fall into two major categories:

(i) Tests determining the child's ability in terms of physical factors, with special reference to speed, strength and endurance.
(ii) Tests determining a child's aptitude for specific sports disciplines, respect of basic essential motor abilities.

In East Germany the use of screening methods to identify children with outstanding talent for sport has been widely reported, though the procedures used are not detailed in any report we could find. The children selected are apparently often sent to sports boarding schools to develop and nurture their potential abilities. However, in spite of the apparent systematic thoroughness of the approach, the specialist sports school system of the Eastern Block has come under attack by writers and researchers in that part of the world. Questions concerning the expenditure involved and the fundamental concepts underlying the schemes have been voiced. The Soviet researchers Zhmarev and Tepper (1975), for example, write:

Statistics refute dialectics, quantity is not turning into quality . . . Experience of work with school children in the German Democratic Republic shows that we should pay maximum attention to creating a reliable system of searching for talent by 'screening' all school-age children. However, an increase in sports schools (even tenfold) will ensure the same size of increase in average results, while the number of discovered gifted athletes will hardly alter. Furthermore, the sports school will be obliged step by step to take its pupil of average ability to his peak, which may well be no higher than a first ranking. Every subsequent step requires expenditure that increases in geometrical progression.

In general the evidence points to the need for early and careful selection of those with undoubted talents, rather than a coarser selection of a larger number, all of whom would receive additional and special training. The economic and educational values of this interpretation are apparent; however, it does focus attention on the vital need for sound predictive tests which are not currently available. Consequently, in many countries the initial criterion for selection is still the child's performance in the various youth competitions, even though this success may be due to additional coaching or experience.

The Soviet Union in particular makes use of the Children's Spartakiade or the Children's Republican Games as an initial indicator of sporting talent. However, there also exists a graded filtering system to identify more precisely the children with special talents, who are sent for further intense training to one or other form of sports school, even though some of these special schools are (as mentioned above) currently under criticism. One example of this process was revealed to one of the authors during a visit in 1975 to a sports boarding school in Leningrad. The school receives approximately 1,000 applications every year for entry in each of the sports in which the school specialises. After preliminary analyses of the candidates have been conducted, 150 are selected to attend summer sports camps, during which 30 are chosen on the basis of performance and results on special tests of the type outlined by Kirsch (1969), to be accepted as pupils in the school.

Some of the particular selection procedures were also revealed, during the same visit in 1975, by the head coach of a special gymnastic school which had never been lower than third in the team competition at the National Spartakiade. The girl gymnasts are selected at seven or eight years and the boys at nine years, although in some parts of the Soviet Union it is apparently the practice to select even younger children for these schools. The physical qualities which are generally considered by this coach to the desirable include a strong torso, slim legs and hips, strong arms, flexibility, and boys in particular should have strong stomach muscles and good spring. A generally harmonious appearance is regarded as essential and a movement pattern which expresses smoothness, flow, mobility and energy. The most important personal qualities are judged to be diligence, will-power, character, inner discipline and eventually 'a responsibility to the group'.

The physical tests which are utilised by this specialist sport school include pull-ups (approximately 10), balance tests and dips (approximately 12) for the boys, while those for the girls reflect a greater concern for plasticity and include movements such as the bridge and the splits. The coach also mentioned the importance of working with 'intelligent' youngsters, and more recently the practice of recording the parents' anthropometric details as an indicator of the pupil's physical growth potential has been reported.[1]

In France, a detailed procedure has also been adopted recently for the selection of gifted youngsters for the 'Sport and Study Section', which operate within the educational system. The criteria for selection for these specialist sport units are devised by the various governing bodies for each sport and a short list of applicants is drawn up. Most of the sections accept pupils at 15 or 16 years old, and each applicant has to submit a file with his application which gives detailed information in three divisions:

(i) Medical;
(ii) Academic;
(iii) Sports.

The selection process commences with the scrutiny of the file by a commission comprised of representatives from such bodies as:

(i) the 'Sport and Study Section' itself;
(ii) the Office of the Secretary of State for Youth and Sport;
(iii) the CNOSF (The National Sport and Olympic Committee of France);
(iv) the governing body of the sport concerned;
(v) the Regional Medical Officer for Health in Schools.

The most likely candidates are subsequently interviewed and examined practically. The structure of the practical test for young soccer players is a good example of the general approach adopted by these specialist sport units in this critical phase of the selection process. The players are subjected to three types of assessment:

(i) General athletic ability — e.g. running ability over distances from 60m to 1000m, jumping ability, throwing a medicine ball, etc.
(ii) Technical ability — e.g. ball control, dribbling, kicking, etc.
(iii) Game assessment — detailed analysis of the player's performance within the game situation.

[1] By Dr J. Riordan, after a visit to the USSR in 1978.

This structured system of selection procedures is similar in several respects to the Soviet pattern described previously, in that it evaluates the youngsters' ability on a number of underlying components relevant to the particular sport, and operates essentially as a filtering process, albeit a fairly unsophisticated one as yet.

The question of the ideal age at which selection for specialised training should be made is a further aspect of the problem which is evident in the research literature of several countries. In general terms one can point to the beneficial effects of an enriched experience at any early age, and Petersen's (1970) researches in West Germany permitted him to conclude that:

> In the movement field it is hardly ever 'too early' to practise a skill, it is more likely to be 'too late' to learn a specific activity really well. In order to avoid the adverse effects of delayed developmental stimuli, endeavours to promote talent should be directed above all towards children of primary school age.

However, the almost wholesale acceptance of this notion in certain sports must be questioned in view of the idiosyncratic nature of children's developmental patterns, nor is there sufficient evidence available concerning the 'ideal' time for acquiring or developing skills. The best children and juniors do not consistently develop into tomorrow's champions, and there are many cases where athletes have been highly successful after taking up their particular sport at a comparatively late stage. Zatsiorsky *et al.* (1973) have illustrated the point with their data on Soviet swimmers who are selected at seven or eight years, as they are in many countries. Analysis of the profiles of the most successful Soviet swimmers in the Olympic Games from 1952–72 (i.e. those who finished in the first six places) showed that not one of them began serious training before the age of 10 and many were 13 years or older.

Zatsiorsky's study also investigated the length of time required to reach international standard, in relation to the age at which training was commenced. The research on Soviet swimmers revealed that an early start tends to be counteracted by a longer developmental period, which decreases in length as the starting age rises.

Research conducted in Poland and reported by Zatsiorsky *et al.* (1973) investigated another problem associated with the selection of youngsters for special sports schools or team squads – namely the difficulty of equating the performances of athletes of different ages in order to decide which individual presents the best prospect of success. Consequently, prior to the Olympic Games in 1972 statistical evidence was collected, (1) to determine the rates of progress of the leading performers in each sport at various ages; (2) to establish the age at which the highest attainments are normally reached; and (3) to fore-

THE GROWING CHILD IN COMPETITIVE SPORT

cast the likely performance levels of the finalists in each event at the forthcoming Games. On the basis of this information it was possible to plot for each event the average rate of progress for athletes commencing serious training at different ages, which could be related to the various targeherformances. In this way the standards expected from potential Olympic performers could be established for various age levels. Thus, for example, in 1968 it was considered that potentially valuable members of the 100m free-style squad for the 1972 Olympic Games would be an 18-year-old with a performance time of 57 sec, or a 14-year-old with a performance time of 1 min .03 sec. In fact, the Polish researchers found that the eventual targets proved to be too low, but the notion of determining standards for Olympic Squad candidates by taking account of their age would seem a useful one.

This brief selective review of some pertinent overseas literature gives some indication of the attempts in several countries to develop a systematic procedure for the identification and selection of gifted children in sport. However, despite the apparent thoroughness of these selection procedures in countries like the Soviet Union and the success of certain sections of the process (e.g. the prediction of physiological capabilities), it is apparent from our evidence that the tests used to identify the potentially outstanding performer in terms of basic abilities or competitive temperament are relatively unsophisticated. It would seem to be possible, on the face of it, using suitably rigorous methods, to develop batteries of tests with high predictive value for particular areas of sports performance and which are better than any so far devised.

References and Bibliography

AEBLI, H. (1969) 'The intellectual development and function of talent, maturity, environment and education.' In Petersen (1970).

BRUNER, J. S. (1973) Beyond the Information Given. London: Allen and Unwin.

BURT, C. (1962) 'The gifted child.' In G. Z. BEREDAY and J. A. LAUWERYS (eds) The Gifted Child: The Yearbook of Education. London: Evans.

CATTELL, R. B. (1967) 'The theory of fluid and crystallised intelligence checked at the 5- 6-year-old level.' British Journal of Educational Psychology, 37.

CRATTY, B. J. (1960) 'A comparison of fathers and sons in physical education.' Research Quarterly, 31: 12–15.

CZIKSZENTMIHALYI, M. (1975) Beyond Boredom and Anxiety. San Francisco, CA: Jossey-Bass.

FLEISCHMANN, R. J. (1971) Cited in Zatsiorsky et al. (1973).

FLEISHMAN, E. (1964) The Structure and Measurement of Physical Fitness. Englewood Cliffs, NJ: Prentice-Hall.

FLOOD, M. and ENDLER, N. S. (1976) The Intraction Model of Anxiety: An empirical test in an athletic competition situation. York University Department of Psychology, Report No. 28.

GAITZARSKA, P. M., SIRIS, P. Z. and GOROZHANIN, V. S. *Psycho-physiological Diagnostics of Sporting Talent for Work, comprising Speed and Endurance.* Monograph, Documentation Centre, Minsk, USSR.

GALLAGHER, J. (1966) 'The Gifted.' *Review of Educational Research,* **36**, 1, February.

GEDDA, L. (1960) 'A study of twins (351 pairs).' *Acta Geneticae Medicae et Genelologiae,* **9**: 387–408.

GERON, E. (1974) *Intelligence and Motor Learning Ability in Gymnastics.* Wingate Institute of Physical Education, Monograph.

GERON, E. (1975) *Sport Giftedness (in Gymnastics) and Intelligence in Children.* Wingate Institute of Physical Education, Monograph.

ERON, E. (1976) 'Psychological problems concerning a comprehensive definition of the search for talent in sport.' *Psychometrik und Sportliche Leistung* (Stuttgart): 178–87.

GREBE, H. (1956) 'Families with a sporting tradition.' *Acta Geneticae Medicae et Genelologiae,* **5**: 3.

GUILFORD, J. P. (1969) 'The three faces of intellect.' *American Psychologist,* **5**.

HILLS, J. R. (1955) 'The relationship between certain factor analysed abilities and success in college mathematics.' *Reports from the Psychology Laboratory,* No. 15. University of Southern California.

ISMAIL, A. H. (1965) 'Predictive power of co-ordination and balance items in estimating intelligence development.' In F. ANTONELLI (ed.) *Psychologie Dello Sport.* Rome.

ISMAIL, A. H. and GRUBER, I. I. (1967) *Motor Aptitude and Intellectual Performance.* Indianapolis, IN: Merrill.

KANE, J. E. (1976) 'Personality and performance in sport.' In J. WILLIAMS and P. SPERRYN (eds) *Sports Medicine.* London: Arnold.

KANE, J. E. (1978) 'Personality research: the current controversy.' In W. STRAUB (ed.) *Sport Psychology.* New York: Mouvement Publications.

KIRSCH, A. (1969) 'The use of aptitude tests and test of suitability in talent searching.' *Die Leiberserziehung,* **18**, 10: 329–31.

KLISSOURAS, V. (1976) *Prediction of Athletic Performance: Genetic Considerations.* Invited paper to the International Congress of Phys Act. Sciences, Quebec.

KROLL, W. (1970) 'Personality assessment of athletes.' In L. E. SMITH (ed.) *Psychology of Motor Learning.* Chicago, IL: Athletic Institute.

LANGER, P. (1966) 'Varsity football performance.' *Perceptual and Motor Skills,* **23**.

LOVELL, K. and SHIELDS, J. B. (1967) 'Some aspects of the study of the gifted child.' *British Journal of Educational Psychology,* **37**.

MARTINSON, R. A. (1973) 'Children with superior cognitive abilities.' In L. M. DUNN (ed.) *Exceptional Children in the Schools.* New York: Holt, Rinehart and Winston.

MILES, C. C. (1954) 'Gifted children.' In L. CARMICHAEL (ed.) *Manual of Child Psychology.* New York: John Wiley.

NEBILITSYN, V. D. (1960) Cited in Gaitzarska *et al.*

NEBILITSYN, V. D. (1966) Cited in Rodionov (1973).

NICHOLS, R. C. and DAVIS, J. A. (1964) 'Characteristics of students of high academic aptitude.' *Personnel and Guidance Journal,* **42**, 8.

PARKYN, G. W. (1948) *Encouraging the excellent: special programs for the gifted*. New York: The Fund for the Advancement of Education.

PAVLOV, I. P. (1927) *Conditioned Reflexes*. Oxford: Oxford University Press.

PETERSEN, U. (1970) 'Concerning the problem of motor giftedness and its significance for the promotion of talent.' *Die Lieberserziehung*, **19**, 5: 156–61.

PIAGET, J. (1950) *The Psychology of Intelligence*. London: Routledge and Kegan Paul.

PONSONBY, D. and YAFFE, M. (1976) 'Psychology takes the soccer field.' *FIFA News*, July.

RENZULLI, J. S. and HARTMAN, D. K. (1971) 'Scale for rating behavioural characteristics of superior students.' *Exceptional Children*, **38**.

RODIONOV, A. V. (1973) *The Psychodiagnostics of Sporting Ability, Physical Culture and Sport*, Moscow.

RUSHALL, B. and SIEDENTOP, D. (1972) *The Development and Control of Behaviour in Sport and Physical Education*. Philadelphia, PA: Lea and Febiger.

TATTERSFIELD, C. R. (1971) *Competitive Sport and Personality Development*. Thesis, University of Durham.

TEPLOV, B. M. (1972) 'The problem of types of human higher nervous activity and method of determining them.' In V. D. NEBILITSYN and J. A. GRAY (eds) *Biological Bases of Individual Behaviour*. London: Academic Press.

TERMAN, L. (1925) *Genetic Studies of Genius, Vol. 1: Mental and Physical Traits of a Thousand Gifted Children*. Stanford, CT: Stanford University Press.

TERMAN, L. (1954) 'The discovery and encouragement of exceptional talent.' *American Psychologist*, **9**.

TERMAN, L. and ODEN, M. (1959) *Genetic Studies of Genius, Vol. 5: The Gifted Group at Mid-life*. Stanford, CT: Stanford University Press.

TORRANCE, E. P. (1962) *Creativity: What Research says to the Teacher*. Washington, DC: American Educational Research Association.

ULBRICH, J. (1971) Cited in Zatsiorsky *et al*. (1973).

VANEK, M. and CRATTY, B. J. (1970) *Psychology and the Superior Athlete*. London: Macmillan.

VERNON, P. E. (1961) *The Structure of Human Abilities*. London: Methuen.

VERNON, P. E. *et al*. (1977) *The Psychology and Education of Gifted Children*. London: Methuen.

WHITING, H. T. A. (1975) *Concepts in Skill Learning*. London: Lepus.

ZATSIORSKY, V. M., BULGAKOVA, N. zh., RAGINOV, R. M. and SERGIENKO, L. P. (1973) 'Giftedness and selections: the direction and methodology of research.' *Teoriva i Praktika Fizicheskoi Kultury*, **1**: 54–66.

ZHMAREV, N. and TEPPER, YU. (1975) 'Talent. What is that?' *Lyogkaya Atletica*, **8**: 26–7.

Pamphlets and Discussion Documents

Education of the Gifted and Talented. Report to the Congress of the United States, March 1972.

DEVON EDUCATION DEPARTMENT (1977) *Find the Gifted Child*.

DEPARTMENT OF EDUCATION AND SCIENCE (1977) *Gifted Children in Middle and Comprehensive Schools* (HMI Matters for Discussion series No. 4). London: HMSO.

18

Giftedness in Music

Sheila McQuattie

I would like to begin by justifying the presence here of a group of
musicians. You may be wondering what possible relevance our subject
can have to the main purpose of this conference. However, it may
intrigue you to learn how many problems we share in the detecting and
correct nurturing of a special talent in the young. I will start by quoting
from a lecture given by Dr John Kane[1] in 1979, in which he said:

> 'Even with the best psychological procedures currently available the
> identification of the gifted and talented is not entirely satisfactory.
> This is particularly so in the area of aptitude testing where tests of
> specific talent or vocational ability have low validities with sub-
> sequent achievement. The exceptions are in the assessment of
> mechanical aptitude and music talent where tests have been shown
> to be particularly useful.'

I shall return to this point later.

No one can argue that there are not marked dissimilarities. In
gymnastics and athletics, age is a critical factor. Not so with music. This
will be discussed later in the chapter.

What we certainly do share in common is the problem of assessing
the potential of our pupils and guiding them accordingly. We have to
distinguish between competence, giftedness and genius. The *Oxford
Dictionary* defines them thus:

- A *competent* student is one who is 'adequately qualified to do'.
- A *gifted* student has 'a faculty miraculously bestowed'.

The quality of *genius* is described as 'special mental endowment;
exalted intellectual power; instinctive and extraordinary imaginative,
creative, or inventive capacity'. On behalf of performing musicians I
would add 're-creative', where the genius may lie in the power to
convey every nuance intended by the composer. Bernard Shaw says, in
one of his 'Essays on Music', that the art of performing is 'a natural gift
of the highest expression which is so rare, and so impossible of
acquisition, that we have no right to complain of its absence'.[2] (We
may certainly, however, appreciate its presence.)

Having quoted from these sources, I would like to consider some of
the points raised. On the question of selecting the potentially outstand-

ing student, who is to recognise genius or talent in its early stages? It takes a particular quality of perspicacity and awareness. Many great musicians have been utterly undervalued in their own time, their significance or skill being unrecognised. We have only to go as far as B in the alphabet to find Bach and Bizet, two such cases. Conversely, others have had far-sighted and wise teachers, of lesser stature than their pupils, but who have correctly judged the importance of the talent in their care. They are the 'also-rans' of music who act as pace setters – the unsung heroes who, recognising promise for the future, perform their function in the race knowing they will be overtaken in the end. You may not have heard of Abrechtsberger, but you will certainly have heard of his pupil Beethoven. Likewise you may not have heard of Franck, but you will know the name Haydn. So one does not necessarily have to compete with one's student in order to be of benefit, but one must have the quality of acute analytical awareness in order to nurture and develop the talent in hand.

This nurturing is the second stage. I maintain that the first is the more difficult: that of correct identification and evaluation. Much time and effort has been devoted to training seemingly promising musicians who have subsequently faded into obscurity. One only has to read an outdated music history textbook to see how artificially upgraded were some composers who have since deservedly vanished in the mists of time. Equally, some whom we will never know must have slipped through the net through circumstance and lack of opportunity. At least with a composer there is the chance of his contemporarily unrecognised genius being discovered posthumously, as has often been the case. No such opportunity is afforded to the performer or sportsman, where time and timing are of the essence. It makes one realise how valuable is the gift of hindsight – useful indeed for the written word or manuscript, but not available in terms of practical activity.

Two interesting instances on the subject of recognition of talent occur in connection with Schubert. If I mention the names Goethe and Huttenbrenner you could be forgiven for assuming that Goethe, one of the great brains of all time and no mean musician himself, would have instantly recognised the works of a fellow-genius. Not so; he did not even acknowledge the receipt of some of the greatest songs ever written. Perhaps he was so preoccupied with his own mental probings that he could not respond to those of another, and inadequate performance of Schubert's offerings may well have played a part in his misjudgement. On the other hand, Anselm Huttenbrenner (whose name may well be totally new to you) rescued many manuscripts from various drawers and cupboards after Schubert's death. (Schubert's filing system was never the most efficient!) He had faith in his instinct as to Schubert's significance. Thus Huttenbrenner, otherwise a fairly ordinary mortal, had his own special talent: that of correctly identifying giftedness in another. He had the special quality of perception necessary for its evaluation. There is an element of selflessness in being aware of the qualities of another, and every good teacher, trainer, or mentor must possess it.

Equipment and environment play an essential part in enabling one to recognised talent. It may seem a simplistic statement, though un-arguable, that a budding artist cannot manifest his ability without the wherewithal with which to draw or paint; similarly, a potential long-distance runner cannot flourish in a confined apartment. What might have happened to the young Mozart had he not been surrounded by music and musical instruments from birth? And when the boy Handel sought refuge from his stern father, what form would that refuge have taken had there not been a keyboard instrument in the house? The presence of basic equipment is vital. In days gone by, musical tuition in education and the presence of musical instruments in the home were accepted essentials. Today it is harder in some ways for a possible musician to realise or even be aware of his ability, as so many junior schools (a crucial stage in the fostering of talent) are virtually without music, and so many homes are totally without it. (I speak, of course, of music which involves participation of a practical or creative nature.)

The effects of environments of two different sorts are illustrated by the case histories of two young musicians present today. One comes from a home where both parents are professional musicians. He has therefore been surrounded by equipment and musical influence since early childhood. The other took up music at the late age of thirteen as the result of a chance encounter at school. Their choice of instrument mirrors their environment: firstly the cello, rarely available to a young child, and secondly the trumpet – less sophisticated, but to hand at the time an interest necessitated action. With regard to the theoretical knowledge needed to back up practical expertise, our trumpeter has had to cram a great deal of learning into a very short time.

Basic equipment applies, of course, not only to the possession of artefacts, whether sporting or musical. It refers also to the physical propensities of the youngster. Some builds are more suited to one specialisation than another. This applies also in dance and music. An ambitious dancer can be told at a very early age whether or not she is going to grow too tall to be of use in the professional world. Would-be cellists must have sturdy fingers with a wide stretch between the digits, whereas large fingertips are a hazard to the violin player who would have great difficulty in achieving absolute accuracy with the fleshy pads of a cellist. Therefore it is wise to study the hand shape of a young string player to ascertain which instrument will ultimately be suitable.

For the wind player, mouth shape or lip formation will be vital. I know of a horn player who actually had to give up his chosen instrument as his lips were too thick and consequently his embouchure was impossible to correct. In the case of violinists, I know of many out-of-tune players who would have been much better off had they been weaned on to the viola or cello. There is also the case of a professional violinist who had to work twice as hard as his peers in order to overcome the fact that his fifth digit was unusually short. Fortunately, sheer determination coupled with a total love of the subject spurred him on to succeed where a host of others would have failed. But the fiercely-competitive world of the professional musician is fraught with sufficient trials and tribulations without inbuilt difficulties having first to be overcome. While on the subject of physique I would like to dispel the myth that a pianist has smooth-skinned hands with delicately tapering fingers. This romantic image is utterly inaccurate. If you ever have the opportunity to examine the plaster casts of the hands of some of the all-time great pianists such as Liszt, Busoni, or Rachmaninov, you will find them to be muscular, sinewed, and quite un-beautiful. A pianist's hands are *working* hands.

Are a musician's ears any different? One so often hears the phrases, 'I'm tone deaf', or 'I can't hear the lower part.' I would discard both these statements. If you can distinguish between the sound of a door banging and a flute playing you have the learning potential to do what the trained musician does – that is, to analyse the difference between like sounds. All that is lacking is early training.

Most people, including musicians, regard 'perfect pitch' as a God-given gift. It is not. It is merely an advanced form of memory. In experiments with students, I have started by asking them to sing a note immediately after hearing it. I then gradually increased the time-lapse between the initial hearing of the note and the repetition of it, and many students have been surprised at their accuracy in correctly pitching the note after a gap of several hours. Almost all string players can pitch an A because of the frequency with which they have to use it to tune up. Their ears are the same as yours, but their memory has been trained in that specialism.

Having dealt to some extent with the basic requirements, both material and physical, for the making of a musician, we now come to a necessary quality which is even harder to judge: mental equipment. Of necessity a young musician is a solitary and isolated being for much of his or her time. Long hours of study and practice are unavoidable. This can be a demoralising process, as more time must be spent on weaknesses than strengths. It is all too tempting to play with great panache all the impressive favourite passages under one's command whilst glossing discreetly over the sections which really need attention. To practise constructively requires a large degree of mental stamina, determination, and a mature and realistic appraisal of the demands to be met.

The young musician therefore has many battles to fight. He or she must persevere against the odds as the chances of real success are rare. He (or she) must often suffer the ridicule of classmates who consider the carrying of a violin case in object of mirth. He must frequently undergo the trial of having to perform to order and give of his best when nerves, a headache, or a fault in his instrument may detract from his usual standard. And as with an athlete, the audience so unkindly remembers what went wrong rather than what went right. Under these sorts of pressures an artistically sensitive youngster may crack.

Frequently the ambitions of proud parents are a destructive force. We have all come into contact with the parents who seek to live their own lost career through an uninspired and unprotesting offspring. There is a fine dividing line between support and push. The dynamic force must come from the child himself. It is always interesting to meet the parents of an interviewee, to ascertain whether they answer for the candidate, or whether the energising force comes from the correct source – that is, the aspiring student himself (herself).

For the persevering musician there are untold compensations. One can enjoy music in isolation even if professional standards have not been attained, by means of an instrument or from electronic equipment, deriving comfort, inspiration, amusement, according to need. There are many and varied social benefits. The community spirit engendered by a group of amateurs struggling through a demanding orchestral work never fails to produce real contact through hard work, mirth and the reward of making music together.

This is the true magic of music – its ability to communicate – and as the tutor communicates his advice and guidance to the student, he must also instil into that pupil the ability to communicate with an audience.

We have at this conference many visitors who speak a variety of languages. We will now hear the first sounds which need no translation, according to Alvin Toffler in his book *The Third Wave*,[3] 'undoubtedly the most famous four notes in music':*

And no language barrier can obscure the genius of Beethoven in the opening of the slow movement from the 'Pathétique' Sonata, opus 13, number 8. A really gifted pianist will recreate that piece of music in such a way as to put the listener in direct touch with Beethoven.

In the gifted student we look for all the qualities so far enumerated, emphasising the willingness to relinquish any idea of a 'normal' life-style. Training, travel, self-discipline of the most unremitting kind, physical and mental stamina are essential requisites of both athlete and musician. The biggest difference is that an athlete must cram a lifetime's achivement into less than half a life-span. But the musician

---

* At this moment every head in the audience was raised; there was no need for transcripts or translations. This dramatically proved my point as to the universal language of music.

has the option of continuing working. Here are some examples of grand old men who were still giving of their all to their art at an advanced age: Klemperer into his late 80s, Rubinstein and Stockowski at over 90, and Sir Robert Mayer at over 100.

And with composing one may make a late start; no muscular flexibility is required, and the receptive musical mind will have been absorbing material, whether consciously or subconsciously, through-out the formative years. It may surprise you to learn that Brahms, one of the great symphonic writers, did not write his first symphony until he was 43. Lully, a towering figure in the history of French opera, was 41 before he first ventured into the medium.

Obviously the performer must start training as early as possible, as young muscles are more flexible than old. Here we come to a danger-ous area: it is very easy to be impressed by a pyrotechnic display of manual dexterity which veils a lack of interpretative power. What can seem amazing in an eight-year-old could be run-of-the-mill in an eighteen-year-old. The question is not of timing but of quality. Music is conveyed by sound: when listening to a record one does not enquire as to the age of the performer – either the performance is artistically viable or it is not. If not, the essential quality of communication is lacking, and the rendering, however technically proficient, is a failure.

It is interesting to know that Yehudi Menuhin, a true expert at spotting exceptionally gifted children, asks violinists to play Mendels-sohn's violin concerto as an audition piece. Significantly, he chooses not the dramatic and impressive first movement, but the slow, lyrical second movement where less technical skill but much deeper musical insight is required.

Our task at the West London Institute is exceedingly hard when selecting students. We have a responsibility to ourselves, but much more importantly, to them. We must bear in mind that a candidate may already have reached his peak and attained all that he ever will. A forced acceleration may have taken place which will give way to a levelling out or even a decline. Our job is to spot potential, and a searching practical interview is essential.

I shall end with a quotation from the Department of Education and Science report of 1977[4] which states that we should be able confidently to predict 'continual rapid progress towards outstanding achieve-ment'.

[At the end of this paper, two of Sheila McQuattie's students from the West London Institute of Higher Education performed for the members of the conference. Matthew Booth (trumpet) played the Recitativo and Allegro by René Defossez, and Bill Butt (cello) played the Prelude from the Suite in D minor for unaccompanied cello by J. S. Bach.]

References

1 Dr John E. Kane, Principal, West London Institute of Higher Education, as quoted in KANE, J. E. and FISCHER, R. J. (1979) *Giftedness in Sport*. London: Sports Council.
2 LAURENCE, DAN H. (ed.) (1981) *Shaw's Music: The complete music criticism in three volumes. Vol. 1, 1876–1890*. London: The Bodley Head.
3 TOFFLER, ALVIN (1980) *The Third Wave*. London: Collins (paperback 1981: London: Pan Books).
4 DEPARTMENT OF EDUCATION AND SCIENCE (1977) *Gifted Children in Middle and Comprehensive Schools* (HMI Matters for Discussion series No. 4). London: Her Majesty's Stationery Office.

19

Selection and its Influence on the Training of Dancers

Richard Glasstone

When I was first approached to present a paper to The British Association of National Coaches, my initial, instinctive reaction was to decline. In my terms, the world of dance and the world of sport have little in common. Serious theatrical dance is above all an art form. There is an apparent similarity in that both dance and sport require high levels of physical skill (with all that implies in terms of co-ordination, strength, fitness, stamina, and so on). But dancers and sportsmen or women require physical skills for very different reasons.

As a dance teacher, I find myself becoming increasingly critical of the current tendency for dancers to stress the athletic aspects of their training, to the detriment of qualities such as musicality and express-iveness, the prime requirements of the dance artist.

Because I hold these views so strongly, the idea of my talking about dance in the context of a sports conference seemed somehow out of character. Yet, on reflection, I began to realise that if the athletic component in dance is being given undue prominence in what is, essentially, a form of artistic entertainment, then perhaps it is equally true that sport, which is essentially an athletic form of recreation, has increasingly become a form of entertainment with, in many cases, quasi-artistic overtones.

Both in sport and in dance we find an ever-increasing emphasis on highly-specialised training. This is leading to more and more stringent selection. The benefits of this are obvious, but the attendant problems are many and complex. This is where we may find areas of experience that are of mutual value to the sportsperson and the artist. That is why it may indeed be relevant for a dance specialist to be addressing a conference of coaches.

My own experience, both as a dancer and as a teacher, has been centred mainly in the world of ballet, although I have had considerable experience of other dance forms. I was for 15 years the Senior Teacher for Boys at the Royal Ballet Lower School, at White Lodge, where my main responsibility was the classical ballet training of boys between the ages of 13 and 16. But I have also taught boys and girls and men and women of all ages, both in highly-selective establishments like the Royal Ballet School, and in much less élite and competitive situations. However, as we are dealing with selection and its influence on the training of dancers, it would seem appropriate to concentrate on the situation at the Royal Ballet School, which is highly selective and competitive and therefore particularly relevant.

There are two sections to the Royal Ballet School. The Lower School, situated at White Lodge in Richmond Park, is a boarding school (with a few day pupils), for children aged 11 to 16, combining dance training with a full educational programme up to GCE O-level. From the age of 16, students attend the Upper School in London. This is a day school where, proportionately, much more time is devoted to dancing and less to education, although those students with academic ability are encouraged to study for their A-levels. Students spend two to three years at the Upper School before either being accepted into the ranks of one of the two Royal Ballet Companies, or auditioning for a job in another professional company in Britain or abroad. Normally, by the age of 18 they will have embarked on a professional career in the theatre.

There is one further area of the Royal Ballet School's programme that I should mention: the Junior Associates scheme. This is for children aged eight to ten years who are, in the main, already at an amateur dancing school. If accepted as Junior Associates of the Royal Ballet School, these youngsters continue classes with their regular teacher (usually once or twice weekly) and in addition attend Saturday school at the Royal Ballet. This involves three to four hours work every Saturday in term time. Their study programme starts with sessions devoted to basic exercises, leading into simple balletic movements. This takes care of the anatomical aspects of their early training, whereas musicality and a sense of movement are developed concurrently through the study of natural dance movement and national dances. For children living too far from London to attend Saturday school there every week, as regular Junior Associates, there are Regional Associate schemes of a similar nature.

The initial selection of the Junior Associates of the Royal Ballet School involves a simple class based on natural movement, to assess co-ordination, musicality and general physical aptitude, as well as an orthopaedic examination. Progress is assessed at the end of the first year. In the spring of the second year, the young Royal Ballet School Associates join children from other schools (including some from abroad) in the final audition for entry to the Royal Ballet Lower School at White Lodge where, at the age of 11, they will commence full-time professional training. Those children who have not been Junior Associates – and they are in the majority – have usually already attended a preliminary audition. These auditions are held regularly throughout the year in London, and at fixed intervals at various regional centres.

What are we looking for at these auditions? It is important here to understand the distinction between talent and natural facility. Ideally, we would like both in equal proportions. In reality, the two do not always go together, and one of the greatest problems in selection is weighing up the abundance of one against the relative lack of the other.

To deal first with what we call 'facility', what we are looking for are natural co-ordination, musicality, energy, an alert personality, and enough intelligence to comprehend and respond quickly to instructions. On the purely physical side, we are looking for a well-proportioned body, with easy joint mobility; strong, well-shaped, flexible feet; a spine that is both straight and flexible; and – a special requirement for classical ballet technique – the ability to rotate the legs outward in the hip socket.

These attributes are essential for a dancer to be able to function satisfactorily at a purely mechanical level, enabling him or her to perform the required movements accurately and without risk of physical injury. But at the physical level, the selection process also involves aesthetic considerations. Whereas less than ideally shaped and proportioned physiques could sometimes be disguised by flattering costumes, nowadays, with so much dancing performed in revealing all-over body-tights, the precise shape of the body and the limbs has become of vital importance and weighs heavily in the balance in our selection procedures. Much too heavily, many would agree with me, but such are the influences and demands of taste and fashion to which, as entertainers, we are inevitably to some degree subject.

Some of the physical attributes I have mentioned can change, be it for better or for worse, with growth and natural physical development. Others can be improved by the training itself or with the help of special exercises.

Some things do not really change. Tendons do not stretch. Stiff toe joints do not become more mobile and are only inflamed by a lot of activity. Throughout the training, specialist orthopaedic guidance is needed (and given) alongside that of dance specialists. For instance, a pupil's body may show signs of becoming tighter in spite of daily exercise. The cause may lie in the bones having grown faster than the ligaments, and it may be that the ligaments need to be coaxed into loosening. Stiff insteps can improve with exercise, but if still insufficiently developed by the age of 13, the prospects of further improvement become increasingly dubious, particularly in relation to girls and pointe work.

In young children, one has to distinguish between actual physical ability and ultimate physical potential. For instance, children will not yet have the muscular strength to control the high degree of joint mobility we look for in them. If the teacher can rotate the child's legs in the hip socket, the child will, with correct training, find and develop the muscular strength to hold the rotation for himself. But if the degree of rotation is itself seriously restricted, no amount of muscular strength will help.

On top of all the physical attributes we are looking for, and in addition to co-ordination, musicality and the other qualities I have listed above, we are also seeking that indefinable thing called 'talent'. Perhaps I can best describe this as a natural, inspirational insight into what dancing is about.

Given sufficient talent and adequate natural physical facility, there is still the question of whether or not the child is going to be capable of exploiting these attributes. This will depend largely on temperament, and it is in order to assess this that a trial period of training is fundamental to the selection process.

The question of intelligence is an important one, and one that is often misunderstood. I have already said that what is needed is sufficient intelligence to comprehend and respond to instructions readily – in other words, a good, average intelligence. The very bright, intellectually-able student often becomes too analytical in his (her) approach to movement and this can impede the flow and ease of his dancing; conversely, the dancer with too low a level of comprehension finds it impossible to deal with the complex demands of advanced work, and in particular with the need to learn how to cope with injury, the dancer's biggest occupational hazard.

These then are the things we look for at auditions. But how accurate is the assessment made by the panel of adjudicators?

We are human and we make mistakes. We also recognise that the pressures of an audition may sometimes affect the child's performance (although, in such circumstances, showing the ability to rise to the occasion can be a factor in the candidate's favour).

Successful candidates are always accepted for an initial trial year. Some children are slow developers, others may experience difficulty in adjusting to the demands and standards of professional training. Still others may be trying to cope with physical difficulties and more time may be needed to assess whether or not they are going to be able to succeed in this. For these, and other, reasons, the School may decide that the offer of a second trial year is appropriate.

Generally speaking, within the first two years of training – when the children are about 12 years old – we will have determined whether or not they should be advised to proceed with professional training to the age of 16, when a further assessment will determine whether or not they continue with the final phase of their training at the Upper School.

To ensure a smooth transfer back into ordinary school life for those children we do not keep on, we try to adhere as far as possible to the main stages in the selection procedure I have outlined above. However, development and progress are monitored continually and this does mean that there is constant pressure on the child to succeed, with all the benefits and all the problems that implies. Let us now look at some of these.

The hard reality of life as a professional dancer is that you are only as good as your last performance. Coping with that is something prospective dancers have to be prepared for from the earliest stages of professional training. This is not a question of imposed discipline or brainwashing, but of teaching pupils to look honestly at themselves and to assess their own efforts and achievements critically. The key to this, of course, is motivation.

Because dancers have to start training so young, it can be very difficult initially to assess, and subsequently to maintain, levels of motivation. Is it the child who wants to be a dancer, or is parental ambition playing too prominent a role? Are there the additional pressures because of divided opinion at home, with one parent or other relative for or against? Further pressures may come about because – for most children – being at a professional school also involves living away from home. All these problems will test and tax the child's motivation, but if he (or she) really wants to dance he will overcome them.

However, it is important that a child's desire to dance be understood as such and nurtured and encouraged accordingly. It is all too easy for teachers to superimpose (albeit unconsciously) adult concepts on a child's perception of dance.

The demands of professional training – particularly with such a specialised and complex technique as that of classical ballet – require seemingly endless repetition of basic exercises, often at a very slow pace, with intense concentration on minute detail of the muscular activity and linear shape involved in each movement made by the pupil. Given these circumstances, how does one maintain the child's initial enthusiasm for the simple joy of dance and bridge the gap between this and the sophisticated control of the trained, adult dancer? Having identified the child's potential, how does one help him or her to realise that potential? The specialists who select the talent can be the very ones who, unwittingly, destroy it. We return then to that other ingredient in selection, talent.

Selection procedures can identify the physiological and temperamental suitability of the prospective dancer. The more selective this process becomes, the more specialised the training it engenders is likely to be. Stringent selection and specialised training add up to greater skill. But talent is the inspirational insight into what the skill is about. We all know of instances where a student's natural talent has overcome limited or mediocre teaching, but are we sufficiently aware of the potential danger of super-specialised teaching methods stifling the inspirational insight, the talent which is, after all, the student's motivating force?

In the true dancer, this springs from innate kinetic energy and rhythmic drive. Therein lies the link, the potential unifying factor which can bridge the gap between a child's spontaneous urge to dance and the disciplined skill of the trained dancer. The prerequisite then of dance teaching at all stages of training is the nurturing of that kinetic energy and rhythmic drive. The danger inherent in certain aspects of some specialised training methods is the emphasis placed on the intellectual analysis of movement, whereas – in my opinion – dance should always be perceived and taught as dynamically-linked patterns of organised rhythmic movement. When analysis of individual aspects of a movement begins to impinge on the dancer's ability to experience it as part of a total kinetic and rhythmic concept, we are entering dangerous territory.

This – and indeed almost everything I have to say on the subject of dance teaching – is essentially empirical. Yet, from the small amount I have read about some of the research that has been done into the workings of the brain, it would seem that what I have observed from practical experience does have a basis in scientific fact. I refer specifically to the concept of so-called right and left brain thinking. My own observations and experience of many years prompt me to believe in this concept of a bi-cameral brain and in its relevance to the teaching of dance. How best to exploit that concept is, for me, the unanswered question.

My own instinctive, but probably only partly adequate, solution has been to place primary importance on the rhythmic, musical and dynamic aspects of any instruction I give to a pupil. A dancer moving with the correct dynamic and rhythmic impulse is much more likely to be achieving the desired postural and spatial requirements in a given series of movements than one who is not. Imaginative and dramatic imagery help to achieve the required dynamic impulses; they are sustained by an internal rhythmic drive. The ability to visualise and experience a series of movements as a rhythmic pattern in space is the essence of dance; this can exist independently of the ability to dissect a dance sequence and analyse its component parts.

The relevance – if any – of all this to the coaching of sport and athletics is something I must leave to specialists in those fields to ascertain. Other problems we encounter in specialist dance training, and which may well have their parallel in those areas, include the reactions of young pupils and older students – and of their parents – to the pressures of selection. I am thinking in particular of reactions to the elimination procedures that exist at various stages of the training. With the younger children (say 11 to 13), this problem is almost invariably greater for the parents than it is for the children. The child will have gradually begun to realise, if only at a subconscious level, that he or she is not making the grade. To be told that they are being advised not to continue professional training often comes as a great release to these children. Youngsters are remarkably resilient and, after the initial upset, usually adjust quickly and happily to a different way of life. For the parents the decision is much harder to accept. Among other considerations, there are problems connected with loss of face at home. For instance, the local paper may have published a feature about their child being accepted into the Royal Ballet School – what will the neighbours say now? It is easy enough to scoff at such seeming trivialities, but these are real concerns that can affect people very deeply. Although the child is to discontinue professional training, even the short experience he (she) has had of it will have to some extent equipped him to understand the (often very technical) reasons the School will have had for advising him to change course. To this extent, the child has already been trained to view the problem from a professional angle, whereas the parents' perception of it will be essentially that of the amateur.

Provided there is parental support at home and proper educational guidance at school, the advantages to a child of a period of professional training far outweigh the problems. The physical and mental self-discipline, learning to understand and control one's body and one's mind, understanding the purpose and value of a healthy degree of competitiveness – above all, learning how to cope with failure and to see it in perspective – these are all important aspects of education that will stand children in good stead in whatever other fields they move on to.

There are less conscious pressures, and these tend to manifest themselves more in the older students, in middle and late teens. Such pressures are often related to differences between their dance expectations and their social expectations. Nowadays this can be a problem, especially for girls training to be ballet dancers. How does one reconcile their changing perceptions of woman's place in society and of the relations between the sexes with the conventional image of the female ballet dancer? One must bear in mind here that the whole structure and dynamic of classical ballet dancing is imbued with concepts of male and female movement and behaviour, rooted in social conventions often radically different from those prevalent to-day. Is there perhaps a parallel between this dichotomy facing the young dancer and that confronting the competitive young sports-woman in a world where the very notion of competitiveness is rejected by many educationists?

The effects of selection on the training of dancers are clearly beneficial inasmuch as selection is a functional part of a training and educative process. Its effect is potentially detrimental in that it can engender super-specialist teaching theories which may become entrenched at the expense of the creative nurturing of the talented child and of the ultimate development of artists who can be fully responsive to the social climate of the times in which they live.

For all its stringent selection and elimination procedures, eight or nine years of training at the Royal Ballet School in no way guarantee a job in the Company. There are tremendous pressures inherent in that fact. Yet it is this ultimate freedom of the directors and choreographers of the Company to audition and select the young artists they wish to employ which is our insurance against the dead hand of institution-alisation. For that is the problem facing us in a free society, where the temptation to standardise the selection and training of artists can lead to the standardisation of the art form itself. I would suggest that this is a very different problem from that facing sports coaches with their sights set on winning Olympic gold medals.

20

The Selection of Top Performers in East European Sport

Jim Riordan

Introduction

Success by socialist nations in world sport since the last war, particularly at the Olympic Games, has excited interest in their sports systems. How do they do it? Yet little serious study exists in the West that would enable us to understand them better or even to learn from them to enrich ourselves. In English-speaking countries particularly, virtually no student of physical education, coach, sports official or writer has sufficient knowledge of either German or Russian, for example, to read the specialist material published in the German Democratic Republic and the Soviet Union.[1] Consequently, the gap between West and East tends to widen in both results and comprehension.

When the socialist nations in the main made their debut at the 1952 summer Olympics, they won 29% of the medals; in 1972, they won 47%; in 1976, 57%. Altogether they took seven of the top 10 places at the last three (1972–80) summer Olympics prior to Los Angeles in 1984 (at which only Rumania, China and Yugoslavia of the socialist states participated). It is noteworthy that the USA and its NATO allies have three times the population and four times the gross national product of the Warsaw Pact states.

The two most consistently successful and versatile sporting nations in the world are the USSR and East Germany.

I *The Soviet Union* has not only 'won' every Olympics, summer and winter, for which it has entered (with the exception of 1968, and the winters of 1980 and 1984), it is also by far the most versatile nation in the history of the Games, winning medals in 19 of the 21 sports at the last 'normal' Olympics (Montreal 1976), and in all sports at the Lake Placid winter Olympics of 1980.[2] The USSR has a population of 280 million.

II *The German Democratic Republic* (GDR) advanced from 15th to 2nd medal position in the summer Olympics between 1956 and 1976, overtaking the USA; and from 16th to 1st in the winter Olympics between 1956 and 1980, and again in 1984, overtaking the USSR. The GDR has fewer than 17 million people.

There is clearly no single key to success. And by no means every key would fit Western sports systems, as many East European coaches working abroad have found; and as socialist nations discovered in grafting selected Western experience on to their own developing systems. In sport, as in much else, each nation has to build on its own traditions, climate, geopolitical situation, stage of economic growth, its priorities.

However, with more information and understanding, it would be less easy to fall back on stereotypes bred of ignorance – such as communist success being founded on 'wonder drugs', hypnosis, or ethical malpractices. Increasingly, demands for more open and serious studies of communist sport are coming from Western coaches and athletes.

Why?

There would seem to be three principal reasons why socialist states display such concern for excellence in sport.

First, athletes are held in high esteem for the skill, grace and strength by which it is hoped they will inspire young and old alike to be active and to join in at all levels of sport. The top performers also encourage a sense of pride in one's team, nationality and country, even in the political system that can produce such world-beaters. They receive rewards, but they also have obligations to undertake forms of public service – e.g. duties as far-ranging as instructing in sports schools to serving as deputies in local and national government.

Second, socialist sport follows foreign policy (since sport is state-controlled, planned and run) and has important functions to discharge. These functions include winning support for the country and its policies, particularly among developing nations; gaining recognition and prestige in the world (of particular relevance to East Germany, Cuba and USSR); maintaining and reinforcing the unity of the socialist states; demonstrating the advantages of the socialist way of life and, more recently, using sport to promote detente and peace. As a consequence, besides winning titles, gifted athletes are expected to be ambassadors of goodwill and models of propriety in the arenas and forums of the world.

Third, there is a strong belief in all socialist states in the parity of mental and physical culture in human development, and a conviction that talent in sport should be treated no differently from talent in art, music or science. In other words, budding gymnasts should be regarded no differently from promising ballet dancers: they must be given every opportunity to develop their gifts for the good of the

individual and the community. Furthermore, unlike the early administrators of amateur-élitist sport in the West, the communist states have
never been constrained by the notion that sport is an unworthy
profession or career.

Where?

Young people who wish to pursue a sport seriously and to develop their
talent may do so at one of several types of school (see Figure 20.1). At
the base of the talent pyramid in the USSR is the children's and young
people's sports school (CYPSS) which young people can attend outside their normal school hours (they are, in fact, 'clubs' in the Western
sense). Until 1981 these were almost entirely for children with some
sort of promise or inclination towards a particular sport. However, as
part of the drive to involve more children in regular and active sports
participation, a distinction was made in 1981 by the government
between such schools 'for all girls and boys irrespective of age and
special talent' and those with the 'necessary amenities and qualified
staff for training promising athletes'. Henceforth, the former would be
known as CYPSS and the latter CYPSS, Olympic Reserve
(CYPSSOR).[3]

Figure 20.1   *Types of Sports Schools in the USSR*

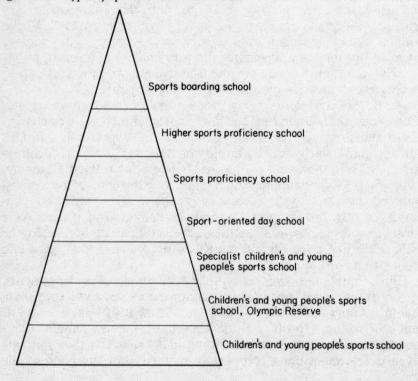

Sports boarding school

Higher sports proficiency school

Sports proficiency school

Sport-oriented day school

Specialist children's and young people's sports school

Children's and young people's sports school, Olympic Reserve

Children's and young people's sports school

Altogether there were 7,426 such schools with a membership of over 3.5 million children in 1983, served by some 50,000 diplomaed coaches and sports doctors.[4] Roughly half the schools come under the Education Ministry and now serve the community and casual enthusiasts, the other half coming under the sports societies (like Dinamo, Spartak, Army) and serving talented youngsters. The aim of the latter is to give special coaching to young people in a particular sport so that they may become proficient, gain a sports ranking (see Figure 20.2) and graduate to a full-time team (Masters of Sport and above become full-time, professional athletes).

Figure 20.2 *Soviet sport ranking scheme*

1 State honorific award — Merited Master of Sport of the USSR

2 Titles — Master of Sport of the USSR International Class — Master of Sport of the USSR — Candidate Master of Sport of the USSR

3 Rankings — Rankings: I, II, III, IV (chess); Junior rankings: I, II, III (ages 10–18)

Some CYPSSs focus on a single sport. For example, each leading soccer and ice hockey club (in the top three Soviet divisions) runs its own school providing a full course of training for talented young lads from the age of seven or eight.

It is also possible from the age of six to attend a full-time 'sport-oriented' school, which combines a normal school curriculum with sports training – on the model of the 'foreign-language'-oriented schools.

Above these schools in specialist training come the sports proficiency schools and the higher sports proficiency schools, which provide extra-curricular training for schoolchildren and students on short-term vacation courses. The distinction between them is normally one of age – students between 16 and 18 attend the former, those 18 and over the latter.

At the apex of the pyramid are the sports boarding schools, of which there were 40 involving 14,211 pupils in 1984 (see Appendix, pages 229–238. They follow other special boarding schools (those designed to cultivate musical and other artistic talents, for example) in adhering to the standard Soviet curriculum for ordinary schools, but their timetables allow for an extra study load in sports theory and practice. Their aim is to permit pupils to obtain the school-leaving certificate in addition to acquiring proficiency in a particular sport. Boarders are normally accepted at about nine, depending on the sport, and stay on at school until 18 – a year longer than at ordinary secondary schools.

While sports boarding schools in East Germany were set up by government decree back in 1951, it was only in 1970 that the Soviet government passed a resolution on their establishment after experimenting with them since 1962. This difference between the two states partly reflects the gap in technological capacity, partly initial parental resistance in the USSR to more 'institutionalised' education than is absolutely necessary and a popular scepticism about the worth of sport as an educational commitment, and partly uncertainty among Soviet pedagogues about the viability of combining sport and education during school years. There is little doubt, however, that today the sports boarding schools are regarded as the key to present and future international sports success, and *only* sports in the Olympic programme are pursued in them (with the sole exception in the USSR of chess, which was introduced in 1983 to the Baku Sports Boarding School in the Soviet Republic of Azerbaidzhan – home of the new world chess champion Garri Kasparov).

In East Germany, from four sports boarding schools (*Kinder- und Jugendsportschule*) in 1952 – in Berlin, Leipzig, Brandenburg and Halberstadt – there were 20 in 1983.[5] Although half the Soviet total, they amounted to eight times more in per capita terms.

In both countries it is regarded as advantageous to bring children with an instinctive aptitude for sport into the 'controlled' environment of a residential school, where they are provided with the best coaches and facilities, nurtured on a special diet, supervised and tested by medical staff, and stimulated by mutual interest and enthusiasm.

How?

Although it would be misleading to imagine that a uniformly-applied programme of tests and standards is employed to select and forecast sporting talent, the USSR and GDR do have carefully-planned guidelines to spot potential talent and guide performers to take up the sport they are most likely to do well in. Such guidelines are constantly being assessed and updated, and the search for talent is based on a centrally-planned system of selecting, grading and sifting over a long period.

The general approach employed to identify talent is based on establishing a *model* for each sport and event. This is made up of statistical data from a large number of domestic and foreign world-class athletes in that particular sport. It includes information on performance at various ages and the rate of progress, the ideal morphological type, and so on. With the biological age taken into consideration, the planners are able to set approximate standards of what can be expected from a potentially talented athlete at a certain age. East Germany widely employs computers to help in this; in addition, it has 'individual computer-aided training analysis based on training records. It is therefore possible to store data on present and long-term training and thus intervene directly in the training process. A diagnosis of performance carried out in this way guarantees sports success and the timing of performance peaks.'[6]

From a recent analysis I made of over a hundred Soviet and East German talent selection and forecasting studies, the data taken into consideration tend to include the following:

– anthropometric measurements (height, weight, arm reach);
– general physical performance (speed, strength, power, endurance, mobility, agility);
– performance levels in a particular sport: swimming, sprinting, long jump, throwing, etc.;
– sport-event specific performance ability (say, in track and field, 100 and 200m – speed endurance; 400 to 1500m – aerobic and anaerobic endurance; 3000 to 10000m – aerobic endurance; hurdles – speed, speed endurance, mobility, agility; jumps – power, speed; throws – power, strength);
– rate of progress in the above indicators.

Once a model has been created for a particular sport, the relevant standards and anticipated rate of progress are used to select potential talent in *three major stages* over four to five years. The age at which a youngster is involved in the system depends on the sport, ranging from seven or eight for swimming, gymnastics, tennis and figure-skating, to 12–13 for boxing and cycling, and 13–14 for weightlifting and shooting.

Stage 1 Basic Selection

This takes place either in ordinary schools during the PE lesson or at the various (non-residential) sports schools. Since the PE lesson is based on the Soviet 'Ready for Labour and Defence' or the GDR

'Ready for Work and Defence of the Homeland' standards, it is relatively easy to measure potential talent at this point. The main standards observed in the Basic Selection stage normally include the following:

- height and weight;
- speed (30m from standing start);
- endurance (12 or 15 min run);
- work capacity (Harvard step tests or Letunov);
- power (standing long jump);
- sport specific tests (performance level and technique efficiency).

Stage 2 Preliminary Selection

This normally occurs some 18 months after Stage 1. Assessment is based on a number of factors: progress made in physical ability and in the sport-specific tests, rate of physical growth, biological age, psychological aptitude, and so on. At this stage it is usual to guide those young people thought suitable for sports schools towards a particular sport or group of sports. There is some reluctance in the USSR, less in the GDR, to specialise very early owing to the erratic rates of motor development.

A number of youngsters will be eliminated after the preliminary selection has been made, but they will be given another chance to prove their worth about a year later when they are reassessed, along with other late developers. Those then found suitable in the second assessment will join the training squads at the sports schools until the final selection takes place.

Stage 3 Final Selection

The final selection occurs about three or four years after Stage 1, most regularly at the age of 13–14, still depending on the sport. For example, in most track and field events it is felt that on average 12–14 for boys and 11–13 for girls are the best ages at which to make performance predictions so as to guide youngsters towards a particular event.

Based once again on the ideal model parameters of a particular sport or event, the final selection takes account of assessment of the following:

- standard attained in specific sports (e.g. times and distances in running, hurdling, jumping and throwing);
- rate of progress in specific sports;
- stability of performance (how regularly good performances occur);
- results of physical capacity tests;
- results of event/sport-specific performance capacity tests;

- results of psychological tests;
- anthropometric measurements (suitability for sports with distinct characteristics – e.g. height for basketball, arm reach for discus throwing, agility for gymnastics).

Evaluation of the standard achieved in a specific sport or event is usually based on observations and data provided by the coach in charge. However, the general physical ability and the sport/event-specific capacity tests are commonly selected according to the requirements of a particular sport/event, from the following:

- strength: back dynamometer, barbell squats, bench press;
- power: vertical jump, standing long jump, standing triple jump, medicine ball throw from the chest, standing five hops;
- muscle endurance: pull-ups, push-ups, sit-ups, parallel bar dips;
- speed: 30m from standard start, 30m from flying start;
- endurance: 12 min run, 15 min run, 2000m run, maximum oxygen uptake (measured by treadmill or bicycle ergometer);
- speed endurance: 300m run, 600m run;
- work capacity: Letunov test/Harvard step test, PWC 170;
- co-ordination tests (closely related to the sport/event);
- mobility tests (closely related to the event);
- psychological tests.

From the literature (both Soviet and East German) it is evident that a number of problems constantly exercise the minds of coaches and planners. One problem is the lack of satisfactory evidence to enable coaches to separate *true* potential from *apparent* potential. Youngsters may attain a high standard of test results at a certain age yet fail to reach forecast performance. This problem is underlined by the high rejection (or drop-out) rate at sports schools: over half of those selected in the early stages of talent identification for sports schools do not attain the anticipated performance levels (a problem not unknown in Western tennis).

A second problem is the varying rate of progress in physical performance indicators, with surges forward in some at certain ages and relatively slow development in others. Some research findings show that such unstable progress occurs in speed and power between 12 and 15, in muscle endurance between 14 and 15, and between 16 and 17, in strength between 13 and 16, and in endurance between 12 and 14.

Third, there is still much disagreement about the most suitable age at which to commence sport-specific training. Youngsters often display good all-round ability in the 10–12 age group, and there appear to be dangers in early specialisation before 13; some specialists, however, insist that guidance to take up a particular sport or event is necessary before 12 in order to ensure efficient skill development in the more complex technical events.

228 THE GROWING CHILD IN COMPETITIVE SPORT

The final point is to warn against believing that either the Soviet or the GDR talent identification system is scientifically tried and tested from start to finish. Many tests would certainly seem relatively primitive to Western coaches. Most tests in the early selection stages are simple field tests, and the coach's or PE teacher's eye often provides the most ready information. Of course, the multi-stage process of testing, with potential talent being subjected to more sophisticated testing at later stages, undoubtedly improves the reliability of physical performance tests. While the reliability of initial testing is reckoned to be about 30%, the reliability of the rate of progress during the first 18 months is said to be about 77%.

Once the young athlete is identified as possessing potential talent and joins a sports school, he or she enjoys certain privileges. Apart from expert guidance from trained coaches and regular examination and advice from sports medical specialists, the young person enjoys completely free tuition and training, all costs covered in training camps (summer camp of 30 days and winter camp of 10 days, plus attendance at such camps before some competitions), and some educational privileges – e.g. being given a longer period to complete educational courses, or receiving an individually-tailored course. As mentioned earlier, in the USSR all athletes who reach the 'Master' grading can apply themselves to their sport unencumbered by a job, though they are not free of studies at school or college.

The system in the GDR is somewhat different: proficient (Class 1, 2 and 3) athletes are normally assigned to a sports club attached to a factory (except the army clubs and Dinamo), and they have jobs or training posts in that workplace. How much time they are permitted to devote to sport then depends on their classification: 'Class 3 athletes must be given occasional time off work. Class 2 athletes must be given 16 hours off per week; and Class 1 athletes do not have to engage in any other occupation.'[7] A reclassification takes place each year depending on results, often against the yardstick of current international standards. As far as students are concerned, 'there are special study plans and extensions of study for special cases'.[8]

This security provided for athletes throughout their active career in competitive sport, and training for a career after sport, are certainly important features of the socialist sports system.

Notes

1 No coaching diploma or PE degree in any English-speaking country includes the compulsory learning of a foreign language (without which specialists have no real access to literature in other languages), whereas in Eastern Europe no licence to coach or teach PE is issued without the recipient having learned a foreign language (420 hours language learning

in the USSR and GDR for all would-be full-time coaches and sports specialists).

2   Although officially no nation 'wins' the Olympics, placing is here based on the system used in the *Olympic Bulletin* of awarding seven points for first place, five for second and so on down to one point for sixth place.

3   See *Sovetsky sport*, 24 September 1981: 1.

4   *Zhenshchiny i deti*, Moscow, 1985: 150–1.

5   EHRICH, DIETER (1981) 'Leistungssport in der DDR unter besonderer Berücksichtigung der Talentsuche und Talentförderung,' in *Die DDR. Breiten- und Spitzensport*, Munich: 32.

6   Ehrich: 35.

7   Ehrich: 36.

8   Ehrich: 36.

Appendix

Sports Boarding Schools in the USSR, 1984

Sports boarding schools	No. of pupils
Moscow No. 9 (Russia)	
Track and field	130
Swimming	120
Gymnastics	70
Diving	50
Fencing	50
Boxing	40
Graeco-Roman wrestling	30
Weightlifting	30
Others	48
	Total 548
Moscow No. 6	
Sculling	90
Rowing and canoeing	60
Cycling (track and road)	65
Soccer	60
Free-style wrestling	10
Judo	10
Others	30
	Total 325
Leningrad No. 62	
Swimming	150
Track and field	95
Sculling	80
Ski racing	40
Skiing (jumping, biathlon)	36

Sports boarding schools	No. of pupils
Leningrad No. 62 (cont.)	
Basketball	50
Volleyball	24
Gymnastics	50
Fencing	40
Pentathlon	15
Canoeing and rowing	20
Others	21
Total	621
Sverdlovsk	
Ski racing	70
Speed skating	75
Figure skating	50
Biathlon	30
Swimming	45
Volleyball	40
Track and field	46
Skiing (jumping and biathlon)	35
Others	10
Total	401
Gorky	
Ski racing	60
Ice hockey	71
Swimming	80
Speed skating	65
Track and field	85
Cycling	23
Others	17
Total	401
Volgograd (no sports specified; all three	Total 240
Cheboksary inaugurated in 1983/84)	Total 240
Stavropol	Total 240
Leninsk-Kuznetsky	
Gymnastics	142
Ski racing	59
Total	201
Rostov on Don	
Track and field	120
Gymnastics	100
Swimming	80
Soccer	60

Sports boarding schools	No. of pupils
Rostov on Don (cont.)	
Sculling	50
Rowing and canoeing	25
Weightlifting	18
Volleyball	20
Handball	26
Graeco-Roman wrestling	30
Basketball	17
Total	546
Kiev Region (Ukraine)	
Track and field	140
Soccer	80
Fencing	70
Gymnastics	40
Swimming	60
Others	30
Total	420
Kiev (City)	
Handball	76
Basketball	75
Volleyball	75
Sculling	57
Canoeing and rowing	28
Free-style wrestling	35
Graeco-Roman wrestling	35
Speed skating	20
Total	401
Brovary	
Track and field	80
Handball	65
Swimming	35
Boxing	30
Ski racing	40
Others	31
Total	281
Nikolayev	
Sculling	115
Canoeing and rowing	137
Others	29
Total	281
Kharkov	
Track and field	103
Soccer	68

Sports boarding schools	No. of pupils
Kharkov (cont.)	
Cycling	78
Swimming	100
Judo	36
Gymnastics	40
Winter sports	76
Total	501
Lvov	
Pistol shooting	55
Track and field	90
Gymnastics	50
Water polo	40
Free-style wrestling	45
Pentathlon	25
Soccer	60
Winter sports	70
Others	40
Total	475
Voroshilovgrad	
Track and field	80
Soccer	60
Graeco-Roman wrestling	40
Volleyball	70
Swimming	75
Gymnastics	45
Weightlifting	25
Others	6
Total	401
Minsk Region (Belorussia)	
Swimming	60
Track and field	90
Diving	35
Gymnastics and Modern Rhythmic gymnastics	55/15
Fencing	35
Soccer	30
Sculling	35
Rowing and canoeing	30
Graeco-Roman wrestling	20
Free-style wrestling	20
Pentathlon	10
Pistol shooting	15
Boxing	15
Basketball	25
Others	35
Total	525

Sports boarding schools	No. of pupils
Mogilyov	
Track and field	50
Swimming	20
Weightlifting	25
Rowing and canoeing	25
Sculling	20
Gymnastics	20
Others	30
Total	190
Gomel	
Track and field	90
Sculling	35
Rowing and canoeing	35
Pistol shooting	35
Graeco-Roman wrestling	35
Swimming	30
Others	21
Total	281
Vitebsk	
Track and field	160
Ski racing	35
Skiing (biathlon)	35
Others	20
Total	250
Bobruisk	
Free-style wrestling	45
Track and field	60
Swimming	45
Others	10
Total	160
Tashkent (Uzbekistan)	
Cycling (track)	40
Gymnastics	71
Soccer	80
Cycling (road)	40
Swimming	75
Fencing	40
Track and field	75
Rowing and canoeing	70
Others	31
Total	522

Sports boarding schools	No. of pupils
Andizhan	
Pistol shooting	30
Archery	20
Free-style wrestling	30
Cycling	20
Boxing	30
Track and field	58
Weightlifting	27
Soccer	40
Others	26
Total	281
Tailyak	
Sculling	80
Rowing and canoeing	80
Boxing	40
Free-style wrestling	40
Others	41
Total	281
Samarkand	
Boxing	52
Graeco-Roman wrestling	53
Track and field	85
Judo	50
Fencing	41
Total	281
Alma Ata Region (Kazakhstan)	
Speed skating	100
Diving	40
Graeco-Roman wrestling	30
Gymnastics	50
Track and field	90
Swimming	80
Soccer	50
Free-style wrestling	30
Others	31
Total	501
Alma Ata (City)	
Basketball	25
Handball	25
Fencing	50
Judo	40
Water polo	40
Cycling	35

Sports boarding schools	*No. of pupils*
Alma Ata (City) (cont.)	
Weightlifting	30
Others	36
Total	281
Karaganda	
Track and field	70
Free-style wrestling	60
Boxing	45
Graeco-Roman wrestling	40
Gymnastics	50
Swimming	50
Cycling	30
Sculling	26
Others	30
Total	401
Baku (Azerbaidzhan)	
Graeco-Roman wrestling	60
Free-style wrestling	60
Soccer	60
Gymnastics	40
Swimming	35
Track and field	60
Boxing	21
Chess	25
Judo	25
Sculling	40
Rowing and canoeing	40
Others	39
Total	505
Tbilisi (Georgia)	
Free-style wrestling	60
Graeco-Roman wrestling	45
Judo	45
Soccer	60
Track and field	60
Fencing	31
Sculling	30
Rowing and canoeing	30
Others	40
Total	401

Sports boarding schools	No. of pupils
Panevegis (Lithvania)	
Track and field	130
Soccer	70
Cycling	65
Basketball	60
Judo	40
Handball (at Siauliai)	50
Rowing and canoeing (at Trakai)	35
Sculling (at Trakai)	60
Others	36
Total	546
Kishinyov (Moldavia)	
Gymnastics	50
Rowing and canoeing	42
Judo	30
Free-style wrestling	30
Graeco-Roman wrestling	30
Soccer	60
Swimming	35
Track and field	60
Volleyball	32
Handball	32
Total	401
Tiraspol	
Track and field	35
Volleyball	30
Basketball	70
Handball	32
Cycling	30
Sculling	50
Rowing and canoeing	25
Others	9
Total	281
Muryany (Latvia)	
Track and field	110
Bobsleigh	65
Cycling	50
Volleyball	55
Handball	45
Sculling	50
Rowing and canoeing	25
Graeco-Roman wrestling	12
Free-style wrestling	13
Total	425

Sports boarding schools	*No. of pupils*
Frunze (Kirgizia)	
Free-style wrestling	40
Graeco-Roman wrestling	36
Judo	40
Track and field	60
Gymnastics	74
Soccer	48
Boxing	37
Cycling	20
Swimming	26
Others	20
Total	401
Dushanbe (Tadzhikistan)	
Free-style wrestling	43
Graeco-Roman wrestling	40
Water polo	40
Rowing and canoeing	40
Track and field	70
Swimming	50
Soccer	38
Cycling	40
Others	40
Total	401
Yerevan (Armenia)	
Soccer	60
Boxing	40
Weightlifting	40
Diving	40
Free-style wrestling	40
Graeco-Roman wrestling	30
Gymnastics	75
Track and field	40
Pentathlon	50
Swimming	50
Others	36
Total	501
Ashkhabad (Turkmenia)	
Cycling	50
Free-style wrestling	50
Sculling	30
Graeco-Roman wrestling	20
Swimming	40
Gymnastics	20
Weightlifting	20
Soccer	25

Sports boarding schools	No. of pupils
Ashkabad (Turkmenia) (cont.)	
Judo	20
Others	6
Total	281
Tallin (Estonia)	
Ski racing	100
Pistol shooting	40
Track and field	90
Basketball	60
Volleyball	50
Graeco-Roman wrestling	35
Swimming	60
Cycling	16
Others	50
Total	501

Source   *Byulleten normativnykh aktov Ministerstva prosveshcheniya SSSR*,
No. II, Moscow, 1983, pp. 36–45.

N.B.   (i) All the sports are *Olympic* except chess (at one boarding school
in Baku). Sailing, however, is not included, nor are several
shooting events. Judo is practised at 10 schools although it is
much less popular in the USSR than the sport of *sambo* (which is
not an Olympic sport).

(ii) The USSR had 40 sports boarding schools in 1984, containing
14,211 pupils – approximately 355 pupils per school, and an
average of 10 sports per school.

(iii) All 15 Soviet republics have at least one sports boarding school;
Russia has 10, the Ukraine 7, Belorussia 5, Uzbekistan 4,
Kazakhstan 3, Moldavia 2, the rest one each – more or less
according to population distribution.

(iv) The schools are run and financed jointly by the USSR Ministry of
Education and the Committee on Physical Culture and Sport
attached to the USSR Council of Ministers. Local supervision is
the joint responsibility of the Republican education ministries
and sport committees.

Expectations and Values

21

Achievement Goals and Drop-out in Youth Sports

Jean Whitehead

I have divided my subject into two parts. The first part reports some work I have done with the help of a small grant from the National Coaching Foundation. The purpose of the research was to discover how children's goals relate to their persistence or drop-out in sport. The second part is a discussion of the results and of wider issues relating to drop-out in youth sports.

Research

The research was prompted by my reactions to the findings of Marty Ewing (1981) who worked under the guidance of Glyn Roberts in Illinois. Her work seemed to have important practical implications for sport coaches, but I had reasons to expect some particular differences in British culture.

Ewing's study was based on the approach of Maehr and Nicholls (1980). They were dissatisfied with research on achievement motivation because traditional approaches assumed that everyone views achievement in the same way. They suggested that such studies of achievement motivation may be invalid outside national boundaries because similar outward behaviour may mean quite different things in different cultures. Maehr and Nicholls regard success and failure as states of mind which depend on people's perceptions of achieving their goals. In this context, reaching a goal implies that some desirable quality about oneself has been shown, but the qualities which are considered to be desirable vary with the culture. In Western society, for example, effort and ability may be regarded as important for success but in other societies the corresponding qualities may be courage, co-operation, or respect.

Maehr and Nicholls devised a new conceptual framework and methodology for studying achievement motivation. They proposed two related methods. The first is based on diversity. It involves a search for the full range of views, from people of different cultures, about success and failure. The second approach, which is the one I have taken, is concerned with universals. It requires a search for 'common' goals for achievement behaviour throughout the world. Maehr and

Nicholls proposed three possible goals that might be found to be universal achievement orientations.

1 *Ability-orientation*   The goal here is to maintain a favourable view of one's ability. The behaviour which might be shown by people with this orientation could include participating in events in which they expect to show high ability, avoidance of events in which they expect to show low ability, and dropping out of situations in which they do not seem to be demonstrating ability.

2 *Task-orientation*   Not everyone is concerned with showing personal ability. There are those who have no apparent desire to do so, but who are concerned with the quality of their work, or the solving of a particular problem. Their goal is to master the task. People with this orientation have no need to avoid specific situations because they have no fear of exposing low ability. This orientation is important developmentally because young children show concern for mastery of their environment although they are unable yet to recognise ability or to distinguish it from effort.

3 *Social-approval-orientation*   When people show high effort this is not necessarily attributed to high ability. It might even be put down to low ability because so much effort must be used. However, the output of high effort does lead to attributions of high commitment or 'virtuous intent'. Maehr and Nicholls regard social approval as the reward for trying hard. Although not strictly an achievement goal, a social-approval-orientation is often found in achievement situations so is included in the studies for this reason.

Ewing (1981) looked for these or other achievement orientations in 452 high school pupils in Illinois. She used a questionnaire which first required the youngsters to recall a sporting experience in which they had felt successful. They then used a 5-point scale to rate 15 reasons for feeling successful on that occasion. (See Figure 21.1, page 243 for a revision of this test.) The ratings were factor-analysed to discover the underlying achievement goals. Ewing found the three orientations proposed by Maehr and Nicholls and also a new 'intrinsic' orientation characterised by a feeling of adventure.

Importantly, Ewing found that knowing the achievement goals of the children enabled her to predict significantly well whether they were sport participants, non-participants, or drop-outs. Surprisingly she found that those who dropped out from sport were more ability-oriented and less social-approval-oriented than those who remained.

The loss of ability-oriented players is disturbing. Speculating about the underlying reasons, Ewing suggests that youngsters whose goal is to show their ability in sport may drop out for two reasons. Either they may perceive that they do not have enough ability, or they may not seem to be getting enough opportunities to show their ability. If ability-oriented youngsters spend a lot of time 'sitting on the bench' in American sports, they are not at these times achieving their personal goal of showing their ability, so they may quit the sport. Conversely, those children whose personal goal is to gain social approval can actually achieve this goal by sitting on the bench and being regarded as loyal and patient team members. Hence they may remain in sport.

This speculation by Ewing was one factor prompting my study because I did not think that the same results would be found in British culture. The major sports in the United States – baseball, basketball and American football – involve a large number of bench-sitters, or a high proportion of time spent on the bench. I considered that the typical sports and coaching conditions in Britain gave children more opportunity to show their ability.

Similarly, I thought that conditions for obtaining social approval differed in Britain, if only because there are fewer spectators and coaches at most games. We are still some way from the regular televising of high school games, or a World Series in Hawaii for nine-year-olds. (On an anecdotal level, I played hockey throughout high school and was rarely watched by anyone other than the travelling reserves of the other team and never by parents. At that time – and it wasn't 1066 – to have had one's parents around would have been to be branded a baby. However, I do appreciate that the world has changed and that the British scene is becoming more like the American one and including heavier parent involvement.)

Achievement goals in Britain

The first phase in my research was to discover whether children in British sport would have the same goals as those of children in Illinois. This is an important study in its own right. Regardless of any relationship with drop-out and persistence, coaches could benefit by knowing the goals of their athletes, and adapting their coaching practices if desirable.

My initial sample consisted of 809 boys and girls in four schools in Bedfordshire and two schools in Northamptonshire. (See Table 1.) The children were selected from three age bands, focused on nine, twelve and fifteen years, because research by Nicholls (1978) has found that children go through four stages in developing their perceptions. It is only after about 12 years of age that they can distinguish between the different roles of ability and effort in producing success and can recognise that ability represents capacity. Before this they believe that effort is the most important component so they do not evaluate their ability. When they do so, and perceive it to be low, they may drop out.

I adapted the Ewing-Roberts Achievement Orientation question-

Figure 21.1 *The modification of the Ewing-Roberts Achievement Orientation Questionnaire*

SPORT QUESTIONNAIRE

Name_____ Age_____ Boy/Girl

Please take some time to think about your background in sport. Think of one time when you felt successful: that is, you felt good about what you had done. Briefly say what happened and how you felt. If you need help, ask us to help you.

_____

_____

_____

What were the things that made you feel successful? Beside EACH statement below, please circle ONE number to show how much you agree or disagree with the statement.

1	2	3	4	5
strongly disagree	disagree	neither agree nor disagree	agree	strongly agree

I FELT SUCCESSFUL BECAUSE

1. I pleased people who are important to me.   1 2 3 4 5

2. I did something few other people did.   1 2 3 4 5

3. I showed my worth (importance) to others.   1 2 3 4 5

4. I showed how clever I was.   1 2 3 4 5

5. I did it on my own.   1 2 3 4 5

6. It was like an adventure.   1 2 3 4 5

7. I did something new and different.   1 2 3 4 5

8. I was seen as a good performer.   1 2 3 4 5

9. I showed I was a leader.   1 2 3 4 5

10. I made other people happy.   1 2 3 4 5

11. I understood something important to me.   1 2 3 4 5

12. I completed something.   1 2 3 4 5

13. Other people made me feel good.   1 2 3 4 5

14. I reached a goal.   1 2 3 4 5

15. My performance made me feel good.   1 2 3 4 5

16. I met the challenge.   1 2 3 4 5

17. Other people told me I did well.   1 2 3 4 5

THREE other reasons (write in below).

18. _____   1 2 3 4 5

19. _____   1 2 3 4 5

20. _____   1 2 3 4 5

naire for British children by simplifying some of the items (see Figure 21.1 Whitehead 1985). I then used factor-analysis in the same way as Ewing to discover the underlying achievement goals. In the oldest age group I found the same four orientations as Ewing: that is, I found the three orientations proposed by Maehr and Nicholls and also the intrinsic orientation characterised by a feeling of adventure. The components of the task mastery factor were almost identical in the British and American studies, and although the components of the other factors showed greater variation they were still very clearly recognisable as representing the same achievement orientations.

Table 21.1   *Composition of the sample*

Group		Age range	No. of subjects
Older Girls	(OG)	14–16*	339*
Older Boys	(OB)	14–15	189
Middle Girls	(MG)	11–13	72
Middle Boys	(MB)	11–13	87
Younger Girls	(YG)	9–10	61
Younger Boys	(YB)	9–10	81

* This sample includes 153 girls aged 14–16 from two schools in Northamptonshire where only girls were tested. All groups include data from two co-educational middle or upper schools in Bedfordshire, one in Bedford town and one not.

When I analysed separately, the boys' and girls' scores in this age group, I found that the boys' results gave two different dimensions of the task mastery factor, one related to performing the task and the other one related to its outcome. I found this same subdivision of the task mastery factor in three of the four younger age and sex groups. It seems that children are differently motivated when thinking of performing the task and when thinking of its outcome.

In general, results for the younger ages showed confused patterns which are not easily interpretable so I will not consider them further here. They confirm the view that clarity and consistency in achievement motivation emerge only as age increases. However, the sample sizes were small for the younger ages, so I put the four youngest groups together and did a combined analysis. This showed ability, intrinsic and social-approval orientations.

This first phase of my study, then, confirmed that different achievement goals exist among British children participating in sport. Not everyone is trying to achieve the same thing or interpreting success in the same way. The major orientations, however, match those found in

America and might be regarded as the universal goals which Maehr and Nicholls proposed.

Relationships between goals and behaviour

In the second phase of my research I further analysed the older age groups only. There were two main questions. First, could the children's goals be used to predict their behaviour in sport? That is, would the information from the questionnaire allow me to identify them as participants or drop-outs? This required a discriminant function analysis and to some extent I found the same thing as Ewing. Using only the achievement goals, I could group the children with significant success as participants, drop-outs, or non-participants in school sport. I could also do this for community sport.

On then to the key second question. Would the drop-out and participant groups in my study show the same achievement goals as the corresponding groups in America? Particularly, would drop-outs be more ability-oriented than participants, as Ewing found? The answer, as I expected, was 'No'. In all but one of my analyses the drop-outs were less ability-oriented than the participants and in that one case the motivation of the two groups was equivalent.

What then of social-approval motivation? The sport participants in Illinois were more social-approval-oriented than the drop-outs. Generally I also found this.

Discussion

The discovery of some cultural differences in contexts which initially seemed the same, reminds me of the saying that Britain and the United States are two nations divided by a common language! Yet it is reassuring that British youth sport – at least in so far as can be determined from my sample – is not characterised by the dropping-out of ability-oriented players. My results indicate that youngsters who want to demonstrate ability are staying in sport to do just that. We need to give them every opportunity to continue in this way.

Much further research is needed to clearly identify the nature and development of the achievement orientations and their influence on behaviour. Glyn Roberts (1984) discusses the ability orientation, which he calls competitive ability or sport competence, in the context of social comparisons. One way to demonstrate ability in sport is to win – or at least to do better than many others. If the essence of the ability orientation is comparison with others, it might be better to call it a superiority orientation, to minimise confusion with task mastery.

The Ewing-Roberts questionnaire did not include any items about winning or defeating others. Glyn tells me that such items did not produce useful results with American children. However, I am now using an extended questionnaire which includes many additional items provided by the children in my sample, and am exploring this and other dimensions. I would welcome the help of anyone in the audience, or who reads this at a later date, who could give my questionnaire to youngsters in organised sport and inform me later which individuals persist in the sport, and which ones drop out.

I think, however, that we must be cautious in assuming that drop-out from adolescent sport is all bad. Children take up many hobbies and interests and cannot pursue them all into adult life. Some drop out for the positive reason that they have achieved their particular goal in sport. They have learned what they want to and had fun and are ready for other things. In the educational context spoken of by Martin Lee in the previous paper – that of developing people rather than developing performance – it seems that it is 'they' rather than 'we' who should decide the level at which 'they' should succeed. It is better for these children to appear in the drop-out statistics than in the figures for those who never participated. Similarly, children who appear in drop-out figures for a particular sport may simply have reduced the range of their participation. Others will drop out for circumstantial reasons, such as prolonged illness or moving house, rather than from any disenchantment with their sport experience. For the important re- mainder, those who quit sport for negative reasons such as too much stress, it would clearly be helpful if we discover the underlying reasons and consider if coaching may usefully be adapted to minimise adverse effects.

Ewing did study the attributions underlying the achievement orientations. Her subjects rated 11 statements about possible causes of their success. She found only partial support for the prediction of Maehr and Nicholls that social approval would be seen to result from trying hard. I found even less support for this prediction. However, the attributions underlying the task mastery goal were amazingly similar in both studies. Of the 11 possible attributions, the top two are identical for both boys and girls in my sample and for the boys and girls in Illinois. The only slight variation is that for Ewing's boys the order of these two items is reversed. The children consider that task mastery occurs because, firstly, 'I met the challenge', and, secondly, 'I tried hard.' Hence they see that their effort is rewarded when they pursue the goal of mastering a task, rather than when they pursue the goal of gaining social approval.

I suggest that it can only be a healthy state for British sport if youngsters devote themselves to mastering the task, and hence to the quality of their performance, rather than to gaining approval from various other people. In this way they will keep control of their own success. Indeed, if I may integrate Glyn's remarks on the need for a focus on performance rather than on outcome with Martin's plea for responsibility rather than expediency, I would conclude that coaches and children would be best served by giving attention to means rather than ends in sport.

References

EWING, M. E. (1981) *Achievement Orientations and Sport Behavior of Males and Females*. Ph.D. dissertation, University of Illinois.

MAEHR, M. L. and NICHOLLS, J. G. (1980) 'Culture and achievement motivation: a second look.' In N. WARREN (ed.) *Studies in Cross-cultural Psychology, Vol. 3*. New York: Academic Press.

NICHOLLS, J. G. (1978) 'The development of the concepts of effort and ability, perception of academic attainment, and the understanding that difficult tasks require more ability.' *Child Development*, **49**, 800–14.

ROBERTS, G. C. (1984) 'Toward a new theory of motivation in sport: the role of perceived ability.' In J. M. SILVA and R. S. WEINBERG (eds) *Psychological Foundations of Sport*. Champaign, IL: Human Kinetics.

WHITEHEAD, J. (1985) 'Sporting achievement orientations of primary and secondary schoolchildren.' Paper presented at the British Association of Sports Sciences, proceedings of the Annual Sport and Science Conference, Chichester.

22

Moral and Social Growth through Sport: the coach's role

Martin J. Lee

Introduction

This chapter is written from the standpoint of one who believes that the training, and coaching, of children in sport is an educational activity. That is to say, those who choose to work in sport with children necessarily have an educational role which demands that they are concerned with the development of children, not only performance. My purpose is to draw your attention to the need for coaches to examine their own values as they relate to coaching children and to consider their role in promoting desirable values in children.

Without digressing too far into the realms of philosophy, perhaps I should say what I mean in distinguishing coaching and training from education. The idea of training implies the development of skills which are applicable in particular situations, or of developing levels of fitness. Coaching seems to refer to the activity whereby people help others to improve their skills. So, in sport, we train for events, or we coach players in skills so that their performance improves. Education, on the other hand, implies more general development of the individual on a number of different fronts. It suggests the understanding of principles, and the development of a set of values which, thereby, have a significant effect on the individual as a person, not just as a skilled performer. While training and coaching may be concerned with developing performance, education is concerned with developing people. However there seems to be no reason why the two should be mutually exclusive; the training process can be educational if it is conducted in such a way that it contributes to the total development of the person (Pring, 1984). Briefly, those who are involved with children's sport are, or should be, educating children as well as coaching activities.

Development of character

Traditionally it has been claimed that sport contributes to personal development by building character. Now, this idea is itself fraught with problems. It leads us to ask a number of questions, such as: What is character? Can we actually measure it? How can we know if sport has any effect upon it? Character is, itself, a neutral word, yet the implication of the claim is that the effects are beneficial – that is, sport builds 'good character'. However, there are many, perhaps in this room, who feel that this belief is at best optimistic, and may be untrue. As sports have become more competitive it seems to become less credible, and we may wonder where the idea came from in the first place.

One of the early references to the claim can be found in Plato's *Republic*; it was reiterated by Rousseau in *Emile* (Meakin, 1981), but its greatest boost may have come from the report of the Public Schools Commissioners under the Chairmanship of Lord Clarendon in 1864. It drew attention to the development of organised games in those schools during the first part of the nineteenth century and expressed the belief that the predominant reason for encouraging games was for the social and moral benefits which were to be derived from them (Smith, 1974, p. 18).

Two approaches to sport: process and product

According to Clarendon, the qualities developed by games included self-discipline, team spirit, courage, and 'fair play'. These represent the radical ethic in sport, in which the worth of success is directly related to the manner in which it is achieved. Advocates of this principle consider that, to play well, players should display respect for others and a respect for the rules of the contest (Kew, 1978). The belief that opportunities to display such qualities exist in sport constitutes the basis for claims of social and moral benefits. The idea of respect for the rules of the contest also embodies the notion of conforming, not only to the letter of the laws, but also to the spirit. Those who take this view expect players to act altruistically when the occasion arises and not to take unfair advantage of the bad luck of their opponents.

A rather different view is that represented by the win-at-all-costs attitude summed up by the apocryphal statement attributed to the American football coach Vince Lombardi: 'Winning isn't everything, it's the only thing.' The only significant value espoused here is that of winning; coaching and training are devoted to that end. It is an outcome-oriented approach in which performance is judged solely by the result, the product, and not by the manner in which it is achieved, the process. Any behaviour which is not directly concerned with winning is superfluous; the intrinsic value of playing the game is de-emphasised and hence much of the play element is devalued. This seems a pity when one hears of children dropping out before they have really got started because 'It's no fun'.

The increase of commercial interest, professionalism and nationalism in many sports may have operated to undermine the intrinsic values of participation and to promote the extrinsic values of various forms of reward. Young people are now subject to procedures designed, first, to make them better performers, and secondly, to encourage them to aspire to ever higher standards of performance, which incidentally may discourage those to whom those standards are unrealistic, and detract from the pleasure of the performance: presumably an important reason for taking part.

Character and values

The term 'good character' is difficult to define if for no other reason than that the use of the word 'good' is a value judgement; what is 'good' to one group of people may not be to another. Derek Wright, of the University of Leicester, has written of character in terms of people's degree of dependence on others, peers or adults, and the extent to which they internalise that influence as determinants of the type of character they exhibit. The implication of his analysis is that the most desirable character is altruistic, capable of putting the welfare of others before self; and autonomous, making independent, considered decisions in respect of moral and social rules (Wright, 1971).

Others have emphasised the development of psychological value systems. Values are those things which are important in our lives. They can be divided into those concerned with the ways in which we live (e.g. logically, honestly) and those concerned with the ends to which we strive (e.g. a comfortable life, a world of beauty). In the first group are moral values, which are interpersonal and arouse feelings of guilt when they are violated; and competence values which are intrapersonal and arouse only feelings of personal inadequacy when we do not live up to them. The second group yields a distinction between social values, which are concerned with others, and personal values, which are not (Rokeach, 1973). In view of what has been claimed about character it would seem that we are actually talking about two types of value, the social and the moral, which are concerned with rather different outcomes, goals on the one hand and ways of acting on the other.

If sport were effective in developing 'character' we should expect to see athletes placing more emphasis on social and moral values than on competence and personal values. My research with college athletes in North America indicates that this does not happen and, insofar as there are differences in the values of athletes and non-athletes, it is only that athletes tend to place more value on being good at what they do (Lee, 1977).

The role of sport

The question of whether sport is character-building is a different one from whether it can be; as with the discussion of the educational value of training, it rather depends upon how it is used. Furthermore, if sports experiences can encourage the development of positive moral and social values, then they can also discourage it.

In sport the rules of the game are prescribed, agreed by the participants, and enforced by a system of penalties for violation. The penalties may be concerned with preserving equity or with deterrence. So, minor infringements which gain some advantage may result in a free kick in football, or a scrum in rugby, while those of a more violent nature may incur sending off. These rules, of course, are subject to manipulation and must be enforced by independent referees. Hence they are subject to interpretation; and who among us can honestly claim never to have reminded a team that they should play to the referee and not to the rules. To do that is to display, first, an instrumental attitude in which the ends justify the means irrespective of the moral value of the behaviour, or the desirability of playing to the agreed rules of the game; secondly, an attitude of divesting oneself of the responsibility for the control of one's behaviour (right is what you can get away with); and thirdly, a belief that the penalties incurred are merely the price you pay for being caught, like the man who parks his vehicle in a restricted area because it is convenient, without concern for other road users who are held up; a fine would be only a parking fee!

Sport can provide opportunities for altruistic behaviour and sportsmanship. They occur when participants refuse to take advantage of the misfortunes of opponents and when they display respect and appreciation for their efforts. The opportunities for this type of behaviour are many, but perhaps we see rather less of it than formerly. The demands of competitive success make altruism counter-productive, and professional players, who are role models for the younger generation, have been criticised frequently for unseemly behaviour. Only quite recently a footballer was fined for making an obscene gesture to the crowd (*Daily Telegraph*, 2 October 1985), tennis players are increasingly disinclined to shake hands in a more than perfunctory manner, and in cricket, which has been the traditional model for fair and respectful behaviour, aggressive acts and language directed towards both opponents and umpires have become more apparent recently.

The moral dilemma

Opportunities to display fair-mindedness, respect for opponents and altruism can arise particularly in situations where there are no independent judges, as often happens in junior tennis tournaments, but the pressure to succeed may prevent it happening. Tournaments can place children in a dilemma. They are required to call the ball good or not when simultaneously trying to play the shot. Even in junior tennis the ball moves very fast and this places a great and, in my view, unnecessary strain on the players. Since their performances in tournaments affect players' rankings, future progress, and opportunities for receiving sponsorship, they may at times have to make close decisions which could lose them the match when it would be possible to call the ball out and gain a winning advantage. It may be easy to make a close decision in favour of the opponent when you are winning easily, but match point against is very different. Yet I recently attended a junior championship where adults were unwilling to umpire because they said they did not wish to sit and receive abuse from youngsters during the matches. The point of this example is that with the increasing pressures of competition children can be placed in situations where the demands for success can result in less than morally praiseworthy behaviours. Moreover, opportunities for developing a sense of moral and social responsibility may not be taken because of the costs.

Promotion of prosocial attitudes: some evidence

The question of whether sports participation develops moral responsibility has not been fully investigated. However, some research has attempted to look into it. One exploratory study conducted by Glyn Roberts and a colleague examined the effect of the sport experience on the prosocial behaviours of co-operation and altruism in an artificial game setting. The limited conclusions they were able to make indicated that the effects of sport experience were negative rather than positive; those who had more experience were less altruistic, and boys were less altruistic than girls (Kleiber and Roberts, 1981). My own research, referred to earlier, suggests that extensive athletic participation is related to higher personal and competence values and not to moral and social values (Lee, 1977). These results are supported by two small studies conducted by students working with me. They investigated the extent to which boys endorsed the commitment of 'professional fouls' in soccer. In the first study (Bolland, 1981), it was clear that professional fouls were more acceptable to them as they became older, and had more experience in the game; furthermore, they were more likely to endorse a foul if it occurred in the context of a cup game than in a league or friendly game. The second study (Waters,

1982) showed that players were more likely to endorse fouls than non-players; however, a measure of moral development suggested that players were no less mature in their judgements of behaviour in non-sporting situations than non-players. If evidence can be gathered to support these findings it would indicate that the instrumental, Machiavellian behaviour which concerns us may be specific to the sport and is not necessarily transferred to other life situations; this is a little reassuring. As the mother of a nationally-ranked junior tennis player recently said to me, 'These boys are really very nice, until they step inside that wire netting, then something happens to them.' If the behaviour is sport-specific, then perhaps it is not a matter of such grave concern for the individual, but it is of concern for the state of the activity and the way it is perceived by others. Further, such complacency denies the opportunity to teach young people that it is possible, and even desirable, to compete with dignity and respect for opponents, and to be gracious both in defeat and victory. Nice guys do not always finish last, as David Hemery and Bill Beaumont have amply demonstrated. Indeed, it occurs to me that the truly superior athlete need not resort to dubious tactics in order to win.

The coach's contribution

In all this the coach is a most important individual. Clearly, coaches perform a wide variety of functions. Not only is there a requirement to teach and improve skills, the coach has also to help athletes to prepare mentally for a competition, to help them through difficult periods both sport-related and otherwise, to be a father confessor, and, I would say, to be an educator of young people. The educational role is a difficult one. It demands an understanding of the world of the child, a willingness to put the welfare of the athlete ahead of one's own ambitions, and the ability to set an example of desirable conduct. The research of Kleiber and Roberts (1981), Bolland (1981), and Waters (1982) leads one to ask why instrumental attitudes in sports increase with age and experience, particularly since one would expect to see a progression towards more morally and socially responsible attitudes. One cannot escape the suggestion that the views expressed by coaches may be very important in determining those of the athletes.

Two pieces of research are relevant here. The first is about the possibility of promoting moral reasoning through sports. In a study carried out with young children in a sports camp, the children were taught by one of the three strategies. The first was the common 'Do as I say' format; the second consisted of teachers providing a desirable model and giving reinforcement for positive social behaviour; the third involved the discussion of moral decisions in the sport when the opportunity arose. The last two strategies resulted in increases in levels of moral reasoning in the children over the period of the research, which suggests that moral growth can occur in sports where coaches deliberately encourage it (Shields and Bredemeier, 1984).

However, given the pressures of competition, coaches may not be inclined to spend the time necessary to do this, nor indeed may they be in sympathy with the principle. The second piece of research is a study of the attitudes of football (soccer) coaches to the laws of the game. Conducted in Canada, it revealed that, while coaches found violence on the field to be unacceptable, there was considerable support for breaking the laws on technical grounds (e.g. encroaching within 10 yards of a free kick, intentional hand-ball, and so on). Only a third of coaches felt that they should forbid foul play and while they felt that retaliation was unacceptable it was on the grounds that having a player sent off would leave the team at a disadvantage rather than for reasons of fair play. School team coaches did differ from others in being less likely to encourage law-breaking to promote team interest, but, importantly, all coaches felt that it was the responsibility of the referee to enforce the laws (Goodger and Jackson, 1985). This represents a relatively low level of moral reasoning in itself, since it externalises the responsibility for the control of the action, and is indicative of a preference for competence values. It would be interesting to see how British coaches fare in comparison.

Conclusion

So here we have some evidence to give answers to the question of character building and moral development through sport. First, there is no reason to believe that taking part in sport necessarily promotes morally or socially desirable behaviour and attitudes either in sport or elsewhere. Indeed, in sports situations the tendency is just the opposite; greater experience is associated with more instrumental attitudes. Second, it is possible to bring about moral growth if, and only if, coaches and teachers deliberately adopt strategies with this in mind; these include modelling desirable behaviour and discussing fairness. Third, there is some evidence to suggest that coaches do not discourage players from breaking the rules of the game in order to win and may not always provide good prosocial models.

As with most things there are no simple answers, the world is full of 'ifs' and 'buts'. It appears that we *can* use sport to help children to become better people *if* we go about it in the right way, *but* we must have a commitment to it and be prepared to recognise the educational as well as the performance role of coaches. If we wish to arrest the declining image of some sports and promote fair-mindedness, respect for opponents, and grace in success and defeat, while at the same time cultivating courage, determination and durability, we must examine our own values and how they are transmitted to children.

References

BOLLAND, C. (1981) *An Examination of the Attitudes of Young Football Players to the Professional/Tactical Foul*. Unpublished manuscript, Trinity and All Saints' College, Leeds.

GOODGER, M. J. and JACKSON, J. (1985) 'Fair play: coaches' attitudes towards the laws of soccer.' *Journal of Sport Behaviour*, **8**, 1, 34–41.

KEW, F. (1978) 'Values in competitive games.' *Quest*, **29**, 103–12.

KLEIBER, D. A. and ROBERTS, G. C. (1981) 'The effects of sport in the development of social character: a preliminary investigation.' *Journal of Sport Psychology*, **3**, 2, 114–22.

LEE, M. J. (1977) *Expressed Values of Varsity Football Players, Intramural Football Players, and Non-football Players*. Eugene, OR: Microform Publications.

MEAKIN, D. C. (1981) 'Physical education: an agency of moral growth?' *Journal of Philosophy of Education*, **15**, 2, 241–53.

PRING, R. C. (1984) 'Negotiation, guidance, and models of social education.' Paper presented at the Conference on Education and Training 14–18: policy and practice, December. Stoke Rochford Hall, England.

ROKEACH, M. (1973) *The Nature of Human Values*. New York: Free Press.

SHIELDS, D. L. and BREDEMEIER, B. J. (1984) 'Sport and moral growth: a developmental perspective.' In W. F. STRAUB and J. WILLIAMS (eds) *Cognitive Sport Psychology*. Lansing, NY: Sport Science Associates.

SMITH, W. D. (1974) *Stretching their Bodies*. Newton Abbott: David and Charles.

WATER, C. (1982) *Attitudes towards Instrumental Behaviour in Youth Football among Players and Non-players*. Unpublished manuscript, Trinity and All Saints' College, Leeds.

WRIGHT, D. (1971) *The Psychology of Moral Behaviour*. Harmondsworth: Penguin Books.

Index